Governance and Public Policy in Canada

GOVERNANCE AND PUBLIC POLICY IN CANADA

A View from the Provinces

Michael M. Atkinson, Daniel Béland,
Gregory P. Marchildon, Kathleen McNutt,
Peter W.B. Phillips, and Ken Rasmussen

UNIVERSITY OF TORONTO PRESS

LIBRARY AND ARCHIVES CANADA CATALOGUING IN PUBLICATION

Governance and public policy in Canada : a view from the provinces / Michael M. Atkinson ... [et al.].

Includes bibliographical references and index. Issued also in electronic formats.
ISBN 978-1-4426-0493-3 (pbk.). —ISBN 978-14426-0766-8 (bound)

1. Provincial governments—Canada. 2. Canadian provinces—Social policy. 3. Canadian provinces—Economic policy. 4. Federal-provincial relations—Canada. 5. Decentralization in government—Canada. I. Atkinson, Michael M.

JL198.G69 2013   352.130971   C2012-908026-8

We welcome comments and suggestions regarding any aspect of our publications— please feel free to contact us at news@utphighereducation.com or visit our Internet site at www.utppublishing.com.

North America
5201 Dufferin Street
North York, Ontario, Canada, M3H 5T8

2250 Military Road
Tonawanda, New York, USA, 14150

ORDERS PHONE: 1–800–565–9523
ORDERS FAX: 1–800–221–9985
ORDERS E-MAIL: utpbooks@utpress.utoronto.ca

UK, Ireland, and continental Europe
NBN International
Estover Road, Plymouth, PL6 7PY, UK
ORDERS PHONE: 44 (0) 1752 202301
ORDERS FAX: 44 (0) 1752 202333
ORDERS E-MAIL: enquiries@nbninternational.com

Every effort has been made to contact copyright holders; in the event of an error or omission, please notify the publisher.

This book is printed on paper containing 100% post-consumer fibre.

The University of Toronto Press acknowledges the financial support for its publishing activities of the Government of Canada through the Canada Book Fund.

Printed in Canada

COVER IMAGES

Top, left to right: Saskatchewan Legislative Building (Regina) by Sandra Cohen-Rose and Colin Rose. Licensed under the terms of CC-BY-SA 3.0; British Columbia Parliament Buildings (Victoria) by Steve Voght. Licensed under the terms of CC-BY 3.0; Prince Edward Island Legislative Building (Charlottetown) iStockphoto; Ontario Legislative Building (Toronto) by Chris Slothouber. Licensed under the terms of CC-BY-SA 3.0; The Alberta Legislature Building (Edmonton) iStockphoto

Bottom, left to right: Parliament Building (Quebec) (Quebec City) iStockphoto; Confederation Building at St. John's (St. John's) by David P. Janes. Licensed under the terms of CC-BY-SA 3.0; New Brunswick Legislative Building (Fredericton) by noricum. Licensed under the terms of CC-BY-SA 3.0; Manitoba Legislative Building (Winnipeg) iStockphoto; Nova Scotia Legislative Building (Halifax) iStockphoto.

Background image: Parliament Hill (Ottawa) by Doug Kerr. Licensed under the terms of CC-BY-SA 3.0.

RECYCLED
Paper made from
recycled material
FSC   FSC® C103567
www.fsc.org

To the memory of Albert W. Johnson and Thomas K. Shoyama

Contents

CHAPTER TWO
Provincial Administrative Institutions 23

CHAPTER THREE
Taxing and Spending 59

CHAPTER FOUR
The Provincial Regulatory State   99

CHAPTER FIVE
Civil Society, Policy Networks, and the Production of Expertise   123

Conclusion   153

Figures and Tables

Preface

Today, provinces play a large role in developing, implementing, and managing public policy. As suggested in this book, in Canada, the provinces have even become the most essential makers of public policy. This is the case not only because of the broad scope of their constitutionally recognized jurisdictions but also because of the direct role they play in most major national policy debates, including those within the jurisdiction of the Government of Canada, in the context of our highly decentralized federal system. Considering the significance of the provincial role in policymaking, it is time to take a systematic look at provincial policy development in Canada. Our short book provides an overview of provincial governance and policy, and we hope it will help students, informed citizens, and researchers pay closer attention to, and further explore, the nature of provincial public policy and administration.

We are determined to make this book the prelude to a new series of volumes on multilevel governance and public policy. This series is sponsored by the Johnson-Shoyama Graduate School of Public Policy, an interdisciplinary centre for advanced education, research, outreach, and training that is also a joint venture between the University of Regina and the University of Saskatchewan. As faculty members of this provincial graduate school, we think the time has come to bring scholars together to further improve our comparative understanding of the administration, development, and governance of public policy in the Canadian provinces. To avoid parochialism, our analysis is grounded in international governance and policy literature. Although the study of provincial public policy is distinct from the study of federalism, we think the analysis of federal institutions is necessary to form a proper understanding of how the provinces formulate policies. Provincial policies, after all, emerge from within a complex relationship that includes the federal government, the governments of other provinces, and other actors that are growing in importance, such as emerging Aboriginal self-governments, local governments, and members of civil society.

This introduction to provincial governance and public policy outlines broad concepts and trends instead of focusing extensively on particular policy areas. We trust that the book will help readers interested in specific policy areas to understand them in the larger context of provincial governance and policy. Due to the limited space available, the book does not address public policy development at the municipal level or in the three northern territories. Municipalities are creatures of the provincial governments, and they are important policy sites, but we believe the analysis of municipal public policy in Canada requires a separate review. As for governance and public policy in the territories, it is a critical yet understudied issue that also requires a distinct analysis, in part because of key institutional differences between the provinces and the territories. Yet we expect that some of the concepts and issues raised in this book are relevant for the analysis of municipal and territorial governance and public policy. Overall, we hope this brief introduction to governance and provincial public policy will help trigger more debates and research about this increasingly crucial topic for the future of Canada.

This book originates from ongoing discussions taking place among the faculty of the Johnson-Shoyama Graduate School about governance and provincial policy. The six authors are faculty members at the school, and the diversity of their disciplinary backgrounds and policy areas adds to the scope of the project. As this book appears, we would like to thank other faculty and staff of the Johnson-Shoyama Graduate School for their support. We also thank Donald Ward and, especially, Karen Taylor for their copy-editing work as well as Ata-Ul Munim for his research assistance. At the University of Toronto Press, Michael Harrison provided much support and advice concerning this project, to which he gave impetus, by suggesting that we write such a concise introductory book before working on a series of more specialized edited volumes on provincial public policy. We warmly thank him for his insight and commitment. Finally, we thank production editor Beate Schwirtlich and the rest of the University of Toronto Press editorial team for their efficiency and professionalism.

We dedicate this book to the memory of Albert W. Johnson and Thomas K. Shoyama, the two outstanding civil servants for whom our school is named. Belonging to a group that earned the label "The Greatest Generation," Johnson and Shoyama devoted almost two decades, from 1945 until 1964, to improving the state of public policy in Saskatchewan. Although they then moved on to become prominent deputy ministers in the Government of Canada, they used their wealth of provincial experience to improve the design, implementation, and management of public policy at the federal level. We aspire to be, and to produce, scholar-practitioners in their image, the next "Greatest Generation" of leaders in Canada.

Introduction

From the cradle to the grave, our lives are shaped by the policies of the state. This is the case regarding numerous domains, including culture, economic development, education, employment, health, inequality, policing, taxation, and the environment. Through fiscal spending and redistribution as well as regulation, the state implements numerous and complex policies that are an integral and fundamental part of our economic and social order. Because the state is ever present in all aspects of society and, as a consequence, of our lives, studying public policy is a true democratic and governance imperative, as knowledge about policies can inform decisions and deliberations that are likely to impact the lives of citizens in direct ways.

In recent decades, global forces have created new policy and governance challenges for states. This is the case in Canada where, despite a decentring of state power and a growing role for civil society in policymaking, governments remain key actors in economic, environmental, and social affairs. As for substate entities such as the Canadian provinces, their role in governance and policy development has increased rather than declined, compared both to the role of the federal government and to the situation prevailing in other federal countries such as Australia and the United States. This growing role for the provinces has occurred because, in Canada, many of the economic, environmental, and social policy challenges involve provincial or shared responsibilities. Health care, for example, is primarily a provincial jurisdiction, and provincial leaders as well as professional and patient associations play the most prominent role in reshaping the country's health system. In other "hot spots" such as the environment—and, more specifically, the fight against climate change—provinces are key actors that either clash or cooperate with the federal government on specific issues. The provinces even play a major role in immigration now. Finally, even regarding international issues, such as the negotiations over a trade agreement between Canada and the European Union, provinces are typically involved, directly or indirectly. Thus, far from declining, the role of the provinces in governance and policy development in Canada is more crucial than ever.

Considering these observations, scholars, organized interests, and informed citizens should pay closer attention to policymaking in the provinces and to how the actions of provincial policymakers shape and are shaped by other actors. Unfortunately, as major sites of policy change, provinces have been largely understudied. In this introductory essay, we show why and how provinces matter in designing and implementing policies that affect the everyday lives of Canadians and the development of our economy and society in a changing world, particularly in a federal system characterized by recurrent tensions between Ottawa and the provinces.[1]

Beyond the enduring and well-known tensions between the federal and provincial governments, this book explores the multiple layers of policy governance in the Canadian provinces, layers that cannot be defined simply in terms of the provinces' relationship with Ottawa. In addition to federal-provincial jurisdictions, these policy layers include the transnational and the municipal levels as well as the increasingly decentred networks of policy experts, think tanks, and other civil society actors. Although this book suggests that the provinces have become the most crucial source of policy development and innovation in Canada, it also points to the decentred nature of contemporary

---

1 Throughout this book, we focus on the provinces, and, thus, we generally exclude the three sparsely populated but strategic territories, which have a distinct constitutional status and deserve separate treatment. At the same time, we recognize that some of the policy trends and tensions discussed here also extend to the territories, which is why we include them in the agenda for future research sketched in the last chapter of this book.

governance, exacerbated by the complex institutional and territorial boundaries inherent in our federal system.

One of the outstanding characteristics of Canada's political order is the growing and often explicit reliance of all levels of government on outside expertise, and, more generally, on civil society partners, without which effective governance is much harder to achieve. For instance, when dealing with most environmental issues, in addition to discussions with Ottawa, provinces typically consult many different stakeholders, ranging from scholars and environmentalists to farmers and business groups. To these realities we must add territorial issues, such as the asymmetrical nature of an increasing number of federal-provincial agreements, the quest for self-government on the part of First Nations, and the growing political importance of cities in policy governance. These realities create new layers of complexity in Canadian governance and policy development. Recent efforts to disentangle traditional federal institutions and simplify policy governance have created fresh challenges, such as the quest for new forms of health care accountability in an age of federal block grants (in contrast with the shared federal funding of the past). More important, the era of so-called "open federalism" has put the provinces squarely at the centre of policy development in Canada.

As these factors converge to reshape governance and policy development in Canada, they create new challenges for citizens and policymakers alike, at all government levels, including—and especially—at the provincial level. We wrote this short book to explore and clarify the meaning of these challenges while analyzing the growing role, and the changing characteristics, of provincial governance and public policy in our asymmetrical and fragmented polity.

Such observations on the fragmentation of our political system should not suggest that it is impossible to improve our understanding of governance and policy development in the provinces. Indeed, this book reviews the key concepts necessary for a systematic analysis of policy and governance issues as they reflect multiple institutional tensions and actor networks that interact to shape and reshape policy development in Canada. Because provinces are now the central site of governance and policy innovation, we assess their role while placing the provincial state in its broader institutional, social, and territorial context. Without this type of broader analysis, we may continue to downplay and misunderstand the crucial role of provinces in policy changes that directly affect the lives of citizens, in areas ranging from health care and social welfare to education and the environment.

Three key themes unify this book. First, it addresses the role of policy convergence and divergence among provinces. Although our analysis stresses enduring interprovincial differences in terms of political culture and institutions, we point to patterns of policy diffusion, according to which policy convergence takes place within specific areas in several provinces.

Second, the book explores the tension between centralization and decentralization in Canada as it affects intergovernmental relations. Undoubtedly, Canada is one of the most decentralized federal systems in the advanced industrial world; yet, while a key trend in Canada has been to increase the role and the capacity of provinces in policy development, discussions with Ottawa on issues such as equalization and health transfers remain crucial to the logic of Canadian federalism. To complicate the situation even further, Canadian cities have mobilized to gain greater fiscal and policy autonomy, in the context of a constitutional order within which municipal governments are mere creatures of the provinces. The quest for Aboriginal self-governance is yet another decentralizing pressure that challenges the power of both Ottawa and the provinces. From this perspective, the centralization-decentralization axis is a major site of political and institutional conflict within Canada's federal system, one that no longer involves simply the provinces and the national government.

Third, although the provinces play a greater role in policy development than ever before, they now face a growing tension between ambition and capacity. This tension is especially clear in the field of fiscal policy, where federal transfers remain a major revenue source for provinces. Similarly, although the provinces have attempted to enact major interprovincial agreements, bodies such as the Council of the Federation have clear limitations. Yet Canadian provinces have sometimes found ways to innovate at a more rapid pace than the federal government to adapt to changing economic, social, and institutional circumstances. This book explores how the provincial state has adapted in the context of these changing circumstances to transcend its limited capacity while engaging with a growing number of civil society actors, policy networks, and intergovernmental bodies.

Before we outline the substantive content of this book, it is helpful to state what it is *not*. First, although written with a broad and interdisciplinary audience in mind, it is not a comprehensive introduction to public policy in Canada. Several textbooks are devoted to this general topic (e.g., Dobuzinskis, Howlett, and Laycock 2007; Howlett, Ramesh, and Perl 2009; Miljan 2008; Pal 2010), and our book complements them through its clear provincial focus.[2] Second, because our book focuses primarily on policy, it is not a general introduction to provincial politics. Although provincial politics is discussed, this is not a textbook on parties and formal political institutions. In fact, the book draws on other disciplines (economics and sociology) and interdisciplinary approaches (policy studies and network analysis) to explore governance and public policy in Canada from a provincial perspective. In general, our goal is to offer a new voice that complements existing disciplinary takes on the provinces as sites of policy development. Finally, we do not discuss in great detail the major policy areas in which the provinces are involved. There are many sources available that map fields such as education policy, environmental issues, and health care programs in Canada. The goal of this book is not to duplicate these efforts but to offer analytical tools to explore these policy areas while looking at the "big picture" of governance and policy development.

At this point, it is helpful to define what we mean by "governance" and "public policy," two key concepts used throughout this book. First, we define governance in opposition to state-centric understandings of public policy, according to which policy development is a purely statist construction. In contrast, a governance approach to public policy is based on the assumption that, in addition to the state, a multitude of actors shape policy development in one way or another. At the broadest level, in the policy world and beyond, governance is about determining *"who has power, who makes decisions, how other players make their voice heard and how account is rendered"* (Institute on Governance 2013). From our policy perspective, studying governance stresses the interaction between the state and other actors involved in policy development, which often takes the form of complex policy

---

2 It is also worth noting that most books dealing with provincial politics are not centred on policy development. For example, the 2001 edited volume by Keith Brownsey and Michael Howlett (2001) is not focused on policy issues. The same remark applies to Rand Dyck's *Provincial Politics in Canada* (1996). As for Christopher Dunn's edited book *Provinces: Canadian Provincial Politics* (2006a), it does feature a number of chapters on provincial public policy, but it does not constitute a systematic introduction to provincial public policy in Canada.

networks. Public policy refers to "the broad framework of ideas and values within which decisions are taken and action, or inaction, is pursued by governments in relation to some issue or problem" (Brooks 1989, 16; quoted in Smith 2003, 5). From our governance perspective, however, the study of public policy should move beyond a traditional, state-centric model to bring in civil society actors and policy networks that help shape policy design, implementation, and outcomes.

To introduce other key policy concepts necessary to frame this analysis of provincial governance and public policy, each of the book's five chapters begins with concise analytical remarks that help produce a "toolbox" for the analysis of policymaking in the provinces. The concepts discussed include constituent units, intergovernmentalism, and decentralization (Chapter 1); the professional civil service, administrative reform, provincial decision making, and departmental organization (Chapter 2); government size and growth, "crowding out" effects, fiscal imbalance, efficiency and effectiveness, deficit and debt, and fiscal rules (Chapter 3); regulation in all its various aspects (Chapter 4); and finally, civil society, policy analysis, collaborative policymaking, network society, and digital government (Chapter 5). These concepts are not unique to Canada, but they take a distinct meaning in its particular institutional context. Once these concepts are both defined and illustrated, each chapter discusses policy trends and challenges in the provinces. Although they address concrete historical, substantive, and analytical issues, the chapters systematically explore the complexities and multilayered nature of provincial governance and policy development.

The first chapter adopts a comparative perspective to explore the prominent role of the provinces in shaping policy governance and intergovernmental relations in Canada. It explores the weight of federal institutions and territorial mobilization in Canadian public policy while stressing the fact that provinces have more policy autonomy than substate entities found in other federal countries. The chapter also discusses the scope of policy interdependencies in our political system before raising the pressing issue of territorial governance and integration in Canada's asymmetrical and multilayered polity. In other words, the chapter explains why the growing policy role of the provinces creates new governance and institutional challenges. Such challenges include the quest for a better balance between diversity and unity, the issue of vertical fiscal imbalance between Ottawa and the provinces, and the push for greater territorial and governance autonomy among

First Nations, larger municipal governments, as well as some provinces, especially Québec and Alberta.

The second chapter explores the administrative capacity of the provinces, an understudied aspect of governance and policy development. Recognizing this, the chapter stresses prominent administrative differences among provinces regarding how they structure their public service and their policy capacity and how they attempt to innovate in terms of policy governance and implementation. After comparing the size and the evolution of provincial civil services and administrative capacities, the chapter points to current administrative challenges such as managerial reform, the changing nature of the civil service in the provinces, and the relationship between provincial and municipal policy institutions.

The third chapter discusses taxation and government spending, two closely related aspects of federalism and provincial policymaking. It explores the trade-offs between perceived economic efficiency and political imperatives that exacerbate the tensions inherent in policy development in the Canadian provinces. Although all provinces play a determinant role in policy development, there are variations from one to another in terms of government size and expenditure patterns. This chapter explores such variations before dealing with fiscal challenges, such as the growing burden created by the rise in health care expenditures and the alleged "fiscal imbalance" between Ottawa and the provinces. Overall, the chapter emphasizes not only the diversity of provincial fiscal realities but also the shared tax and spending challenges facing the provinces.

The fourth chapter analyzes the role of the provinces in the crucial policy area of regulation. Stressing the fact that regulation is now at the core of modern government, which is more likely to steer and guide rather than drive the economy and civil society, the chapter discusses the changing nature of provincial governance through regulation, the scale and scope of the provincial regulatory state, and the key ways in which provinces can become true sites of experimentation for regulatory innovation in Canada.

The fifth chapter turns to civil society and knowledge production in the provinces, which often takes place outside formal state boundaries, notably through the development of multilevel policy networks comprised of both state and civil society actors. We see how policy knowledge in the provinces is produced and disseminated and how government and non-governmental actors interact to foster such policy expertise. Here the focus is on improving efficiency and policy control through decentred sources of expertise, which once again reflects the multilayered nature of governance and policy development in Canada.

Overall, our book shows that provinces play a growing role in policy governance and that, to grasp this role, we must focus on both government and civil society actors, who interact in multilayered ways, in the provinces and well beyond. In our conclusion, we return to these issues and propose an agenda for future research on provincial public policy in Canada.

CHAPTER ONE

Intergovernmentalism and Provincial Policy Setting

Introduction

One of the key contributions of this book is to show how the provinces have become the most crucial generators of public policy in Canada. This chapter focuses on provincial policy in the context of the changing role of the federal government and the shifting nature of federal-provincial relations. Key concepts, including the nature of constituent units, intergovernmentalism, and decentralization, are introduced in the context of developed federations in general and of Canada in particular. Shifts in leadership and responsibility from the federal government to the provinces are illustrated through key public policy domains such as Medicare, immigration, and internal trade, including labour mobility. Although the federal government once played a major if not determinative role in these policy domains, in recent decades, provincial governments have come to play an ever more significant role.

This development is a consequence of several factors, but one stands out: globalization has weakened the role of the modern, sovereign state. Although it has not necessarily precipitated a demise of state power overall, globalization has typically diminished the role of the national state relative to suprastate (e.g., the European Union) and substate (e.g., provincial or state) levels of governance. In the Canadian case, the trend to decentralization has been exacerbated by factors endogenous to the Canadian federation, factors that will be examined in more depth in this chapter. The struggle for future provincial governments, acting with or without the federal government, is to balance regional diversity—which is the advantage of a decentralized federation—with the necessary unity required to remain a country with a meaningful, shared citizenship. The tension between the two has been the inescapable and permanent conundrum of the Canadian federation.

In this chapter, three key concepts are examined: constituent units (and their role in a federation), intergovernmentalism, and decentralization. Each of these concepts is central to an understanding of the contemporary provincial state in Canada and of the manner in which the direction in key policy domains, such as Medicare, immigration, and internal trade, are set. This discussion is followed by an examination of two of the major challenges facing the provinces as constituent units in the Canadian federation. The first is the struggle to find a balance between diversity and unity—between self-rule and shared rule —in a decentralized federation, one in which new pressures are being exerted by large municipal governments as well as by the movement for indigenous self-government. The second challenge is to address more effectively the vertical fiscal imbalance not only between the provinces and the federal government—which in the past has focused on unconditional transfers such as equalization payments and conditional transfers for social policies such as universal Medicare—but also between the two constitutionally recognized orders of governments and other orders of government, including local governments and Aboriginal governments. Based at least on recent trends, it seems likely that provincial governments are going to continue to expand their role in managing these challenges and reshaping the political and fiscal future of the federation.

Key Concepts and Their Application to Canada

CONSTITUENT UNITS AND THEIR ROLE IN A FEDERATION
What is a federation? This seemingly simple question opens up a range of answers, few of which are either simple or satisfying. Indeed, in a recent book on federalism, the editors stated that any "attempt to confine such a complex and dynamic concept as federalism to a

single authoritative definition is deeply problematic" (Ward and Ward 2009, 1). This may be so, but the fundamental difference between a federal state and a unitary state is the role of the constituent units and the extent of the constitutionally protected power and authority they exercise. As Watts (2008, 8) points out, in contrast to a unitary state, a federal state has "two (or more) levels of government" that combine "elements of *shared-rule* (collaborative partnership) through a common government and *regional self-rule* (autonomy) for the governments of the constituent units." The phrase "constituent unit" is used because the names for these constitutionally recognized substates— states, provinces, *Länder*, autonomous communities, regions, cantons—vary from country to country.

Because such a definition can still encompass a broad range of political systems, from constitutionally decentralized unions to more loosely bound confederations and associated states, criteria have been identified to help separate federations from other political systems. The following six criteria are derived from Watts (2008, 9), but they are consistent with those proposed by other students of comparative federalism. A federation has

- At least two constitutionally recognized orders of government, one acting for the whole federation and the other for the constituent units;
- Formal constitutional distribution of legislative and executive authority and allocation of resources between the two orders of government, thereby ensuring real autonomy for the constituent order;
- A written constitution that is the supreme law of the land that can only be amended by a significant proportion of the constituent units;
- An umpire to resolve disputes between the two orders of government, most often through an independent judiciary;
- Some provision for formal representation by region (as opposed to population) within the federal policymaking institution, usually provided in a second federal chamber; and
- Processes and institutions to facilitate intergovernmental collaboration in policy and program areas where government responsibilities are shared or overlap.

Constituent units such as provinces are democratically account-able to the people who live within their defined territories.[1] *Globally*, the population size and geographic area encompassed by constituent units vary considerably, from almost 200 million in Uttar Pradesh (India), as of the 2011 census, to about 50,000 in island nations in the Caribbean (e.g., St. Kitts and Nevis) and about 738,000 in the Union of the Comoros, an archipelago island nation in the Indian Ocean. In Canada, provincial populations vary from more than 13 million in Ontario to about 146,000 in Prince Edward Island, a ratio that is not much different than that of the largest and smallest state populations in the United States, where you have more than 37 million residents in the state of California compared to almost 570,000 in the state of Wyoming.[2] However, as Watts (2008) points out, if most population is concentrated in one or two constituent units, it is more likely that this will generate tensions within the federation, as these units will play, or will be perceived by the other constituent units to play, a dom-inating role in the federation. In Canada, the provinces of Québec and Ontario contain 62 per cent of the population of the country and have often been seen by those living outside central Canada as dominating the federation, a perception of "inner" Canada vs. "outer" Canada that has periodically triggered tensions (Milne 2005).

Federations have a written constitution setting out the division of powers between the central government and the constituent units, but the authority of constitutions as the supreme law of the land is lim-ited. Long-term societal trends as well as the exigencies of politics and economics can influence a federation's political culture more than its constitution (Livingston 1956; Cole, Kincaid, and Rodriguez 2004; Erk and Koning 2010; Erk and Anderson 2009). Indeed, the politi-cal cultures in some federations have strayed far from their originat-ing constitutions; for example, the United States today has a more

---

1   There are some exceptions. Belgium, for example, is made up of six overlapping con-stituent units: three are territorially defined regions and three are ethnolinguistic communities, though the Flemish region and community recently merged their insti-tutions (Gérard 2002).

2   Population statistics are the most recent available as of December 2012 and come from the official government websites of Uttar Pradesh and of St. Kitts and Nevis, from the online *World Factbook* entry for Comoros, and from Statistics Canada (http://www.statcan.gc.ca/tables-tableaux/sum-som/l01/cst01/demo02a-eng.htm) and the U.S. Census Bureau Annual Population Estimates for 2011 (http://www.census.gov/popest/data/state/totals/2011/index.html).

centralist political culture and set of institutions than its more decentralist Constitution of 1787 would indicate, and the contemporary practices reflected in today's federation stray far from the legal intent of Canada's quasi-unitary constitutional document—the British North America Act of 1867.

Written constitutions themselves produce grey areas in terms of the division of powers. In addition to areas of jurisdiction that are deemed to be within the exclusive authority of either the central government or the constituent units,[3] there are also areas of concurrent and shared authority. Concurrent jurisdictions are those areas where the framers of the constitution formally recognized what they perceived as a necessary policy overlap between the two orders of government. In contrast to nations with constitutions (e.g., Australia, Germany, and the United States) where there are numerous areas of concurrent jurisdiction, Canada has a very limited list of concurrent jurisdictions: agriculture; immigration; old age pensions and benefits; and export of non-renewable resources, forest products, and electrical energy (Watts 2008). Shared authority refers to a situation in which governments have related (though not identical) jurisdictions in a general policy area. This situation exists for environmental policy in numerous federations, including Canada, where the provincial and federal governments both require their own environmental reviews before they approve major projects.

Finally, there are residual as well as emergency or override powers. Although a larger number of federal constitutions have tended to give residual power (defined as jurisdiction over a policy domain that is not enumerated as exclusive, concurrent, or shared) to constituent units, the Canadian constitution gives residual power to the federal government, a legacy of its quasi-unitary origins. Again, consistent with the objectives of the constitution's original authors, the Government of Canada has the right to intervene to ensure peace, order, and good government; the power to declare that certain public works are in the national interest (and, once having invoked this declaratory power, to have jurisdiction over these works); and the power to overrule provincial legislation (called the powers of reservation and disallowance).

---

3 Some federations enumerate lists of powers for only one order of government and leave everything not specified as the exclusive purview of that order of government as falling within the jurisdiction of the other order of government.

However, the powers of reservation and disallowance have not been used in the postwar era and are constrained by federal and provincial political cultures that would make it extremely difficult for a federal government to employ such powers in the future (Cole, Kincaid, and Rodriguez 2004).

Since the essence of a true federation is the partnership between two orders of government—the balance between regional self-rule and national shared-rule—federal constitutions require that both orders of government consent to any changes that affect the division of powers. Most constitutions also specify a formula as to the process of change and the threshold required for agreement among the constituent units for consent. As a consequence, constitutional change is generally difficult to achieve, and Canada's history—from the failed Victoria Charter in 1971 to the defeat of the Meech Lake Accord and the Charlottetown Accord in the early 1990s—highlights the many obstacles that stand in the way of initiating change through this instrument (Russell 2004). Although a revised Constitution was finally passed in 1982, its legitimacy has been questioned because it was not endorsed by the government of Québec (Romanow, Whyte, and Leeson 1984; Banting and Simeon 1983).

When constituent units get into disputes with a central government concerning the division of powers and the appropriate exercise of jurisdiction, they generally negotiate until they reach a solution. If the two orders of government cannot find a solution or compromise, then the most common avenue of appeal is judicial. Since 1949, the Supreme Court of Canada has been the final court of appeal on any constitutional matter. Provincial appeal courts and the Supreme Court of Canada have since ruled on critical issues involving the division of power, the emergence of Aboriginal self-government, and even the right of a province to secede from the federation (Saywell 2002). In addition to adjudicating the constitutional division of powers between the federal and provincial governments, the Supreme Court has been critical in interpreting and extending the individual rights of Canadian citizens based on the Charter of Rights and Freedoms that became part of the Canadian constitution in 1982 (Graefe and Bourns 2009; Banting 2006).

Virtually all federations have two chambers at the central government level: one that provides for representation by population and a second that provides regional representation by constituent units as an offset to the first. For example, every state in the United States, regardless of population size, is represented by two senators in Congress. With a Senate appointed by the Canadian prime minister based on an outdated constitutional formula,[4] Canada has among the least legitimate and effective legislative chambers among all OECD federations in terms of regional representation.

The weakness of the Canadian Senate has, over time, produced a dynamic in which provincial governments end up performing the regional representation role through intergovernmental processes such as First Ministers' Conferences. Consequently, the burden of finding a political balance between self-rule and shared rule common to all federations has been largely borne in Canada at the executive level. Although executive federalism is a feature common to Westminster parliamentary systems, it is particularly pronounced in Canada. In these less-structured or informal intergovernmental processes, decisions are made on the basis of consensus and convention without the benefit of clear decision rules or legal frameworks. This situation puts a premium on intergovernmental relations among the individuals who occupy the most senior positions in the political and bureaucratic tiers of government (Smiley 1987). As a consequence, the word "intergovernmentalism" is used in this book to describe relations between federal and provincial governments as they are conducted through the executive branch of government.

INTERGOVERNMENTALISM

Most federations have a dense network of intergovernmental mechanisms and institutions involving varying degrees of cooperation, competition, and coordination to deal with policy interdependencies and overlaps (Agranoff 2004; Bolleyer 2009). Along with Germany and Australia, Canada has one of the more extensive sets of intergovernmental mechanisms and conventions, at least in terms of the executive level of government, amongst the 9 federations of the 34-member Organisation for Economic Co-operation and Development (OECD). However, most intergovernmental decision making in Canada proceeds on the basis of soft consensus rather than hard decision rules.

---

4 Of the 105 seats in the Canadian Senate, Ontario and Quebec have 24 seats each; the Western Provinces of British Columbia, Alberta, Saskatchewan, and Manitoba share 24 seats, as do the Maritime Provinces of New Brunswick, Nova Scotia, and Prince Edward Island, and a further six seats are assigned to Newfoundland and Labrador as well as one seat for each of the three northern territories.

Historically, particularly in the four decades following World War II, almost every area of social policy in Canada has been highly influenced by intergovernmentalism (Marchildon 1999). Intergovernmental relations have ranged widely on the cooperative-competitive spectrum though, relative to countries such as Switzerland and Germany, which have a stronger culture of intergovernmental cooperation, Canada (as well as Australia) has leaned toward the more competitive, if not conflictual, end of the spectrum (Watts 2008; Meekison, Telford, and Lazar 2004).

Intergovernmental relations (IGR) can be divided into two groups: 1) vertical IGR between constituent units and the central government and 2) horizontal IGR among the constituent units. In Canada, vertical IGR involves a network of federal-provincial-territorial[5] councils, conferences, working groups, and agencies, which, at the apex, involves the country's first ministers—the prime minister of Canada, the 10 provincial premiers, and the 3 territorial leaders (now renamed premiers). The First Ministers' Conference (FMC) is often perceived as the peak organization in vertical IGR, and FMCs continue to receive extensive media attention whenever first ministers meet. Although the first FMC was held as early as 1906, it is only after World War II that the FMC came into its own as a major instrument for constitutional change, administrative devolution, welfare state development (including health, welfare, education, and pensions), and addressing fiscal questions of taxation, transfers, and equalization. To support the network of FMCs and ministerial conferences and councils, the Canadian Intergovernmental Secretariat was established in 1973 to assist the conferences and ensure services in both of Canada's official languages (CICS 2004). More recently, however, the policy influence of FMCs has, at times, been overshadowed by other IGR institutions, including horizontal (interprovincial) IGR venues, especially the regularly scheduled meetings and initiatives of provincial premiers now known as the Council of the Federation (Meekison 2004a).

To some extent, conferences and councils led by provincial premiers and ministers mirror the vertical FMCs and ministerial councils and conferences. The first Annual Premiers' Conference (APC) was held

---

5 Over time, the territories have come to occupy full seats in these intergovernmental bodies despite their lack of constitutional status—in part because of the assumption that the territories are gradually evolving into full-fledged provinces, a change that will require formal constitutional amendment.

in 1887. The prime mover was Premier Honoré Mercier of Québec, who described this first APC as an opportunity for the provinces "to solve, in the general interest of the whole of Canada, such difficulties as experience has shown to exist in the relations between the General and the Provincial Governments" (quoted in Meekison 2004, 142). While the primary objective of provincial collaboration—more accurately described as forging a united front against the federal government—has remained a constant through the APCs' long history, these periodic meetings of premiers have, on occasion, been used in a proactive manner to set a national agenda either without the federal government or with the federal government playing a subsidiary role to that of the provinces. In contrast to FMCs, which have been held on an irregular basis, APCs have been held annually since 1960. In 2003, as proposed by Québec, the APC morphed into the Council of the Federation, an institution performing the same functions as the APC but now supported by a full-time secretariat (Adam 2005). The Council of the Federation excludes the federal government and performs the same functions as the APC (Tiernan 2008; Leclair 2006).

There are also regular regional meetings of provincial premiers. The Council of Atlantic Premiers and the Western Premiers' Conference (which includes the three territorial premiers in addition to the four provincial Western Canadian premiers) hold annual meetings to cooperate on regional policies and programs. Premiers also use the opportunity to forge a common provincial position relative to the federal government on a host of pressing fiscal and policy issues (Meekison 2004b; Smith 2008).

Specialized bureaucracies have been established at the provincial and federal levels to facilitate this extensive intergovernmental machinery, while specialized intergovernmental personnel provide strategic advice to first ministers in advancing and defending their respective agendas (Inwood, Johns, and O'Reilly 2004). In the years leading to the patriation of the constitution in the early 1980s, as well as during the second round of constitutional talks triggered by the desire of the federal government to have the government of Québec formally agree to the constitution, these intergovernmental specialists were focused on formal constitutional change (Leeson 1987). After the failure of the Charlottetown Accord in 1992, they eventually concentrated on administrative rather than constitutional change. These changes included the devolution of labour market training and some aspects of immigration policy and programming; the working out of a pan-Canadian accord on environmental harmonization; the establishment of a national child benefit; and an agreement and dispute resolution mechanism on the federal-provincial governance of social policy known as the Social Union Framework Agreement, or SUFA (Simmons 2004; Fortin, Noël, and St-Hilaire 2003). These bureaucracies at the provincial level have been instrumental in moving from an earlier pattern of federal leadership to a culture of the co-determination of national policies by both orders of government (Cameron and Simeon 2002). In some cases, such as the social union initiative in the latter half of the 1990s, the provincial governments took a leadership role (Marchildon 2000).

DECENTRALIZATION AND PROVINCIAL GOVERNMENTS IN CANADA

Decentralization is the third concept reviewed in this chapter. At its essence, decentralization in the context of federations involves the dispersing of decision-making governance—political, fiscal, and administrative—from the central government to the constituent units. The more decentralized a federal system, the less the central government can rely on hierarchical structures and the more it must rely on horizontal—intergovernmental—structures, relationships, and consensus-based decision-making processes to achieve national policy and direction.

Based on a broad measure of decentralization developed by Requejo (2010) that benchmarks federations in terms of substate powers over foreign affairs, social policy, culture, internal affairs, infrastructure, communications, the judiciary, the economy, and fiscal resources, Canada is ranked the most decentralized federation in the OECD (see Table 1.1). Using a narrower measure of fiscal control based on the substate share of revenues (when intergovernmental transfers are not included), Canada is the second most decentralized federation in the OECD (see Table 1.2).

In all federations, there is an imbalance between the revenues and expenditures of central governments and constituent units, and every central government transfers funds to the constituent units. Through such transfers, central governments exercise their spending power to achieve various goals, including national standards and objectives (Watts 1999). Consequently, the share of provincial revenues obtained from central government coffers can be used as a crude measure of the fiscal dependence of constituent units. If one assumes that constituent governments should have the capacity to raise most of their own revenues, then the extent to which constituent units are reliant on own-source revenues as opposed to transfers can be used as a proxy measure of their fiscal capacity. As shown in Table 1.3, the Canadian provinces are the most fiscally autonomous substates in the OECD.

Despite this comparatively low level of transfers in Canada, the spending power of the central government has been highly controversial, largely because of Québec's long-standing position concerning the illegitimacy of federal spending in policy areas within provincial jurisdiction (Telford 2003; Bourgault 2004). Other provinces, in particular Alberta, have also periodically criticized the conditional nature of some federal transfers and their impact on reshaping provincial policy priorities. This federal spending power is controversial, in part,

TABLE 1.1 Broad Measure of Decentralization

OECD Federation	Degree of decentralization (20-point scale)
Mexico	5.0
Austria	8.3
Spain	10.5
Australia	12.0
Germany	12.0
Belgium	14.0
Switzerland	14.0
United States	14.5
Canada	16.5

Source: Data from Requejo (2010), 287.

TABLE 1.2 Central Government Revenues of OECD Federations as a Percentage of Total Government Revenues before Intergovernmental Transfers, 2000–2004

Mexico	91.3
Australia	74.8
Belgium	71.0
Spain	69.2
Germany	65.0
Austria	61.8
United States	54.2
Canada	47.2
Switzerland	40.0

Source: Adapted from Watts (2008), 102.

TABLE 1.3 Intergovernmental Transfers as a Percentage of Constituent Unit Revenues in OECD Federations, 2000–2004

Mexico	87.9
Spain	72.8
Belgium (Regions only)	57.4
Austria	47.4
Australia	45.6
Germany	43.8
United States	25.6
Switzerland	24.8
Canada	12.9

Source: Adapted from Watts (2008), 105.

because of the federal government's greater revenue generating capacity and, although it has chosen not to exercise its spending power to the extent of this capacity, it remains a potential policy instrument for federal administrations in the future.

Of course, Tables 1.1–1.3 provide a snapshot of the relative degree of decentralization at one point in time, but past studies of fiscal decentralization have shown that the provincial share of total fiscal resources has increased dramatically since the 1960s (Marchildon 1995). The real question is why there has been such a pronounced trend toward decentralization in Canada while, in other federations, there has been limited change, or even the opposite trend.

Erk and Koning (2010) found that federations divided into two groups. In those where there is linguistic homogeneity, the trend is toward greater centralization over time. In multilinguistic federations, the trend is toward greater decentralization because of the central importance of language to cultural identity and the ability of a national linguistic minority, which forms a majority in a constituent unit, to nation build using language as a differentiating feature within the federation. Québec's role in the Canadian federation, and its historic efforts to gain greater autonomy over numerous public policy domains, closely fits this hypothesis (Bourgault 2004; Béland and Lecours 2006, 2007). Although Quebec has taken the lead in gaining greater control over numerous policy domains, other provinces have followed its lead (Cameron and Simeon 2002). Three key policy areas have been selected to illustrate how provinces have assumed more provincial policy responsibility in recent years: 1) health policy, in particular universal Medicare; 2) immigration policy and the provincial nominee programs; and 3) internal trade and labour mobility policy.

MEDICARE

Although health care is largely a provincial responsibility, the federal government played a key role through its spending power in encouraging provincial governments to implement single-payer, universal hospital and medical care insurance plans (now known as Medicare) in the 1950s and 1960s. The provinces adhere to basic national conditions, and Ottawa can potentially reduce transfers to provincial governments that transgress the five criteria of the Canada Health Act, which are public administration, comprehensiveness, accessibility, universality, and portability. However, since the mid-1990s, when it unilaterally cut funding transfers to the provinces, the federal government has preferred to avoid confrontation with provincial governments on alleged breaches of the Canada Health Act. Instead, the Government of Canada increased transfers to the provinces for health care through agreements reached at the First Ministers' Conference of 2000, 2003, and 2004. The provinces were expected to report on specified health system indicators, perhaps because the federal government had been influenced by the use of benchmarking by central governments in other federations to improve the policy performance of constituent units (Fenna 2010). In the 2000 agreement, for example, 14 indicators in 3 areas (health status, health outcomes, and service quality) were identified, and an intergovernmental Performance Indicator Reporting Committee (PIRC) was established, which then generated 67 precise measures out of the 14 performance indicators. Two years later, federal, provincial, and territorial governments finally released a report on most of the 67 measures, but very limited progress has been made on this initiative since that time (Fafard 2012).

This model of joint accountability became a major flashpoint during the 2003 first ministers' negotiations when it became tied to the establishment of the Health Council of Canada. Québec and Alberta refused to participate in the new intergovernmental agency, but they nonetheless received their full share of the extra federal transfers ($34.8 billion over five years), which were ostensibly aimed at primary health care, home-based care, and catastrophic drug coverage. Having already opted out of the Health Council of Canada, Québec opted out of the 2004 agreement, but with its share of the transfer intact. A separate communiqué issued by the governments of Canada and Québec accepted that provincial government's "desire to exercise its own responsibilities with respect to planning, organizing and managing health services within its territory" (quoted in Fafard 2012, 39). Despite a significant increase in provincial transfer funding from Ottawa, little has changed in terms of the vertical (federal-provincial) accountability for Medicare or the horizontal (interprovincial) management of Medicare.

Since his election in 2006, Prime Minister Stephen Harper has moved the federal government even further from a joint governance role in Medicare. His government's unilateral decision to set the level of future Canada Health Transfer funding without any conditions leaves the provinces more clearly in the driver's seat in terms of setting the future direction of Medicare than at any time since its inception. Perhaps as important, the "Harper Doctrine" of downplaying executive federalism by eschewing any negotiation with the provinces over the future direction of Medicare and insisting on the provinces exercising their own responsibilities under section 92 of the Constitution, opens new possibilities in terms of interprovincial initiative (Norquay 2011). However, the institutional weakness of the Council of the Federation combined with the preference of most provinces to work alone rather than together means that the future of Medicare is more likely to be decided on a province-by-province basis than through interprovincial negotiation.

IMMIGRATION

According to the Constitution, immigration is a shared jurisdiction between Ottawa and the provinces (with federal paramountcy), but, until recent decades, this policy field was almost entirely occupied by the federal government. In the 1960s, Québec became an early advocate for greater provincial control over immigration, in large part to promote and protect the French language. In the past decade, other provinces have entered this field to fill key skill shortages as part of increasingly ambitious economic development policies. Although the federal government continues to set the criteria for immigrants in the family and refugee classes, the economic class now has two streams with two sets of criteria: the federal stream and the provincial nominee programs (Baglay 2012).

The provincial nominee programs (PNPs) have permitted provincial governments a major role in selecting economic-class immigrants to their respective jurisdictions, and most provinces have invested substantially in these programs in the past decade. Although some PNPs have been successful in recruiting skilled labourers, technicians, professionals, and entrepreneurs, they have been less successful in retaining them. Only the Manitoba PNP has been able to retain more immigrants than those residents who were originally federal economic-class immigrants (Pandey and Townsend 2011; Lewis 2010). However, the PNP programs have spurred the growth of immigration into Canada, and provincial governments now see immigration as a vital tool in their economic development policies.

INTERNAL TRADE AND LABOUR MOBILITY

Although there are no tariffs obstructing the flow of goods between provinces, provinces have often generated regulations and policies that have acted as barriers to the flow of goods, services, people, and labour among provinces. It was these non-tariff barriers that were the target of the Agreement on Internal Trade (AIT), signed by the provincial premiers and the prime minister in 1994 and implemented in 1995. However, the AIT was limited in its capacity to reduce or eliminate interprovincial barriers to trade until the 2009 amendments, which bolstered the labour mobility and dispute settlement provisions (Hansen and Heavin 2011).

At the same time, the AIT allows for provincial governments to enter into agreements with each other as long as they actually enhance trade, investment, and labour mobility among the parties. Thus far, there are at least three such agreements. The first was the Trade, Investment and Labour Mobility Agreement (TILMA) between British Columbia and Alberta, which was implemented in 2007 (Macmillan and Grady 2007). The TILMA has since been superseded by a tripartite agreement—the New West Partnership Trade Agreement (NWPTA)—implemented by British Columbia, Alberta, and Saskatchewan in 2010. An additional though more limited bilateral agreement is the Ontario-Québec Trade and Cooperation Agreement, which was implemented in 2009. These provincial efforts have had little or no federal government involvement.

The AIT and the bilateral and multilateral agreements that have supplemented it have facilitated a greater mobility of workers with a professional designation or occupation certified by a provincial regulatory body and of tradespersons that have undergone a provincial apprenticeship training program. Although other aspects of the

Canadian economic union are under firmer federal control, this is an area that is clearly the responsibility of the provinces, particularly since the funding and administration of labour training programs was formally "transferred" from Ottawa to provincial governments.

However, in areas where individual provinces are not willing to relinquish control, the AIT and the supplementary agreements have done little to reduce non-tariff barriers. The most obvious example of the limits of the AIT is in the policy area related to agricultural commodities. Provincial supply management schemes have consistently been protected by provincial governments, despite the fact that they act as barriers to trade among provinces and between Canada and other countries. Thus far, the AIT and the supplementary agreements between regional groupings of provinces have done little to liberalize cross-border movements in agri-food products covered under provincial supply management regulation (Coulibaly 2010).

Issues and Challenges

In looking at the next decade, provincial governments face two major policy challenges. The first is the gap between, on the one hand, provincial policy responsibilities and ambitions, which have grown in recent decades, and, on the other, provincial fiscal and administrative capacity. The gap includes the capacity (and willingness) of provincial governments to plan and act together to deal with the challenges and opportunities posed by policy overlaps and interdependencies. The second challenge is how provincial governments will respond to the demands of Aboriginal governments and municipalities, particularly larger urban governments, for greater autonomy, although the salience of this challenge varies considerably across the country. Although decentralization may appear to be a one-way ratchet between the provinces and the federal government, the dynamic is considerably more complex, and provincial governments may eventually be required to give up some power in restructuring their relationships with these emerging "local" governments.

FIRST CHALLENGE: RESPONSIBILITY VS. CAPACITY
As noted, federalism is the shared rule between two or more constitutionally recognized orders of government. In a decentralized federation, this shared rule is achieved not only through vertical

intergovernmental collaboration between the provinces and the federal government but also through horizontal collaboration among provincial governments. Despite the establishment of the Council of the Federation and the potential of interprovincial collaboration to address policy interdependencies, provincial governments have shown limited desire to work together in complex policy areas, although the recent initiative by the Council of the Federation in health care may yet prove to be the first significant policy initiative by the provincial governments since the social union initiative of the 1990s (Council of the Federation 2012). Although this historical weakness of the Council of the Federation and of its predecessor, the Annual Premiers' Conference, is no doubt a product of the voluntary, consensus mode of decision making followed at the interprovincial level, it is also a consequence of the large investment made by provinces in vertical (federal-provincial) processes, mechanisms, and institutions in the building and expansion of the welfare state. In recent years, there has been a determined effort by the federal government to avoid meetings of first ministers. If this trend continues, then provincial governments will no doubt invest correspondingly more in interprovincial processes, mechanisms, and institutions, such as the Council of the Federation.

The fiscal capacity of provinces to carry out their extensive policy responsibilities depends on their actual tax base. Although all provincial governments have extensive taxation powers under the Constitution, their tax capacity depends on individual and corporate income as resource taxation. Because this capacity varies considerably across the country, the federal government, through an equalization program created back in 1957, provides unconditional transfers to less well-off provinces to supplement their lower-than-average tax capacity. As stated in section 36(2) of the 1982 Constitution Act, the purpose of equalization is to enable less prosperous provincial governments to provide their residents with public services that are reasonably comparable to those in other higher-income and more resource-endowed provinces, a policy statement that has been entrenched in the Constitution since 1982 (MacNevin 2004). Thus, the fiscal capacity of these below-average provinces to exercise their extensive responsibilities will continue to depend, to some considerable extent, on the federal government's future willingness to use a portion of the revenues it collects to "equalize" the taxation capacity of the provinces (more on this in Chapter 3).

There is also the question of whether provincial governments have adequate leadership and intergovernmental skills to work more constructively with each other. Despite the fact that Canada has become a more decentralized country, some provincial governments—particularly those provincial governments that are most fiscally dependent on federal transfers—continue to expect Ottawa to take the lead in many provincial policy areas, at least in terms of funding and standards. Interprovincial policy leadership requires a change in this mindset, as well as a new style of political and bureaucratic leadership. In addition, new institutions and mechanisms are required, as well as the adoption of decision-making rules that allow collaboration in policy areas with majority rather than complete consensus support. Of course, these developments will be complicated by the demands of other governments within the provinces, including local and Aboriginal governments.

NEW CHALLENGES FROM MUNICIPALITIES AND ABORIGINAL GOVERNMENTS

Provincial governments have faced considerable challenges in coping with the self-government demands of Aboriginal communities within their territories and with the emergence of a third constitutionally recognized order of government. Fortified by a series of constitutional decisions by the Supreme Court of Canada and by the recognition of the rights of the "aboriginal peoples of Canada" in the Constitution Act, 1982, First Nations and Inuit have negotiated with several provincial and territorial governments various new treaties and land claims, as well as redress for the non-compliance with existing treaties (Abele and Prince 2006).

Perhaps as important as the courts have been the policies and resultant actions of both federal and provincial governments on Aboriginal treaty and land claims. Over time, it is their actions, and the resulting institutions that have been created, that have entrenched the right of Aboriginal self-determination within the Canadian polity (Dalton 2006). In most cases, the negotiated results of these land claims and treaties—with examples extending from the James Bay and Northern Québec Agreement to the Nisga'a treaty in British Columbia—have added additional asymmetry to an already asymmetrical federation, unleashing a debate about the merits and demerits of continuing down this course (Cairns 2000; Flanagan 2000; Palmer and Tehan 2007; Graben 2007). One significant exception to this asymmetry is the territorial government of Nunavut. Carved out of the eastern portion of the Northwest Territories, Nunavut was established in 1999 as a public government, but with its majority (85 per cent) Inuit population, it was also created as an Inuit self-government, an experiment that may end up having a trajectory similar to that of Greenland's establishment of self-rule as an autonomous country within Denmark (Loukacheva 2007; Henderson 2007). With the status of a territorial government, Nunavut is a full-fledged partner in federal-provincial and interprovincial structures and processes, including any First Ministers' Conferences and the Council of the Federation.

With the notable exception of Nunavut, Aboriginal governments, the most common of which are First Nations band governments under the Indian Act, are not integrated into the structures and process of Canadian federalism. As a consequence, they do not participate in shared-government forums and mechanisms except on an ad hoc basis (Abele and Prince 2003). Moreover, there is no concentration of other First Nations people or Inuit similar to that in the eastern Canadian Arctic that would allow for another large, geographically determined province or territory to be created similar to Nunavut. For this reason, the future of Aboriginal self-government would likely be viewed as a zero-sum solution by provincial governments, one in which provincial land, natural resources, and population would be removed from provincial jurisdiction to be administered as a part of a self-governing Aboriginal jurisdiction.

To some extent, this diminution of provincial jurisdiction has already occurred, but continuing federal responsibility for funding most of the services in such zones—the band governments of First Nations and their respective reserves, for example—has served to soften the blow. These funding arrangements have increasingly involved block transfers to Aboriginal governments as part of the process of self-government, and these transfers have permitted Aboriginal communities considerable autonomy in the allocation and administration of this funding. However, it is important to note that these are the early stages in the movement toward Aboriginal self-government, and any future policy shifts by the federal government, including changes to federal legislation such as the Indian Act or to the transfer system, would have a major impact on provincial governments and their approaches to the self-governing Aboriginal administrations within their territories.

At the same time, provinces are under significant pressure to provide more adequate funding to their own municipal governments. Constitutionally, municipal governments lack autonomy and, at least in legal terms, are creatures of the provincial governments, even if they play an important role in affording some degree of self-government at a local level (Sancton 2008; Magnusson 2005a, 2005b). Historically, their revenue sources have been limited—largely restricted to property taxes. In recent years, municipal governments and, in particular, larger municipal governments such as the large city governments of Toronto, Montreal, and Vancouver have become much more vocal in demanding tax transfers from both the federal and provincial governments to fund their considerable responsibilities. Although there has been only limited movement by the two constitutionally recognized orders of government in meeting the demands of city governments, it is likely that these demands will intensify in the future (Sancton 2011).

Strengthening this demand is the fact that local governments in Canada have less fiscal capacity than in almost all other OECD federations. In fact, the fiscal imbalance between the provincial and local governments may be as significant, perhaps even more critical, than any fiscal imbalance between the provinces and the federal government.

Conclusion

In all federal countries, there is a constant struggle to balance the shared rule of the provincial and federal governments—most often expressed as intergovernmentalism—and the autonomous rule of substate governments. This struggle is particularly evident in Canada, which has experienced rapid decentralization in recent decades. For the most part, the institutions and processes of Canadian federalism have not kept pace with this development, causing inevitable stresses and strains. Moreover, after years of public reinvestment and fiscal surpluses, the economic downturn and the reappearance of government deficits can only serve to increase the tension in an already tense federation, including exacerbating existing tensions of the relationship between provincial and municipal governments and between, on the one hand, federal, provincial, and municipal governments and, on the other, Aboriginal governments, organizations, and communities. Upcoming negotiations over equalization and federal transfers will reveal the extent to which provincial interests conflict with the interests of the federal government.

In this chapter, we have reviewed key concepts in intergovernmentalism, including the nature of constituent units such as provincial governments and their role in a federation that has a written constitution setting out the division of powers between them and the central government. As part of this, we have reviewed the balance between provincial self rule and national shared-rule that is common to all federations.

Although most federations have a dense network of intergovernmental mechanisms and institutions that address policy interdependencies, provincial governments have taken on the role of representing their "regions" due to the lack of an effective legislative instrument for regional representation in the federal order of government. As a consequence, intergovernmental relations through the executive level of government have played a major role in the Canadian federation. More recently, as the federal government has chosen to play less of a role in the social policy domains that it considers within the jurisdiction of the provinces (e.g., health care), there has been more emphasis on interprovincial organizations and mechanisms, such as the Council of the Federation, rather than on the traditional and more vertical organizations and mechanisms involving the federal government.

This movement reflects the growing trend toward decentralization, the third concept reviewed in this chapter. As is evident from a broad array of measures, Canada has become one of the most decentralized federations in the OECD, and the authority of the provinces over numerous policy domains has been a pronounced feature of the federation for some time. The reason for this trend to decentralization likely originates with the fact that one province, Québec, is home to the country's largest linguistic minority, a population with a strong collective identity that constitutes a majority within the province. In this province, public policy, particularly social policy, has been used as a tool for nation building. At the same time, other provincial governments have joined the Québec government in the demand for greater provincial autonomy and have taken advantage of the additional powers and policy responsibilities exercised by Québec, over time, in areas such as immigration and internal trade.

This chapter identified two key policy challenges for the provinces. The first is the gap between the provinces' increasing policy responsibilities and their fiscal capacity to carry out these policies and programs. One aspect of this challenge is structural—the limited taxation capacities of at least some provinces, as well as the institutions and programs, including the Council of the Federation, equalization, and the health and social transfers, that address these limitations. The question remains whether the skills and mindsets acquired at a time when the federal government played a larger role in the federation can be reoriented to a more provincially driven intergovernmental system.

Although provincial governments are in the ascendency in terms of the federal-provincial balance, they face challenges from other governments within their own borders. Aboriginal governments will continue to demand greater autonomy and greater fiscal independence from provincial authorities. These demands have a legal basis, supported as they are by the Constitution and treaty rights. Historically treated as "creatures of the provinces," local governments, particularly the larger city governments, have pursued greater autonomy and more fiscal capacity in the form of tax credits, transfers, and greater own-source taxation authority from provincial governments. As cities become ever larger, and as their importance as centres of economic, cultural, and social development and as magnets for immigration becomes more evident, provincial governments will have to be more responsive to the demands of local governments.

CHAPTER TWO

Provincial Administrative Institutions

Introduction

Contrary to the wishes of some of the key founders of Canada, the provinces have not withered away; indeed, they have proven to be capable and innovative policy and administrative actors. But as Canada becomes more decentralized, there is a need to better understand the role provincial states are playing as policy actors, administrative innovators, and deliverers of services to their citizens. Provinces have demonstrated again and again that they are eager to acquire more authority from the federal government and that they are capable of using it effectively. Not only can they succeed in their primary role as service deliverers but also they are capable of developing public policy. Yet provinces remain reluctant to shift power downward to the municipal level, whose governments find themselves in a situation not dissimilar to that of the provinces a generation ago, when provincial responsibilities were increasing but they did not have adequate revenues. This chapter examines provincial states as dynamic systems that are changing in response to the many pressures and tensions highlighted throughout this book. These changes are worthy of close examination; they will have a significant impact on how Canada will be governed in the near future.

There is a long list of dynamic forces that are having an impact on all of Canada's provincial states. This list would begin with Canada's Constitution and its countless federal-provincial agreements, partnerships, bilateral agreements, and informal understandings. In addition, there are the dynamic processes of federal-provincial relations, intragovernmental relations, and, increasingly, tripartite relations between the federal government, the provinces, and cities. Indeed, in the absence of any interest in constitutional amendment, administrative forms of action are more and more dominating coordination and cooperation between the various levels of government in Canada. As Ted Hodgetts (1964) noted three decades ago, our constitutional framework is very rigid, and it is within the public bureaucracies themselves, both provincial and federal, that we find much of the adaptation to changing conditions and the needs of Canadians that has provided the flexibility we need to function effectively as a country.

In this regard, Canada is different from most other federal states because so much of the growth of the modern state has taken place at the level of the provincial state. As suggested in Chapter 1, provinces regulate in a wide variety of fields, including housing, labour, and agriculture. They deliver most health services, education, and social services, and they own and operate their own utilities and other public enterprises, including banks, liquor distribution outlets, and auto insurance programs. One of the most significant elements in the growth of the provincial state has been the expansion of the welfare state, which requires provinces to be the actual service providers. As a consequence of this role, the provincial public services, especially in larger provinces such as Ontario and Quebec, now rival the federal government in terms of policy capacity. This development involves more than a dramatic increase in the size of provincial bureaucracies; the provincial governments have also undergone qualitative changes as they have sought to adapt to changing political, socio-economic, and technological conditions. As a consequence, they have taken on many more policy-related functions. Internal structures and processes have been transformed, along with the relationship between public servants, politicians, and citizens. Despite these alterations, long-standing questions of accountability, responsibility, and responsiveness remain primordial concerns and do not seem to be easily resolved in the face of growing pressures for new constraints on public services in the provinces.

Three dynamic forces have shaped the development of provincial institutions in Canada. The first is comprised of the issues around convergence among the provinces and their related role as policy laboratories. Provinces, of course, learn as much from failures as from success, but they tend to imitate one another and compete, such as for film production through generous tax credits, in tourism promotion, or through environmental regulation. Although each has a different regional economy, they are similar when we examine the overall pattern of provincial expenditures (see Chapter 3). The model of convergence continues in the similarity around institutional features such as decision-making processes and public service regulations, not to mention the similar array of government services. Though provincial political cultures vary widely and the pattern of political parties differs substantially, the overall range and arrangement of provincial state services are increasingly similar, coordinated, and regionally integrated.

Despite this convergence, differences can be observed among provincial institutions and service delivery structures. The one area in which we are witnessing significant change is in how decentralized the provinces are vis-à-vis their overall governance and administration arrangements; that is, some provinces have created more arms-length agencies, rely more on non-profit organizations, have privatized more, and make use of markets to bring about new forms of decentralized and non-departmentalized service delivery. Each province's place on the centralization-decentralization continuum tends to be unique, with history, tradition, and political forces resulting in a situation in which every province tends to have different governance priorities. Yet small provinces are more likely to have a more centralized system of service delivery, and larger provinces are more likely to rely upon a more diversified set of policy instruments in the delivery of their services. Provinces have been caught up in the currents that are shifting from direct government service delivery to a decentralized form of administrative practice (Frederickson and Smith 2003). Likewise, provinces have been caught up in the move toward collaborative forms of governance or toward a more networked approach that is part of a broader move in the direction of more involvement for stakeholders and a consequent increase in public scrutiny (discussed further in Chapter 5).

Finally, each province has a similar array of policy responsibilities, and each has local ambitions that are equally well understood, yet provincial states are caught up in a bureaucratic-political dynamic that requires increases in capacity building due to the pressures associated with growth resulting from both convergence and decentralization.

That is, provincial governments are acquiring more responsibilities (often due to the demonstration effect of other provinces) at the same time as they are expected to find new ways to deliver existing services. Provinces have thus begun to develop capacity in areas such as international trade, immigration, and environmental regulation, but they are unable to put enough resources into developing the necessary policy capacity within their individual public services due to ongoing issues such as fiscal sustainability, debts, and perceptions of their ability to manage existing programs without the addition of new and expensive burdens (Alberta 2007; Nova Scotia 2007).

This chapter will explore these three interrelated themes: 1) the growing convergence of provincial states and the factors that promote convergence, 2) the pressures toward greater forms of decentralized and collaborative public service delivery, and 3) the ongoing sense that provinces still struggle to match the policy capacity of the federal government as they are each faced with dynamic pressures to keep the provincial state as small as possible in the face of public resistance to both deficits and increases in taxation, either of which would be needed to expand provincial activity and capacity.

Key Concepts

We will begin by exploring several key concepts related to the provincial state that help define its role in broad questions of public policy and governance. The features of convergence, disaggregation, and capacity will inform each concept. This discussion will help us understand the dynamic features of provincial state institutions, which are now at the interface between governments, citizens, and interest groups. These institutions include the bureaucratic and political institutions providing the necessary support, advice, and policy and administration capacity that allow provincial governments to carry out their varied programs, develop their policies, and engage with civil society in unique ways. More specifically, the key concepts related to provincial institutional structure include the development of a professional public service in the provinces based on merit hiring; the presence of new, decentralized organizational forms to help deliver public policy in ways more open to citizen engagement and input; and the evolution of provincial decision-making structures from the classic departmental focus to an institutional or aided-cabinet process and, more recently, to the current premier-dominant model that exists in many provinces. This examination of the nature of provincial administrative and decision-making machinery will help to establish a common terrain, but it will also point to similarities and differences in the ways provincial state institutions function, to patterns of convergence and divergence, and to the ongoing struggle that provinces experience in managing their own ambitions and expectations. Although provinces converge on many policy fronts, differences remain as a result of the scale of their public service, their economies, their urbanization levels, and the scope of their dependency on federal transfers, to name some of the most prominent factors.

THE PROFESSIONAL PUBLIC SERVICE

Provincial public services are each the product of unique constitutional, political, economic, and social demands. But at the heart of each province's public service system rests a set of core principles that define the responsibilities and obligations of public servants, on the one hand, and politicians, on the other, and that continue to evolve in a common direction. Although they took a long time to reach their current level of sophistication, provincial governments had to adopt similar practices and values as a necessary precondition for their growth. Thus, in all provinces, there currently exists a sharp division of labour between permanent public servants providing ongoing advice and support and policy capacity and a changing cast of politicians who are expected to lead and animate the policy process (Aberbach, Putnam, and Rockman 1981). At the base of this system are a series of constitutional conventions that have come to be interpreted in a broadly similar manner in all provinces, and which set out the behavioural and policy roles of public servants. These conventions, most notably, include ministerial responsibility and public service anonymity and neutrality. This system's great asset is that it preserves the political neutrality of public servants, who can then serve successive governments without anyone being concerned about political bias on their part.

The origins of this particular approach can be traced back as far as 1854 and the Northcote-Trevelyan report in the UK, which first articulated the basic principles delineating a professional and independent public service designed to be the key source of policy support and advice for the governing party. In its ideal form, this system was to be self-regulating, with no political interference in the appointment of public servants. Ministers were to take all the policy decisions and be accountable for the activities of the entire ministry, and the public service was to provide independent advice and implement the policy decisions taken by cabinet. In this model, public servants are neutral and permanent and serve any government that comes to power with equal dedication and loyalty. Indeed, the neutrality of the system is based on the possibility of separating politics from administration, something that has come slower to some provinces than to others. Yet all provinces accept that public servants are to remain anonymous and politically neutral—and are not to be blamed publicly for the policy or administrative failures of ministers. Likewise, this model of professional public service requires that public servants refrain from partisan political activity or any public criticism of government and that they serve with equal vigour any political party forming the government. The role of the public service is to provide expert and frank advice to ministers in confidence in return for anonymity. It is expected that they will implement the policies of the government loyally, regardless of the political views they may privately hold (Kernaghan 1976).

The goal in creating a neutral and impartial public service has always been to create a sphere of non-partisanship that would allow all public servants to do their jobs more effectively and efficiently. To emphasize this fact, most governments initially restricted public servants from any form of political activity, including party membership, campaigning, political comment, and even voting (Juillet and Rasmussen 2008). Citizens would then have confidence that the public service was functioning in a neutral way and was dealing with the public fairly, equitably, and without favouritism. Creating a nonpolitical public service requires a commitment on the part of incoming governments not to fire senior personnel after their party takes office because to do so would create suspicions about the impartiality of the public service, which could potentially erode the trust between the public service, politicians, and citizens. Therefore, public servants in this model are granted tenure as long as they do their jobs well, and, in return, they use all their resources and policy capacity to respond to the legitimate political directions and policy preferences of the government of the day (Heclo 1977, 20).

Historically, provinces lagged behind the federal government when it came to creating this model of the professional public service, and they remain behind to this day. But provinces are clearly converging toward a similar model, one that preserves the administrative leadership of departments in the hands of career bureaucrats but allows some political appointments to the senior ranks of the public service. As a result of these political appointments, changes in the provincial governing party often result in turmoil in the senior ranks of the public service. Although provinces are moving to a less partisan model in which this sort of turmoil is less severe than in the past, there nonetheless remains a conflict between the more traditional requirements for the public service to be *neutrally* competent and the growing desire on the part of political leaders to have a public service that is more *responsively* competent—more eager to implement their particular agenda. Provinces have traditionally erred on the side of responsive competence and thus been less concerned with formal structures of bureaucrat independence than is the federal government, which has erred on the side of neutral competence. Each approach is problematic and creates its own set of difficulties for political leaders at either level of government. However, the model chosen by each province embodies these various values to a different extent and plays a role in the public policymaking and governance of that particular province. That is, some provincial public service systems embody greater levels of neutrality, and others accept higher levels of politicization (Gow 1976; Bernier, Brownsey, and Howlett 2005).

In some provinces, for example, British Columbia and Saskatchewan, where there are more patronage appointments after an election, it is generally felt that these new individuals are necessary to bring fresh policy ideas and approaches, that they help impose political control on the public service, and that their advice to governments will be more sensitive to the political implications of public policy. On the other side of the equation, other provinces believe that, by avoiding the principles of the professional, non-partisan public service, you lose experience and expertise, risk having public servants dragged into partisan debates, and lose much vital continuity with past decisions (Thomas 2010; Rasmussen 2000)—not to mention damaging the morale and motivation of public servants, who would be blocked from the senior ranks. So, despite their convergence on the *idea* of a professional public service, provinces legitimately disagree over the nature of the policy role of the professional public service, with some questioning whether the public service is capable of serving governments in anything other than an administrative role (Cameron and White 2000).

At the core of this debate is a balance that each province must structure, and the tendency is to allow greater political interference in senior appointments to the public service. Few provincial governments wish to insulate the public service entirely from political influence; they want to see it become responsive to the political preferences of the government. Thus, the notion that a neutral public service is capable of responding rapidly to new policy directions has never been fully embraced by Canadian provinces, where the concern is that bureaucratic growth has made public servants resistant to external influence. The other factor that insulates the public service from external pressures is the fact that the complexity of public programs and public policies in the provinces has created a situation in which the expertise in the public service is more specialized but also more central to the making of public policy. In most provinces, the large role that is played by public servants in policymaking, coupled with the stability provided by social and economic rules and regulations, has created concerns about the political biases of public servants and their role in the overall direction of the public services, leading politicians to search for a host of alternative sources of advice.

The concept of the professional public service is intimately tied to the adoption of the merit principle in each of the provinces. The merit principle came later to the provinces than to the federal government, but it is now well entrenched and protected by both public service legislation and strong collective agreements. Merit is a key concept in creating a system of good governance, as it allows for the order and stability that the provinces need to pursue their expanding public policy agenda. Provinces remain committed to this system for similar reasons, and their commitment began to develop in the 1960s, when they started to need skilled public servants able to take on more complex functions, so the provincial government could exercise the full range of its jurisdictional authority and expand into new governance areas as well.

Policy adoption is rarely uniform across provinces, and almost every aspect of the growth of merit hiring has seen some provinces act quickly and others lag behind. What were the reasons behind the lag in the adoption of the merit system, which was adopted as early as 1918 in British Columbia and as late as 1962 in Prince Edward Island (Hodgetts and Dwivedi 1974)? As with any convergence, both province-specific as well as national factors likely fuelled its speed; thus, we should not expect to find a regular and predictable pattern in the adoption of merit across the provinces. Not all provinces will accept a particular reform, nor will all those adopting it do so at the same time or for the same reasons. There is no simple pattern of reform that touches one province and then moves like a virus to the rest: it is something that has an internal logic, based as much on local factors as on national trends.

None of this is to suggest that patronage has been eliminated in provincial states, all of whom deploy a vast array of local patronage in the form of appointments to boards, commissions, crown corporations, and countless other agencies across provincial jurisdictions. However, some attempt has been made to increase the transparency of this process. This is particularly the case in British Columbia, which created a Board Resourcing and Development Office in 2001. Yet this provincial attempt to bring about board appointments based on merit, transparency, and constancy remains unique in Canada.

The one common factor that all provinces share has been a need to ensure that their development of merit-based employment practices did not conflict with the rise of public sector unions and new collective agreement obligations. Public sector unions came on the scene in Canada in the 1960s, and, again, followed the familiar pattern of provincial emulation and policy transfer. Aside from Saskatchewan, which was the first province to allow public sector unions in 1947 under the umbrella of the existing Trade Unions Act, all other provinces have created a special legislative framework for dealing with public sector unions, and each has made similar provisions regarding merit and other aspects of the employment environment, such as essential services.

Another significant causal factor in the adoption of a merit system is related to the presence of electoral competition, and, in a province such as Alberta without a strongly competitive party system, there was little incentive to abandon patronage in favour of improved services to constituents (Johnson and Libecap 1994). The economy is also a key factor in predicting reforms to the public service, as well as the level of urbanization. But reform is also political, in that when you are shifting your governing arrangements, you are also picking winners and losers. Thus, the fact that provincial leaders managed to eliminate some forms of patronage and yet have managed to maintain patronage at more senior levels shows their ability to adopt an idea that has broad popular currency such as merit, while retaining important patronage levers to help them remain in control.

ADMINISTRATIVE REFORM

The rise of public service unions in the 1960s and 1970s, which continue to be a strong and vocal presence in all provinces, has produced a counter-reaction aimed at improving the quality of the public service and a general awareness of the need for its improved management. Since the 1980s, there have been urgent concerns expressed in most provinces centred on how to ensure that this new, more assertive workforce would maintain both its professionalism and its commitment to efficient, citizen-centred service delivery. Although provincial administrations accepted the arrival of unions, they have equally embraced the managerial revolution that has swept through the world since at least the 1970s. Provincial governments became very interested in giving more authority to public managers, including authority over personnel matters, and finding new, decentralized, and arms-length means of policy implementation. This mantra of the "New Public Management" (NPM) movement from the early 1980s wanted public managers to be given more responsibility to manage and politicians to focus more on their policy and strategic planning role. What this ideology has meant in practice is a shift in the responsibilities of the central personnel agencies, which now became more important leadership actors in the entire area of personnel management and management reform. They were not only to eliminate patronage but also to facilitate and implement a better system of personnel management to ensure that the public service had the skills, leadership, and capacity to deliver on the (often contradictory) commitments of politicians in an increasingly performance-conscious environment.

At the core of this concept is the need to balance efficiency with effectiveness in a more decentralized system of public policy implementation. As provincial governments grew, they also experienced changing assumptions about how to deliver programs to their citizens, and, although they were concerned with efficiency, this concern came to be only one of the many competing values they had to pursue. The effort to pursue efficiency in the delivery of services is a key aspect of administrative reform in each province, and, likewise, each province has, to varying degrees, looked toward decentralized models, often derived from private-sector experience, as a way forward. There has been an ongoing concern about measuring outcomes and outputs, yet provincial governments have struggled to find ways of measuring efficiency and productivity. This search has, if anything, become even more frantic as the costs of government continue to escalate, as many provinces see deficits rise, and as ever more efforts to contain costs come forward.

Equally problematic has been the issue of the effectiveness of policy implementation. Many of the complex, multidimensional problems provincial governments have to deal with—such as health care, homeless strategies, youth-at-risk initiatives, or support for urban Aboriginal populations—are difficult and unpredictable. Provincial governments must offer services to multiple clients effectively, but this requirement means that each client group will have different demands and a different sense of what is satisfactory. Provinces, much more so than the federal government, are on the forefront of making trade-offs between these various clients and values, and they face growing demands in Canada's most complex policy domains. These complexities are reflected in the administrative machinery, which is itself growing in complexity because of the growing number of partnerships and contracts that provincial governments manage as well as the increasing need for collaboration, community engagement, greater transparency, and interest group scrutiny.

Administrative reform is a key concept in public management, and changes have occurred in all provinces with regard to the structure and integrity of the public service. Common changes have occurred in human resource management, public service renewal, accountability regimes, and reorganization and restraint initiatives, and a variety of new arms-length organizational arrangements have been instituted, including public-private partnerships. Indeed, by some standards, significant downsizing, such as the "Common Sense Revolution" in Ontario, qualifies as public service reform, and all provinces have done this, often multiple times. Of all the reforms mentioned, retrenchment tends to be something that affects all provinces at various times, and, indeed, more often than not, many other positive reforms fall victim to massive expenditure reduction plans that provinces are compelled to engage in. Retrenchment usually involves some combination of staff cuts, restructuring that emphasizes greater authority at the top of the public service coupled with decentralized administrative organizations, and substituting technology for people with the aim of improving service delivery (Loreto 1997). Retrenchment can take a toll on ideas to improve service innovation, apply new technology, and seek out synergies among ministries because of the heavy front-end investments these activities require. On the other hand, the sustained pressure to find savings and to maintain service levels has itself led to innovations in line ministries and central agencies. Owing to the magnitude of these changes, provinces are often compelled to improve less-central administrative processes, such as communications within ministries, to help ensure the effective development and implementation of complex public policies.

Public services in the provinces have been buffeted by many pressures and remain in the midst of tremendous change and flux. In the 1990s, even governments without much commitment to NPM-style reforms or to the retrenchment of public expenditures, such as the NDP in Saskatchewan, backed comprehensive administrative reform and promoted retrenchment aimed at responding to economic pressures and furthering their policy priorities (Rasmussen 2001). At other times, provinces such as Alberta and Ontario have been much more proactive on the reform agenda, promoting the "Alberta Advantage" and the "Common Sense Revolution," respectively, which had tremendous consequences in both provinces and provided a great opportunity for other provinces to learn from their successes and failures (Tupper and Gibbons 1992; Cameron and White 2000; Taft 1997).

Although we may have seen the end of the major reform efforts of the past, smaller-scale innovations continue to occur, including new ways in which public service professionals exchange ideas and information among specific units using, for example, tools such as "best practices," a theory and technique developed to delineate standard and effective ways of doing things, and developing a "community of practice" through which to share experiences and knowledge. There are now a variety of forums in all provinces that are used to promote communications among those charged with developing policy and innovation within ministries. These often extend across jurisdictions and result in learning and imitation. Yet provincial public servants are often perplexed about the extent, direction, and diversity of the reforms with which they must cope. Surveys indicate that they are overloaded with demands and receive little guidance about what is important and how to balance trade-offs. This situation leads to an important question about public service overload and its consequences for policy development and service delivery. Early in the 1990s, provincial officials often argued that overload was the price of managing in the public service: good managers had to juggle many balls, and the best could keep most in the air while accomplishing the tasks critical to the missions of their ministries. As a result of this overload, of course, many innovations and ideas would not be taken up unless they were connected with the most urgent priorities. Moreover, some senior officials have suggested that continuous change and overload, though jarring and confusing, is the only way to make bureaucracies move. Yet the consequence of this activity has been growing insecurity and low morale throughout provincial public services, particularly after the announcements of consolidations and expenditure control plans—which are made under the continual mantra of doing "more with less" (Clark and Swain 2005).

Public service reform can occur for very different reasons: it can be driven by policy objectives, budgetary imperatives, or conceptions of sound management practice. But, in the end, most public service reform has not been management driven but has largely been aimed at meeting policy and budgetary priorities. Most critical decisions about the trajectory and shape of the provincial public services have been made by the central agencies most responsible for policy and budgetary concerns, namely, executive councils and departments of finance. The opportunity to put management concerns, both within and across ministries, on the table at the front end of the process seems to have been lost, though this loss may have been inevitable given the magnitude of the changes set in motion by the expenditure reductions and budget crises of the 1990s. Although provincial governments are devoting more attention to management, they continue to draw on ideas that have been circulating for years or on ones having good currency in the private sector.

All of this implies relinquishing a control posture on the part of central agencies who now must work cooperatively with line ministries, facilitating the exchange of information and best practices across the entire public service while still keeping line ministries attentive to corporate and government priorities and, sometimes, intervening to ensure that departments are addressing these central priorities. Besides creating the capacity to adjust and finding new ways to manage change, provincial governments can reduce the uncertainty and tension engendered by significant change by articulating a new vision of the professional public service. Many provinces have begun to do just this, calling for the renewal and rejuvenation of the career public service. In the case of provincial public services, most of which will be getting by with a smaller core over the next few years, this revitalization need not mean the public will be short-changed or that a professional public service will be weakened.

PROVINCIAL DECISION MAKING

With government growth and public service reform ongoing, cabinet decision-making systems have also been radically adapted, reflecting not only the personal style of the incumbent premier but also the past decisions and structural reforms that have accumulated to produce new structures and processes. In all provinces, the cabinet is the final decision-making body, but, aside from in a crisis situation, the cabinet, as a whole, only considers decisions after they have been reviewed and vetted by departmental staff, central agency staff, designated deputy minister task forces, and various cabinet committees, not to mention the senior staff of the premier's office. In most provincial decision-making systems, ministers and their officials begin the policy elaboration process and then take their policy ideas to cabinet—or to a committee of cabinet in order to have this committee further elaborate the policy before its submission to cabinet for a final decision. Often, the deputy minister to the premier and the premier's chief of staff have a prominent voice in who should be included in the decision-making and vetting processes.

Issues of a financial nature are most often referred to a treasury board, which, in most provinces, is the cabinet committee with responsibility for financial matters. Indeed, each province has a financial administration act, which requires that certain issues must be presented to the treasury board for approval. In every province, the treasury board is chaired by the minister of finance and is generally supported by members of the department of finance. Most other issues are considered by a planning and priorities committee of cabinet, but there are other committees of cabinet in all provinces that deal with social issues and economic development issues, respectively. Often, these committees have some form of ongoing secretariat support from permanent public servants.

One new feature of cabinet decision-making structures is that they are now more elaborate and very much infused with visible public consultation and engagement exercises that are supplemented by groups of deputy ministers providing bureaucratic support; by executive council officials, including cabinet secretariats; and by cabinet committees. Of course, traditional tools such as regulations and orders in councils also affect cabinet decision making. The increased use of mandate letters is an additional constraint that shifts power toward the political arm of government and especially to the premier. These letters are now used by incoming premiers to guide new ministers by outlining the premier's expectations of the minister and ministry; they are the first minister's attempt to create a sense not only of accountability and purpose but also of control. This overall complexity produces a decision-making process that is opaque to many outside and inside government, including even cabinet ministers, who feel that they are often left out of some decisions. This new emphasis on engagement and consultation adds to a structure of public policy formation that is increasingly elaborate, often centred on the premier as the final arbiter, and, in most cases, very slow and cumbersome. Yet this unwieldy structure does not diminish the ability of cabinet to establish regulations and orders in councils as ways to move its agenda forward.

Along with the more elaborate decision-making structure has also come a broadened understanding of which officials constitute the chief executives of a provincial government. These include the secretary of the cabinet, the deputy minister to the premier, the chief of staff to the premier, the director of communications for the premier, the ministerial members of the treasury board, and the top intergovernmental affairs officials. In addition, the executive branch can use several tools, such as orders in council and appointments to semi-independent agencies, in order to add to its power and that of the premier.

Not surprisingly, the growing institutionalization of provincial cabinets has had a major effect on the executive branch in all provinces, particularly on how public policy is formed and decisions are made. Cabinet structure has both changed and been changed by power relations within cabinet, often with the consequence, both intended and unintended, of more powerful provincial premiers. The full cabinet appears to have been overshadowed as a decision-making centre, but planning and budgeting have also grown in both complexity and complementarity, firmly concentrating decision making at the top of the hierarchy. This strengthening of the decision-making role of the top executives is greatly aided by the growing importance of the chiefs of staff in ministerial departments, all of whom are appointed by and report to the premier.

Yet what is telling about these reforms has been the way that innovative provinces have seen their ideas move quickly to other jurisdictions, including the federal government. Early reforms that have occurred in one province often have been adopted by the federal government and other provinces. Innovations such as central planning offices, treasury board systems, and streamlined budgeting processes all followed this route (Johnson 2004; Dutil 2008).

DEPARTMENTAL ORGANIZATION

Because of their enormous constitutional obligations, provincial governments have grown more rapidly in the past 20 years than the federal government when we include those public servants employed in health care, universities, and K-12 education (see Table 2.1). The same constitutional arrangement that caused the growth of the provincial public administration also resulted in a distribution of functional departments that is remarkably similar in all provinces. Although it might be hypothesized that we would see differences in the departmental organization of the various provincial governments, based on different provincial economies, regional factors, and size, the fact remains that there is a remarkable similarity in provincial organizational architecture. That is, the provinces, though varying in size and population, have all assumed a similar organizational structure, which, at its core, means they have a large number of small departments.

Despite the similarities in overall structure, provincial governments have developed some organizational differences in response to individual provincial policy needs and different levels of growth. At one time, it would have been possible to state that PEI and Ontario had roughly the same number of ministries (Hodgetts and Dwivedi 1976, 345), but this is clearly no longer the case. Less populated provinces have fewer ministries than more populated provinces: for example, PEI now has some 14 departments and 11 cabinet ministers and Ontario has 30 departments and a cabinet of 28. A mid-sized province, Saskatchewan has 18 ministries and 18 cabinet ministers (see Table 2.2). Yet the basics of a consistent departmental structure exist in each province and mirror the growth of various political constituencies with different policy demands.

The need for provincial governments to respond to a growing number of policy demands has resulted in more or less continuous reconfigurations of government units, even in the smaller provinces. What has happened as a result of this growth is that cabinets have not grown beyond an upper limit, but some ministers hold multiple portfolios that extend across departments and agencies. That is, to keep the size of the cabinet relatively small, the premiers have given their ministers multiple departmental responsibilities and additional staff to coordinate. Even so, in many provinces, the size of the cabinet is often large in proportion to the party's legislative caucus. A relatively large cabinet has some positive consequences because it is a good thing to have small departments that are more manageable; this arrangement can give real meaning to the concept of ministerial responsibility. Yet larger departments have some advantages too: if governments locate common activities within a single department, some planning and

TABLE 2.1 Government Employment, 1991–2011

	1991	2001	2011
Federal Government	415,387	351,331	427,069
Provincial Government	378,716	342,746	356,830
Health and Social Services	746,190	711,476	859,889
Universities	276,826	299,977	382,871
Local Government	362,221	459,549	607,746
School Boards	525,512	605,308	680,297
Crown Corporations	149, 331	131,158	148,340

Source: Statistics Canada, Table 183-0002—Public Sector Employment, Wages and Salaries, Seasonally Unadjusted and Adjusted, Monthly, *CANSIM (database).*

TABLE 2.2 Total Number of Provincial Government Ministries and Total Number of Ministers in Provincial Cabinets, 2012

Government Ministries (Departments)	BC	AB	SK	MB	ON	QC	NB	NS	PEI	NL
Total # of Ministries	17	24	16	19	28	26	18	18	11	16
Total # of Ministers in the Cabinet	17	23	18	19	28	28	18	14	11	18

overall coherence can occur and some forms of performance management can have a realistic effect and lead to positive outcomes in terms of accountability. Smaller departments, on the other hand, are a bit more human scaled and can appear accessible to citizens as clients of the services.

Departments, no matter what their size, also tend to seek independence. Thus there has been a growth in the number of strong control agencies that reduce the capacity of departments to govern their own affairs and, as a result, increase the likelihood that these departments will preserve a sense of their own responsibility. All departments, but particularly small ones, can become captured by stakeholders and clients that are well organized and effective in lobbying, and thereby lose sight of the broader public interest. Again, this danger of capture is part of how the departmental structure and governance arrangements affect the nature of policy outcomes in all provinces, and reflects the growing policy ambitions of all provinces, including small ones.

Having many departments means that a government needs several policy coordination mechanisms, among which, at the top of the organizational chart, would be cabinet itself. Cabinet is always the primary decision-making body in government and controls the executive branch of government. Although cabinet dominates the executive branch (as well as the legislative branch if the government holds a majority), the growth of activity in all provinces means that cabinets cannot realistically remain genuine decision-making bodies for all matters and have been supplemented by elaborate committee systems. Committees of cabinet can allow for the more efficient allocation of cabinet resources and help expedite the agenda of government.

There is also the issue in each province of the more or less continuous shuffling of departments as governments attempt to respond to changing demands. Thus, we witness constant dismantling, reshuffling, renaming, and restructuring of provincial government departments. Governments are not institutionally adapted to this sort of rapid change, and the public service system has proven resistant to it. When reform does occur, it is often in the form of new requirements for additional reporting and accountability and, as such, creates new constraints associated with change and the need to develop new organizational loyalties promptly to help resist the change.

All provincial governments have departments in areas of exclusive jurisdiction that often have no federal corresponding unit. One obvious area is municipal affairs. All provinces have departments of municipal affairs, but the federal government has no equivalent and has chosen to maintain no institutionalized presence in this area, despite pleas from cities to get directly involved in urban affairs. Aside from an experiment in 1970 with a ministry of state for urban affairs, the federal government has decided to avoid having any ongoing coordinating mechanism. Another example is the area of education and post-secondary education. All provinces have a department of education, and most have one that is exclusively focused on K-12 education and another that focuses on the post-secondary system. The federal government, again, has no institutional or organizational presence in this policy area, and Canada is one of the few OECD countries that does not have a central department of education (Wallner 2010).

As suggested in Chapter 1, there are other areas in which jurisdiction is shared, such as agriculture and immigration (Constitution Act, 1867, section 95) and old age pensions (Constitution Act, 1867, section 94A), which have an overlapping of departmental organization between the federal and the provincial level. That is, each provincial government has some version of a department of agriculture, as does the federal government. Until recently, provinces outside Québec did not have a department of immigration, but all provinces are creating larger immigration branches, and some of these branches have moved to full departmental status, such as the one in Ontario. But, in most other areas, departmental patterns are very similar in the federal and provincial governments, and there appears to be a principle of informal concurrency at play.

In general, there are differences among provinces related to key economic and geographical features. For example, British Columbia and Newfoundland and Labrador, coastal provinces, have provincial ministries of fisheries, but Saskatchewan and Alberta, landlocked provinces, do not. Tourism and recreation, forests and natural resources, the environment, and energy are seen as important portfolios in most provinces, but the focus obviously varies from province to province. Industry and commerce ministries exist in all provinces. Transportation departments concerned primarily with roads and highways exist in all provinces, but they have been supplemented in recent years by ministries of infrastructure.

Yet provinces have also added to their institutional burden by interpreting the Constitution's property and civil rights clauses in a manner that means they have accepted large burdens on their budgets for health, social services, and labour. Because of the federal government's lack of constitutional authority and, often, its diminishing interest in policy areas such as housing, provinces increasingly have had to come up with new departmental responses, sometimes through the coordinated efforts of multiple departments, to deal with complex horizontal policy problems such as homelessness.

Because of the ongoing difficulty in finding adequate policy responses to many complex problems, horizontal agencies with the responsibility for coordinating cross-cutting policy issues have developed. Thus, aside from public works and the traditional finance or treasury functions, each province now has a large and increasingly powerful department of executive council with the premier at its head. At least as significant has been the growth in horizontal coordination in areas of cross-cutting responsibility, such as Aboriginal and Métis affairs and women's initiatives; increasingly, offices dedicated to health promotion, to seniors, and to children and child welfare now have coordination secretariats (Malloy 2003). But perhaps the oldest and most prominent structure for provincial policy coordination is found in the formal intergovernmental machinery, which requires an examination of its own, as it is perhaps the key reality on the ground for provincial public policy formation and coordination.

THE GROWTH OF INTERGOVERNMENTAL FUNCTIONS IN THE PROVINCES

In 1954, the first agency to deal with intergovernmental issues was established in the federal government, and it was situated in the department of finance (Pollard 1986). Likewise, the first provincial intergovernmental units were found in departments of finance. Often, these units were created in response to perceptions that the federal government was threatening provincial interests (Leeson 1987). It is no surprise, then, that Québec was the first province to develop an intergovernmental agency in 1961. By 1971, all the other provinces had established an intergovernmental unit to manage federal-provincial fiscal negotiations (see Table 2.3). The 1970s witnessed an acceleration of this pattern, when provinces established individual ministries or central agencies of intergovernmental affairs outside of the departments of finance. Smaller provinces have their intergovernmental affairs branch or agency report directly to the premier (see Table 2.2). And, although the provinces have developed these agencies at different times for different reasons, they are often the consequence of the demands put on governments because of conflicts over resources or agriculture and, increasingly, over responsibilities in areas such as social services, health, immigration, and international relations.

Initially, intergovernmental tensions were driven primarily by a series of fiscal matters, which were outlined in the previous chapter. But, beyond the issue of fiscal disputes and coordination, there is a growing and compelling need for both intergovernmental and intra-governmental collaboration and coordination, as a response to the problems of overlapping jurisdictions and the need for regional and national policy coordination. There are many formal financial and administrative agreements between the provincial and federal governments and, as already noted, by the 1960s, it was apparent that a permanent mechanism needed to be created to address the necessity of more federal and provincial cooperation. Yet, in the area of interprovincial relations, provinces have been less successful and, indeed, have rarely been able to find a united front in dealing with the federal government or collectively advancing common interests. In policy areas such as education and the environment, governments have managed

TABLE 2.3: Number of Departments with Intergovernmental Units of Jurisdiction, 1985 and 2003

	1985	2003
Alberta	2	9
British Columbia	1	8
Manitoba	2	3
New Brunswick	1	2
Newfoundland and Labrador	0	6
Nova Scotia	0	2
Ontario	1	4
Prince Edward Island	0	3
Quebec	7	16
Saskatchewan	1	1
Canada	8	11

Note: Intergovernmental Associations (IGAs) and finance departments are excluded, and Nunavut was not created until 1999.

Source: Johns, O'Reilly, and Inwood (2007).

to develop some institutional capacity, but, generally, efforts of inter-provincial cooperation have been carried forward by small groups of regional ministers supported by a small number of public servants.

Despite a modest institutional presence, from a policymaking point of view, intergovernmental activities have often overshadowed the role of legislatures and Parliament and have given premiers and prime ministers and senior departmental officials a considerable amount of influence, often shutting out interest groups as well as legislators in the formation of many important policies in key areas (Meekison 2004). Thus, elite or executive federalism still remains a reality and represents a closed door that shut outs not only citizens but also interest groups, who are often presented with final settlements and accords negotiated in secret. Though this top-down approach is slowly changing in areas such as Aboriginal policy, it remains a preferred mechanism of policy development in areas of overlapping jurisdiction, such as the environment, for example.

A trend that is having significant influence on the provinces is that federal programs and services are more and more frequently being directed to individuals rather than through their provincial governments. The federal government provides support to students, parents, seniors, and others directly and no longer relies on provincial partners to administer programs. Likewise, issues of national interest such as the economy, resource development, trade, transportation, and communications can be advanced by federal unilateral action, with the federal government often using regulatory power. What this means is that provinces will be trying to maintain and, indeed, expand their jurisdiction while resisting the growth of unilateral federal action.

If anything, there continues to be a desire to expand the machinery of intergovernmental affairs in a variety of ways. Most recently, the tendency is to include international affairs as part of the mandate of intergovernmental affairs offices. Another interesting development in this area has been the growth of intergovernmental units in traditional departments of government (Johns, O'Reilly, and Inwood 2007). Because there are so many multilateral and bilateral intergovernmental agreements and partnerships, there is more inter- and intragovernmental activity in many areas of exclusive provincial jurisdiction, including health, education, and trade. We are also witnessing the development of regional cooperation in some of the most intractable areas, for example, interprovincial trade, with the establishment of new agreements such as the New West Partnership Trade Agreement (NWPTA) between BC, Alberta, and Saskatchewan. Thus, intergovernmental offices have been gaining new, wide-ranging policy responsibilities, ones extending well beyond traditional federal-provincial and intergovernmental activities, and these offices can be expected to grow in importance and influence in the years to come. With increased pressure for regional coordination on the environment, the economy, and labour mobility, provinces will all be ramping up this part of their organizational machinery.

Issues and Challenges

THE DISAGGREGATION OF PROVINCIAL ADMINISTRATIVE ACTIVITY

As noted, provinces engaged in a variety of reform activities over the years, and they continue to engage in reforms that often have as their goal disaggregation of the provincial organizational apparatus. In the end, however, these reforms have meet with relatively little success. The first and most influential wave of this activity entailed privatization in the 1980s, and provinces were often the leaders in this movement. Many controversial privatizations took place in provinces, including the sale of the agricultural and environmental laboratories, mining operations, airlines, and so on. This trend began to slow down in the 1990s as provinces came to see the limitations of privatization and, specifically, of the privatization of elements of government regulatory functions. Privatization problems in particular: first, private sector contractors often faced conflicts of interest; second, complex and costly contract-monitoring arrangements were required to ensure the quality of work performed by contractors; and, finally, failure of the contractual arrangements had implications beyond the contract itself, ultimately affecting the provincial government's ability to achieve its regulatory and or policy objectives (Winfield 2002).

That provinces should have been leaders in the area of privatization is not surprising—they were also leaders in the creation of the first generation of Crown corporations. Provinces established Crown corporations first for natural monopolies such as utilities before expanding their use into more generic province-building activities in areas such as banking and the development of resources, industry, and infrastructure. These Crown corporations also represented a ripe target for right-of-centre governments in the 1980s who saw them as opportunities for state disaggregation because they were already structurally differentiated by their arms-length status from core government activities and were engaged in competitive sectors of the economy and had numerous rivals.

Yet, despite the temptation to privatize provincial Crown corporations, a notable feature of the privatization process at the provincial level was its tentative nature—its reluctance to follow the lead of the federal government and one of the tenets of the privatization orthodoxy, which was simply to sell the entity to the highest bidder or have a public share offering. Beginning in the 1980s, provincial governments offered various inducements to government employees to get them to become private-sector contractors or to take over the enterprise outright. To further this goal, provinces even accepted uncompetitive bids from employee groups, contradicting their own primary objective of privatization—to increase efficiency based on competition.

What the efforts in the direction of the privatization of government-owned corporations reflected was a continuing trend toward a greater reliance on the market and an attempt to better manage the resources of the provincial public sector. But advocates of privatization, often provincial governments themselves, assumed that it would yield quick gains in efficiency and windfalls in cash, neither of which occurred. Provincial governments have had difficulty in completely disentangling themselves from the corporations they privatized. In fact, there were often complicated links between the government and the entity being privatized. These links were built up over time and were essential to the performance of the entity, either as a public or as a private corporation. For example, for fear of public backlash, governments continued to protect provincial employment even after privatization (Munro 1989).

After the initial push toward greater privatization in the 1980s, we can observe a relative cooling off of this impulse. There has, in fact, been a stable level of public enterprise employment among the provinces over the past 20 years. From a peak of 172,835 employees in this sector in 1981, employment has stabilized, with employment in 2011 at a similar level as it was in 1991. As for the various privatized corporations, the provinces continued to use these for similar reasons as in the past, including the facilitation of economic growth, the redistribution of income, and overt province-building activities associated particularly with utility ownership (Chandler 1982). When we examine the transformation of Crown corporations at the provincial level, it is perhaps not surprising to find that they remain a popular tool for provincial governments who, due to their limited levers for macroeconomic management, look to a variety of instruments that they can control to help manage their economies. Despite the many governments that have been friendly to free enterprise in Canada over the past 20 years, Crown corporations remain a key aspect of provincial public policy and appear posed to remain so for the foreseeable future.

THE PREMIER AS THE FOCAL POINT OF POLICYMAKING

Provincial governments have for decades been described as "premiers' governments" to reflect the very broad set of powers that premiers have always had, in contrast to those of the prime minister, which, until recently, were considered more circumscribed, especially in the event of a minority government, by greater media and interest group scrutiny and so on (Morley 1996). There is, then, a continuing awareness within all provinces that the premier's role is a focal point for the development of policy and for decision making. This rise of the preeminent premier is part of a descriptive argument that sees provincial decision making moving historically from a departmentalized cabinet, in which the cabinet was the only decision-making body, to an institutionalized cabinet divided up into a variety of committees with strong bureaucratic support and finally culminating in a premier-centred cabinet (Dunn 1995; Bernier, Brownsey, and Howlett 2005). According to this argument, all provinces have witnessed the replacement of the unaided (or traditional) cabinet by the institutionalized (or structured) cabinet, which has, in turn, been replaced in many jurisdictions by the dominant-premier model. In other words, unstructured and relatively uncoordinated central executives in all provinces have given way to those that are more structured, more collegial, more prone to emphasize planning and coordination, and more focused on the decisive role of the premier (Tennant 1977). The factors promoting initial cabinet institutionalization in all provinces were a mixture of ideology, pragmatism, and historical precedent unique to each province. Indeed, some provinces moved farther toward the dominant-premier model than others. Both endogenous factors (those growing from within government) and exogenous factors (those emerging from the outside environment) affected the persistence of institutionalized cabinets. They were common to more than one province, but their relative weight differed among provinces and premiers.

Premiers have always had a great deal of authority, and a rapid examination of the powers they currently exercise makes this clear. They appoint deputy ministers and the heads of crown corporations, as well as other key officials in executive government, and they have a veto on the appointment of many other employees. They set the agenda of cabinet, determine the composition of cabinet, and dominate the party apparatus and even the party nomination process. In addition, the premier and his or her staff can oversee public administration and a very large range of policy priorities and can monitor the policy activities of cabinet ministers. It is obvious that the premier will continue to be the focal point for decision making in the provinces, even more so than the prime minister is at the federal level.

PROVINCIAL-MUNICIPAL RELATIONS

One of the vexing issues faced by all provinces is the issue of municipal-provincial relations, which has undergone several transformations, including, recently, the move away from a conditional grant structure to a more stable funding process in which some provinces are providing tax revenue in the form of a proportion of the provincial sales tax (PST) to municipal governments as part of transfer arrangements. Yet provinces continue to dominate municipalities through either overt control mechanisms or conditional grants, and the relations are often quite tense due to the fiscal gap between a province and the poorer local governments (Graham and Phillips 1998; Feldman and Graham 1979). Although municipalities raise almost 80 per cent of their budgets from their own sources, primarily through property taxes, there are increasing expectations that provincial transfers should increase as they take on a larger role in service delivery and face enormous infrastructure costs (Siegel 1980, 2006).

One dominant theme since the 1990s has been greater municipal autonomy. Several provincial governments have undertaken legislative changes to provide greater autonomy for municipalities, which has allowed these municipalities the discretion to act on local matters without specific provincial authorization. In spite of these moves toward more municipal autonomy—local government in Canada remains heavily dependent on the legislative, program policy, and financing decisions of provincial governments. All provincial governments have ministries primarily devoted to municipal affairs with responsibility for overall municipal legislation and the conduct of relations with municipalities, and most provinces have programs that directly affect municipal activity (Steunson and Gilbert 2005).

Other players in municipal-provincial relations are the associations of municipalities, which have long been on the scene. These municipal associations act as a common voice for municipal governments when they deal collectively with the province, and, traditionally, they have been a very influential policy voice. Because larger and more urban municipalities have different points of view than the smaller, more rural ones, some provinces have two or more municipal associations. In New Brunswick, Ontario, and Manitoba, there are separate associations for primarily francophone municipalities (Steunson and Gilbert 2005). Provincial government personnel and cabinet ministers frequently attend the annual conferences or other meetings of these associations to explain provincial policies, obtain feedback, and roll out policy announcements. Some forms of consultation are even more institutionalized. For example, Ontario has an Advisory Committee of the Municipal Engineers Association, which meets on a regular basis with the minister and officials of the Ministry of Transportation and Communications. These sorts of arrangements exist in most provinces and continue to reinforce the elite or expert policymaking behaviour in areas of provincial-municipal policy development. Despite all this access, larger municipalities are left facing serious infrastructure gaps and increasing social service demands on top of stagnant or declining revenue capacity.

Nowhere is the gap between municipal fiscal capacity and new policy responsibilities more apparent than in the issue of immigrant settlement, which is increasingly landing on the doorstep of municipal governments. Municipal governments see immigrants as an opportunity for economic growth, but they also represent a threat to budgets if municipalities are expected to finance adequate housing, solid economic prospects, and an opportunity for a high quality of life. Many of these basic responsibilities fall to urban governments, but municipalities feel increasingly isolated from the new focus on collaboration between provinces and the federal government, which they feel excludes them from a meaningful role in crucial decisions that pertain to their jurisdictional responsibilities. And they are probably right to worry, as most provinces now have in place significant and ambitious immigration strategies that focus on provincial needs but that rarely articulate a significant role for municipalities and provide little in the way of resources.

POLICY DEVELOPMENT AND THE CAPACITY OF
THE PROVINCIAL PUBLIC SERVICES

As explored earlier in this chapter, the question of the role that the provincial public service should play in policymaking is highly contested, and, increasingly, provincial governments are looking for ways to reduce their previous dependency on the public service in policy development while simultaneously recognizing their lack of capacity in dealing with other provinces and the federal government. In larger provinces, this capacity issue is often solved by using consultants, public affairs firms, lobby groups, and other policy advocates who can provide policy advice directly to the minister and cabinet. There is clearly an evolving relationship between the public service, the policymaking process, and the external policy environment in each province, and this dynamic context is creating an ongoing challenge to find the appropriate policymaking role for the public service, one that balances the provision of policy advice with its primary responsibilities for policy implementation. Changes to institutional structures are important indicators of the ferment within the governance agenda as it affects provinces. There is a clear challenge to the traditional model of decision making, which often had public servants at the centre. The new model is marked by the growing presence of political staff in ministers' offices, a growing number of arms-length bodies and organizations with independent authority, the use of management and audit boards, and the provision of services through alternative agencies, such as non-profit organizations. Although smaller provinces might have difficulty in creating this sort of a machine, in all of the larger provinces, we can see the decline of a public-service-prominent system and the rise of a more politically centred system, a change that reflects the growing competitive nature of provincial politics and the need for policymaking to reflect greater political sensitivity.

Yet the declining policy capacity within the public service can be blamed only partly on this more ideological and politicized style of making policy. Provincial politicians have always had more conflict in their relationship with the public service, owing, in part, to the fact that provincial politicians feel that they are much closer to policy problems and are more likely to assert their knowledge and understanding of the facts on the ground. They believe they have as much capacity and more legitimacy than public servants when it comes to assessing policy problems. Another potential cause of the decline of policy capacity is simply the deteriorating fiscal position of provincial governments, which increasingly lack funds for new policy initiatives. Still others might argue that the combination of growing public scepticism and increased reliance on public consultation has made policymaking more difficult and limits the latitude given to provincial governments when it comes to taking autonomous action.

There is a clear perception that the public service's overall ability to provide advice and to be a significant source of *trusted* policy advice have both eroded, and this view presents a significant challenge to a provincial government that still seeks to adopt and implement "good" public policy (IPAC 2011; CPRN 2009; Baskoy, Evans, and Shields 2011). Indeed, it can be easily speculated that the factors that are eroding the policy development capacity of the public service have, ironically, made the capacity to deal analytically with policies even more important. At a time when provinces are facing budgetary shortfalls and interconnected problems, the ability of the public service to engage in policy analysis is vital to achieving political goals. Likewise, if governments are being bombarded by policy advocacy from the private and non-profit sectors, not to mention the federal government and other provinces, then they should want to deploy more resources and better tools to sort through the conflicting positions presented by self-interested organizations. But this is not the direction in which most provincial governments appear to be moving.

Provinces are looking for new sources of policy advice to deal with capacity problems while they devalue the role of their own policy advisors. As a result, provincial governments have driven some of their more talented individuals either out of government or to the federal arena. Even if provincial politicians were interested in better policy advice from public servants, there are now questions about the ability of the public service to find the necessary personnel resources to deliver this advice. As one recent study of provincial policy capacity noted,

> Provincial and territorial analysts, like their federal counterparts, are highly educated. . . . But they do not tend to have a great deal of formal training in policy analysis and mainly work in small units deeply embedded in provincial and territorial ministries. . . . They lack substantive knowledge in the areas in which they work and of formal policy analytical techniques and tend to bring only process-related knowledge to the table. They also tend to work on a relatively small number of issue areas, often on a "firefighting" basis. . . . [They] can be thought of as working in an interactive "client-advice" style somewhat removed from the traditional "rational style" promoted by . . . policy schools. (Howlett and Newman 2010)

A final general consideration about the policy role of the provincial public services centres on the importance of policy development associated with the horizontal dimension of government policy. Provinces are still organized around "stovepipes" that link functional experts at all levels of government with interest groups and with other advocates within the policy area (Atkinson and Coleman 1992). This ongoing isolation of policy issues and the separation of one set of programs from others have long impeded effective governance, and there are growing concerns about coordinating policies within and across provincial borders (Aucoin and Bakvis 1993). Policymaking capacity, therefore, increasingly implies being able to work across the conventional functional definitions of policies and being able to make strategic and redistributive choices among programs. Provinces appear to be making only tentative steps in these directions, despite their best intentions.

Provincial governments as diverse as the Devine government in Saskatchewan in the 1980s, the Rae government in Ontario in the 1990s, and the Charest government in Québec have all moved to shift the focus of policymaking away from the public service toward elected officials. Thus, professional policy capacity has been diminishing at the same time as provincial policy ambitions have continued to grow. The result is that the previous trend of relying on professional policy analysis appears to be weakening. This reduced reliance on professional policymakers is associated with the weakening role of expertise generally and with the weak causal relationship between analysis and good policy more broadly. These concerns lead to questions about whether more policy capacity and more deliberative policy processes are related to the level of policy innovation that is a current preoccupation in most provincial capitals. Indeed, the answer that most provinces appear to be offering is that, because of greater centralization at the political level and in light of the goal of smaller core governments generally, the role of provincial governments as incubators of innovation at the provincial level should continue and, indeed, become even more rapid in the future, despite their diminished policy capacity.

PROVINCES AS ADMINISTRATIVE AND POLICY LABORATORIES

One of the issues at the forefront of provincial economic and social development will be the continuing ability of provinces to innovate in terms of how they organize their service delivery activities and how they relate to their citizens and other constituencies via consultation and dialogue. In the past, they have been very innovative. They pioneered the use of Crown corporations as a tool of government policy; modernized cabinet decision-making structures; initiated programs of disaggregation and decentralization that included initiatives such as alternative service delivery, privatization, public and private partnerships, and contracting out; and led the way in the use of information technology and citizen-centred service delivery. There has also been a great deal of policy diffusion and convergence in this agenda across provinces and even up to the federal government (Carroll and Jones 2000). Though there are significant differences between and among provinces, they have arguably been able to innovate faster than the federal government, and with fewer resources, and we have witnessed a flow of innovation, often from the provincial level to the national level in certain areas of public administration and service delivery (Borins 2001). The question for the future is, how much innovation of the policy development and service delivery functions are we likely to see from provinces?

Most provinces are now more conscious of the need to innovate than they were in the past, and each has a broad innovation agenda, both for itself as an organization and, more broadly, for the economy as a whole. There is an acceptance that innovation is a key factor in future economic success in our knowledge-based economy, and most provinces are promoting a combination of initiatives centred on research, workforce development strategies, infrastructure development, greater competition, improved access to government services through innovation in program delivery, and a host of programs to attract educated and entrepreneurial immigrants. Likewise, they are developing strategies to leverage money from both the federal government and the private sector. These federal and private development initiatives are attractive for most provinces, as they focus on increasing skills, increasing interactions between business and government, and strengthening communities—all of which are things that provincial governments feel they can influence with their existing machinery of government and which focus on their citizens and their economies. Thus, we see a common pattern, with provinces creating targeted initiatives centred on existing departments such as the recently renamed BC Ministry of Jobs, Tourism, and Skills Training or Manitoba's Ministry of Innovation, Energy and Mines. Whether or not the focus on innovation will bear fruit remains to be seen, but this trend clearly has a significant attraction for all provinces.

Provinces have often been innovative and deserve to be recognized as the pioneers they have been. Whether it was in the use of Crown corporations such as Ontario Hydro (Freeman 1996), the establishment of cabinet decision-making structures in Saskatchewan (Johnson 2004), or the extensive use of public-private partnerships in Ontario (Mylvaganam and Borins 2005), provinces have been vigorous innovators of service delivery and policy development, despite lacking the capacity of the federal government. Likewise, they have been shamelessly willing to accept ideas developed in other provinces and will imitate successful policy developments and avoid obvious failures.

This trend will undoubtedly follow the usual pattern of policy development that is based on imitation and convergence. When we look at the traditional pattern of policy diffusion across provinces, we witness a series of beggar-thy-neighbour policies in which provinces feel compelled to offer similar tax breaks, economic incentives, and money for research and development so as not to lose out to other provinces. Whether they offer tax credits for film production, mining incentives, or small business development grants, the result in the past of much provincial intervention is inefficient, wasteful, and, ultimately, a futile attempt to hold back the tide of market forces. It can be argued that, in the past, provinces have more often ended up striking poor deals with corporations, supporting incompetent firms, and grasping desperately at investment opportunities regardless of their fit with the provincial economic milieu (Borins 1986). One can hope that polices aimed at promoting innovation and the knowledge economy will be better managed and, indeed, more innovative than those previously followed.

Conclusion

The provincial state is undergoing a great deal of transformation, and the pace of change shows no sign of letting up. Whether the issue is institutional decision making, public service delivery, or evolutions in the role of the premier, provinces in Canada remain innovative and, compared with the federal government, quite nimble and daring. The provincial state and its component institutions make up a dynamic and changing set of relationships among public servants themselves, the organizations in which they work, the politicians for which they work, and the public to which they provide services. These relationships occur within the context of a single national system with predictable subnational variations.

What we have seen is that, although there is considerable convergence taking place at the provincial level in Canada, at times encouraged by an aggressive federal government, more recently, convergence is occurring through a more natural process of policy transfer and learning. In areas as diverse as performance measurement to health reform, provinces are clearly emulating each other. This convergence of approach in policy and policymaking is taking place in an environment in which provinces are more capable policy actors, but their ambition to master their own destiny is limited by constitutional realities, limits in analytical capacity, and ongoing competition with the federal government and other provincial governments. In addition, provinces have responded to ongoing fiscal pressures through a series of disaggregating measures involving greater reliance on arms-length bodies, non-profit organizations, and public-private partnerships, all of which exacerbate coordination problems.

When we examine changes across time, it is clear that the Canadian provincial state has changed tremendously since the early 1960s, when the growth of the welfare state was beginning to gain momentum. All provinces have undergone growth in size and purpose and, as a consequence, have been under almost continual managerial reform and restructuring. Bureaucracies within the provincial state have also suffered a series of attacks by politicians of almost every political stripe who have accused these bureaucracies of being wasteful, inefficient, and unable to deliver good value to citizens. Despite this stark assessment of the capacity of the state apparatus, provincial politicians have continued to take on more and more responsibilities for new and emerging social and economic problems. Within this changing dynamic, public servants have lost their privileged status in the policy process, yet they nevertheless continue to maintain a crucial role in policy development and service delivery, despite the varied efforts to reduce this influence (Hood 2005).

The implementation of public policy is the essential other half of the public policymaking process. It is the final stage of the policy process in which, after the policy debates and ratification by the legislature, policies are handed over to the various public and quasi-public organizations that implement them, including universities, schools, regional health authorities, and countless agencies and departmental units. However, at this stage, public policies get altered and are adjusted to meet the circumstances on the ground. Also, evaluations take place to determine if the policies are actually meeting their goals, and measures are established to report back to legislatures on the progress toward goals. Although it is possible to define the delivery of services to citizens as merely the product of the administrative state, this definition does not adequately grasp the role that the provincial state plays in the ongoing evolution of public policy in some of Canada's most crucial policy sectors.

Future research on the growth and operation of provincial state institutions should focus on the relationship among the democratic institutions associated with policymaking, most notably, the executive and, to a more limited extent, the legislature, civil society actors, citizens, and, of course, public servants. What is of concern for the purposes of this book is the provincial state as an organization that pursues the objectives of provincial governments, particularly the development and implementation of public policy. Consequently, we focus on the organizational and personnel structures of provincial governments, both of which have been under almost constant pressure to reform since the mid-1980s. Future research should also recognize the democratic role of public servants and their continuing relevance as part of the provincial state that supports broader definitions of democratic engagement.

To understand successfully the role the various institutions of the provincial state play in public policy requires that we see each particular province as a distinct system that is responding to the local economic and social dynamic. Thus, we begin with one basic assumption—that institutional systems vary across provincial jurisdictions and that this variation is worthy of study in and of itself. The fact is, we have provincial administrative cultures that shape policy outputs and form part of the practice of governance in various provinces (Bernier, Brownsey, and Howlett 2005). In this sense, we argue that the different provincial state systems affect policymaking and policy outcomes in ways as profoundly as do the different economic characteristics of the provinces.

This chapter has examined the proposition that provincial governments have structured their institutional arrangements to further their policy goals and pursue their agendas within their borders. There are both substantial differences and growing convergence among the provinces in terms of how they structure their administrative and decision-making institutions, how they use their administrative capacity, and how they innovate in the organization of their executive branch, especially in terms of how traditional their organizational structures continue to be. Growing attention has begun to be paid to the provincial state in Canada as these questions begin to appear more urgent and in need of more careful analysis and systematic examination (Lindquist 2000; Bernier, Brownsey, and Howlett 2005). However, the empirical basis of comparative study is relatively weak and undertheorized in Canada. Most of the existing research has been vaguely comparative, while another stream of research has investigated how and why provinces have innovated or otherwise done creative things regarding public administration in Canada. Yet it is evident that provinces have been continuous innovators in the development of public policy as well as in the use of new administrative structures designed to develop and deliver those policies (Poel 1976; Chandler 1982).

In the end, provincial institutions are difficult to analyze because they are parts of a distinct political system. This fact imposes the problem of whether and how to aggregate the 10 provinces. For example, when we seek to measure the policy and organizational capacity of provinces, is it meaningful to speak of the total number of provincial public servants or crown corporation employees, or is it necessary to break down all data by province? Do aggregated findings reveal general trends, or do they obscure significant differences among provinces? A related question is whether quantitative variations result in qualitative differences. Is the policy process in smaller provinces fundamentally different from that in larger provinces? Can we safely assume, for example, that New Brunswick's public service operates similarly to Ontario's, which is 10 times as large, or are its operations fundamentally different? Answers to such questions will go a long way toward helping us understand the dynamic role that the provincial state plays in developing responses to some of Canada's most complex policy dilemmas.

CHAPTER THREE

Taxing and Spending

Introduction

As Chapter 1 explains, fiscal arrangements are critical to the federal bargain. To understand the taxing and spending powers of the provinces, one must appreciate Ottawa's powers and responsibilities. Yet provincial fiscal policy is more than a direct reflection of federalism. The provinces and territories have considerable autonomy in meeting citizen demands, and provincial patterns of taxation and expenditure reflect different requirements, opportunities, and challenges.

Taxation and expenditure are powerful policy instruments. Taxation obliges citizens to surrender their assets for benefits that are unlikely to match their preferences perfectly. For this reason, suspicion accompanies all public budgets. Some think that governments tax and spend to maximize votes. Others believe that transfers of funds cannot be justified because terms such as "the public interest" are empty concepts. Still others are cynical because each budget represents simply an incremental adjustment on the preceding budget.

These suspicions often give rise to other concerns. Because governments set budgets into law, what is to stop provincial governments from seeking to meet an endless list of demands? Will some interests appeal to the finance minister and claim an increasing share of provincial spending without justification? Or, perhaps, governments will mismanage their taxation powers so that private investments dry up, people stop spending or invest elsewhere, and the provincial economy contracts. And what about the federal government? Will it decide that its problems are more important than those of the provinces and decline to transfer funds to help balance the books?

To reassure citizens, guide policymakers, and ensure that taxes do not generate inefficiencies, economists have suggested principles to help form an optimal tax regime. As important as it is, efficiency is not the only criterion in creating such a system. Economists generally agree that the tax system should also display vertical equity: people with different abilities to pay should be expected to make different contributions to societal welfare. Similarly, the tax system should also be fair regarding horizontal equity: those who are in equal or virtually equal positions should be treated equitably (Musgrave 1959).

The search for an optimal tax regime has helped clarify the trade-offs between efficiency and equity, but it has not produced a consensus. The provinces, for example, with their dissimilar economies, have neither the same tax systems nor the same spending requirements. In addition, there are legitimate political disagreements on how much efficiency to trade for how much equity and on the ways in which different tax regimes affect macroeconomic conditions. The provinces are now considering how to reduce corporate taxes, for example, in part because they are widely interpreted as a drag on investment. But not everyone is prepared to accept that general trends in taxation, for example, lower corporate taxes, represent long-term positive developments.

The quest for optimal taxation is complicated by the desire to provide tax exemptions to certain groups of taxpayers or for the purchase of certain commodities or services. Often referred to as tax expenditures, these deductions or tax credits change savings and spending patterns, but they also reduce revenue by shrinking the tax base. For those who decry loopholes, tax expenditures are anathema; but for those who believe taxes promote charitable giving, for example, or encourage physical activity or education, tax expenditures are legitimate tools of public policy.

As a result of these different perspectives, economists have declined to produce a blueprint for taxation and most are circumspect regarding how taxes should be spent. Provincial finance ministers would not follow such a taxing and spending blueprint even if it were available. Much depends on the ambitions of governments. Some are inclined to allow markets to set the conditions for the provision of public goods such as health services and car insurance. Others see a larger role for governments in improving public welfare. Balancing spending and taxing is the goal of most finance ministers, but the opportunities for disagreement are significant. And then there are economic management considerations: for example, should provinces balance their budgets annually, or should they use their taxing and spending powers to smooth out fluctuations in the economy?

Can we really expect provincial governments to satisfy all the demands associated with taxing and spending and avoid the temptation to indulge special projects or to focus on re-election? It is easy to be cynical. But public finance in the provinces is not just about politics. It is about economics as well, and about how provincial governments, with growing economic power, balance the requirements of sound public finance and sound politics. Taxing and spending are at the heart of this balancing act. They involve myriad judgments, and on each budget day these judgments are bundled into a single document. Over time, they have created some discernible patterns and have given rise to some specific long-term concerns.

Key Concepts

Several key concepts, some of which are contentious, are crucial to our understanding of the theory and practice of public finance. This section introduces these concepts and examines their underlying (and different) meanings as well as the measurement issues they raise.

GOVERNMENT SIZE AND GROWTH

An important issue in public finance is government size and growth. Oddly enough, little disagreement exists on how to measure government size. Most studies use the ratio of government expenditures to total economic activity, either GDP (gross domestic product) or final domestic demand, which removes net exports from the GDP calculation. Government growth is due not only to increased ambition but also to higher input costs (Berry and Lowery 1984, 745–46). Governments do not face the same cost structures as the rest of the economy because their purchases of labour and services do not occur in markets with clearly discernible outcomes. Finally, what counts as government spending is debatable, especially when one government is transferring funds to another. In that case, who is spending? And should universities and hospitals be counted as government spending (as they are in this chapter) when provincial government cost control is relatively limited? If they do not make stipulations and corrections, researchers can assess government size very differently using what is ostensibly the same basic measure.

FISCAL IMBALANCE

The term fiscal imbalance is used to describe the relationship between the taxing and spending profiles of federal and provincial governments. One feature of this alleged imbalance, usually referred to as vertical fiscal imbalance, is premised on the idea that the federal government's tax sources are much greater than its expenditure responsibilities whereas, in the provinces, precisely the opposite is the case. Whether this is the right way to conceive of vertical imbalance is addressed later. Note, for now, that, in the past several decades, provincial expenditures have grown more than federal expenditures. At the same time, the federal government has increasingly disentangled itself from funding provincial programs.

Two other fiscal imbalances are horizontal imbalance and structural imbalance (Dahlby 2005). Horizontal imbalance refers to the differential capabilities of the provinces to raise revenues. The disentanglement of provincial and federal affairs and the decentralization of power and responsibilities that increases provincial autonomy are welcome developments as long as provincial economies grow fast enough to keep up with demands. Unfortunately, this growth has not occurred everywhere, leading to demands for compensation by the poorer provinces. Horizontal imbalance has led, in particular, to equalization payments in recognition of different provincial tax bases. Failure to address this problem would likely result in the migration of labour to areas of high fiscal capacity with consequent efficiency losses. Horizontal fiscal imbalance has also been criticized for offending the principle of equity. If, as many have argued (e.g., Boadway 2003), citizenship norms and the Constitution Act, 1982 (section 36[2]), give Canadians the right to receive the same level of services no matter where they live, then equalizing spending capacity is a necessity.

Structural fiscal imbalance refers to the tendency of different provinces to rely disproportionately on different revenue sources. These differences set up incentives to purchase and invest in one province rather than another—incentives that have nothing to do with the price and quality of goods and services. Efficiency costs are made worse because major spending areas, such as health, are not funded with equalized dollars, providing provinces with fiscal incentives to spend in some areas rather than others.

EFFICIENCY AND EFFECTIVENESS

All provincial policymakers want their taxing and spending decisions to be efficient and effective. Efficiency is the most recognized criterion for evaluating the uses of tax dollars. Efficient organizations produce more desired outputs with less costly inputs, which implies that the efficiency criterion is based on the assumption that conservation is preferable to waste. It is possible, of course, to waste resources by efficiently supplying public goods that people do not want. Normally, the efficiency criterion is invoked on the assumption that what is produced is valued. But that need not be true, which is why it is legitimate to ask if the taxing and spending decisions of government are effective; that is, do they result in outcomes that people want?

While efficiency describes the best use of money, time, and effort, the effectiveness criterion focuses on how to conceive of the goal to be achieved. Efficiency, an historically constructed norm closely associated with economics, is virtually synonymous with economizing. Effectiveness, on the other hand, is a political criterion. Governments want to be effective in achieving the goals they have chosen. Choosing what to tax and what to spend involves judgments about both efficiency and effectiveness. Although they often go together, sometimes they work at cross purposes, such as when political goals trump efficiency or when the only legitimate goals seem to be those that can be realized with relatively few resources.

DEFICIT AND DEBT

Deficit is the difference between what a government raises and spends in a given year, and debt refers to the borrowing that a government undertakes to support its expenses accumulated over the years. Debt can be short-term (treasury bills with maturities between one month and a year) as well as long-term (10-, 15-, 25-year provincial and municipal bonds) and represents governments' liabilities. Excessive debt sends a negative signal to the markets, as it represents a future burden and the diversion of resources even in a flourishing economy. The federal government's attempts to reduce its deficits in the late 1980s, for example, floundered because it underestimated the cost of debt obligations in an environment of increasing interest rates.

Experts distinguish between cyclical and structural deficits, the former being associated with intentional stimulus to the economy and the latter with a situation in which program costs are, at equilibrium, persistently underfunded. A structural deficit means that even at the end of a cyclical downturn, when the economy returns to former productivity levels, a deficit continues to occur. In Canada, the federal government's structural deficit is negligible or non-existent; at the provincial level, several provinces have structural, not merely cyclical, deficit problems.

FISCAL RULES

Broadly speaking, fiscal rules are all the rules and regulations that govern how budgets are drafted, approved, and implemented. More narrowly, they refer to deliberate restrictions placed on the possible outcomes of budget making. These restrictions are agreed to by legislatures and are intended to govern all budget making, thereby constraining current and future politicians and bureaucrats. Fiscal rules place restrictions, including constitutional constraints, on fiscal indicators such as the budgetary balance, debt levels, spending, or taxation (Kennedy and Robbins 2003, 2). They typically stipulate a numerical target for a fiscal indicator (for example, spending must not exceed specified levels), and these targets are easy to operationalize, to communicate, and to monitor (IMF 2009). Among the most common of rules are those that require all budgets to be balanced, tax increases to be subject to a referendum, and increases in debt levels to be authorized by legislatures.

The idea behind fiscal rules in the creation of budgets is that the political process does not reward governments for behaving in a socially optimal manner. A competitive political process is sometimes accused of inducing certain tendencies, such as a short-term focus to improve the immediate chances for re-election or a deliberate increase of the public debt to discourage successors from embarking on alternative policy agendas. Fiscal rules apply external pressures on decision makers, depriving them of political flexibility in exchange for fiscal stability.

"CROWDING OUT" EFFECTS

"Crowding out" refers to the supposed harmful effects of government debt, which can crowd out private investment by raising interest rates or by replacing private investment with government expenditures. Whether these effects exist, how large they are, and whether government spending might actually improve private sector productivity are the subjects of ongoing debate. Crowding out has also been used to suggest that public spending in one category, such as health care, reduces expenditures in others. Appreciating expenditure categories and their potential for crowding out other public services helps us to understand the dynamics and dimensions of government growth.

"RACE TO THE BOTTOM"

It is widely assumed that provincial governments, or any subnational political units, will be tempted to engage in competition with one another to attract human and financial capital. One possible result has been described as a "race to the bottom," in which competing jurisdictions reduce taxes, relax environmental standards, and shrink social assistance payments (Harrison 2006). This type of competition results in downward spirals that, even if they do not converge on the policies of the most aggressive and least generous government, at least produce suboptimal equilibria. These include outcomes that would not have been chosen by the electorate, do not meet efficiency criteria, and are widely perceived as unfair to vulnerable populations.

It is not clear, however, that governments will invariably seek to undercut one another or that firms and individuals will always be attracted to jurisdictions with the most lucrative packages of goods and services. Moreover, central government policies, especially those that stipulate minimum standards of service or that make funding conditional on meeting established benefit levels, can mitigate provincial competition. In Canada, provincial taxes on business, for example, have increased over time, undermining the popular view that tax competition inevitably leads to smaller government (McKenzie 2006). Provincial social assistance, which generally trended downward during the 1990s, was more generous in some provinces than in others. Yet its uneven provision showed no evidence of creating strong "neighbour" effects, whereby generous jurisdictions become "welfare magnets" for low-income citizens living in nearby provinces (Boychuk 2006). There is reason to pay attention to the danger that provinces may converge on suboptimal policies but not a lot of evidence that the "race to the bottom" is currently the dominant dynamic.

Realities on the Ground

THE GROWTH OF PROVINCIAL GOVERNMENT

If government size is the ratio of government spending to gross domestic product, what constitutes government spending? Most students of public finance (Petry et al. 2000; Imbeau et al. 2001) use an inclusive definition that begins with *net current government expenditures.* These are outlays for goods and services, including wages and salaries, and are the largest component of government spending. They comprise approximately 60 per cent of government spending across the provinces. *Transfers to individuals,* the next largest category, include payments such as employment insurance, scholarships, compensation benefits, and pensions. *Government gross fixed capital formation* includes capital expenditures on buildings, roads, machinery, and equipment. Finally, *transfers to business* include subsidies on wages, interest, and the purchase of equipment. Rounding out estimates of government size are *debt-servicing* payments, which are included in calculations of government size because they are part of the cost of delivering public services.

The ratio of government spending relative to the size of provincial economies remained fairly constant between 1989 and 2008. The peak value occurred in 1991 when government represented 23.1 per cent of the final domestic demand. In 1996, after the federal government had restructured provincial transfers in the previous year, the provinces experienced a trough in terms of their size. For the next five years, almost all the provinces reduced their expenditures in absolute terms. As Table 3.1 shows, in all provinces except Newfoundland and Labrador, per capita spending decreased between 1994 and 1998. Since then, government size as a percentage of final domestic demand has remained fairly constant, although the composition of government spending has changed. Note, as well, that provincial governments differ in size. As Figure 3.1 reveals, Ontario, the most populous province, has traditionally had the smallest public sector relative to the size of its economy. The next smallest governments are those of Alberta and British Columbia. Likely, these larger provincial governments operating in provinces with growing economies can achieve both managerial economies of scale, efficiencies resulting from opportunities for division of labour and specialization, and lower costs of borrowing (financial economies of scale).

TABLE 3.1 Per Capita Expenditures (2002 = 100) and Gross Total Expenditures as a Percentage of Total Provincial GDP, 1990–2008

PROVINCE	1990	1994	1998	2002	2006	2008
NF	7077.2	7421.2	7589.3	8469.9	9286.2	7489.7
	35.0	35.2	32.5	26.8	26.3	19.3
PEI	6794.8	8869.7	7014.0	7967.5	8296.3	8781.9
	33.0	40.5	28.3	29.5	28.3	29.3
NS	6366.7	5969.3	5918.1	6425.5	7086.4	7764.0
	28.1	26.4	23.8	22.2	23.5	24.8
NB	6088.8	6803.6	6732.0	7314.4	7860.6	8925.5
	28.5	30.3	27.5	25.9	25.2	28.2
QC	6345.1	7177.4	7012.0	7985.9	8548.1	9197.6
	24.1	26.9	24.4	24.6	25.2	26.5
ON	5281.0	6152.6	5577.2	5692.9	6698.3	7130.3
	16.1	19.1	15.8	14.4	16.2	17.2
MB	6870.9	7200.1	6886.2	7464.5	7519.8	7877.9
	25.6	26.8	23.2	23.6	22.0	22.3
SK	8018.3	8288.9	6769.8	7655.6	7342.5	6169.8
	29.1	27.8	20.3	22.2	18.7	15.1
AB	7747.6	7610.5	6769.0	7536.4	6243.9	6307.3
	19.9	18.0	14.5	15.6	11.7	12.0
BC	5823.6	6547.9	6614.9	7142.2	6323.5	6604.0
	18.8	21.4	21.5	21.2	16.8	17.6

Source: Authors' calculations based on data from Statistics Canada, Table 384–0002: Gross Domestic Product (GDP), Expenditure-Based, Provincial Economic Accounts, Annual (Dollars), CANSIM (database).

Although government employment is not generally favoured as a means of assessing government size, it is worth noting that wages and salaries constitute about 75 per cent of net government current expenditures. The cost of public sector employment is a concern for all provincial governments, and public sector employees are the traditional targets of cutbacks as governments attempt to signal fiscal prudence. Those efforts have not had a dramatic impact on the size of provincial public services, but remember that these services have not grown very much in either absolute or relative terms.

FIGURE 3.1: Average Provincial Government Size as Percentage of Final Domestic Demand, 1981–2007 (per capita, real 2002 $)

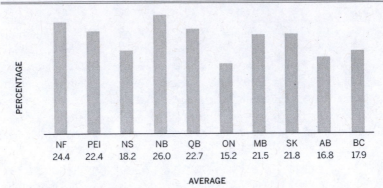

	NF	PEI	NS	NB	QB	ON	MB	SK	AB	BC
	24.4	22.4	18.2	26.0	22.7	15.2	21.5	21.8	16.8	17.9

AVERAGE

Source: Authors' calculations based on data from Statistics Canada, Table 385-0002: Federal, Provincial and Territorial General Government Revenue and Expenditures, for Fiscal Year Ending March 31, Annual (Dollars), *CANSIM (database).*

REVENUES

At Confederation, it was assumed that the provinces would have little need for an independent tax base. The major tax sources of the day—customs and excise revenues—were assigned to the federal government, which could tax "by any means," while the provinces were given "direct taxes," those that were imposed on individuals. This distinction made sense in the 19th century, but it makes no sense today. Payroll taxes, income taxes, and sales taxes—all direct taxes—were unknown at Confederation, but they now make up 95 per cent of federal revenues and over 80 per cent of provincial own-source revenues (Rosen et al. 2008, 6). Custom and excise revenues are negligible by comparison. In terms of access to tax fields, only a few constitutional differences exist between the federal and provincial governments, and they draw on the same basic revenue sources. The main federal tax sources are also the main provincial sources, except for the royalty revenues derived from natural resources, which are the exclusive preserve of the provinces.

Periodically, efforts have been made to disentangle taxing powers. The Rowell-Sirois Commission, for example, recommended in 1940 that the federal government take over all personal and corporate income taxes as well as succession duties. The federal government would assume provincial debt, and the provinces would receive

sufficient transfer payments to allow them to discharge their constitutional responsibilities. Transfer payments have become part of
Canada's constitutional tradition (see the Constitution Act, 1982, section 36), but the provinces did not permanently cede their taxing
authority. In 1954–55, Québec introduced its own provincial income
tax in response to the federal government's direct funding of universities, a provincial responsibility. This initiative alarmed Ottawa and
set off a flurry of fiscal negotiations that saw the federal government
transfer tax points to the provinces and introduce equalization payments to compensate for differential tax bases. Tom Courchene (2012,
4) describes the Québec government's move as "easily the most significant post-war development in the evolution of Canadian federalism." From that point on, the provinces have enjoyed increased fiscal
flexibility, which currently manifests itself in different tax rates and
tax credit schemes from one province to the next.

Supporters of decentralization are enthusiastic about the high level
of autonomy the provinces have achieved, and economists agree that,
in a federation, it is normally efficient for the central government to
define the tax base and collect taxes on behalf of the provinces. Tax
harmonization avoids the deleterious effects of tax competition (see
the section "Race to the Bottom")—inefficiently low tax rates and capital misallocation (Mintz and Smart 2004; Wilson and Wildasin 2004).
In the case of income taxes, a great deal of harmonization has been
achieved in Canada. Before 2000, provinces other than Québec simply levied their income tax as a percentage of the federal tax—a "tax
on tax" arrangement. Beginning in 2001, all the provinces shifted to a
"tax on income" system, which allows more latitude in the definition
of "income." The federal government continues to collect provincial
as well as federal taxes, except in Québec, where the government collects its own personal income taxes using its own definition of what
constitutes taxable income. It should be observed that tax experts
consider the income tax in general to do a mediocre job of achieving
equity, in part because the provincial tax rate structure has become
flatter in recent years (Boadway 2011, 169–71).

No issue of tax harmonization has been more contentious than
the Harmonized Sales Tax (HST). The federal government wants the
provinces to scrap their sales taxes and levy an HST based on the
federal value-added base. This tax base is broader than the sales tax
base, but it does not levy taxes on intermediate transactions, so-called
"hidden" taxes that are passed on to consumers in the form of higher

prices. The HST also ends the practice of levying provincial sales taxes on the GST, another "tax on a tax." In 1996 three Atlantic provinces—Nova Scotia, New Brunswick, and Newfoundland and Labrador—took up the federal government's offer, and early indications were that consumer prices did fall, although the impact of the tax on different income groups remains to be determined (Murrell and Yu 2000). Revenue fell as well in New Brunswick and Newfoundland and Labrador, although Nova Scotia fared much better (Blagrave 2005). In all cases the transition was made easier by federal funds that were slowly phased out after implementation. Ontario joined the HST in 2010 and received compensation for conducting the inevitable audits that accompany tax collection. In addition, provinces are now able to set their own HST rates, unlike the original arrangement with the Maritime Provinces. In Québec's case, the HST goes into effect in 2013 following an extended period of discussion. Endorsing the principle was easy enough, but negotiating the details became a colossal task. In British Columbia, even the principle was a difficult sell. In 2011, most voters in a provincial referendum rejected the HST, thereby setting the stage for a comparison of how economies fare with and without tax harmonization.

The provinces' revenue sources have not changed much in the past 20 years (see Figure 3.2). Income taxes, the largest component of own-source provincial revenues, contributed slightly more in 2008 than in 1989, while consumption taxes contributed slightly less. Enthusiasm for provincial tax increases grew immediately after the 1995 federal budget, which dramatically reduced transfer payments to the provinces. The "other taxes" category has grown modestly in the interim, as provinces have increased gambling revenues in their search for new contributions to their consolidated revenue funds.

Compare this picture of relative collective stability with the highly differential reliance of particular provinces on different tax sources. For example, although income taxes have been the most important tax source in aggregate, in only half of the provinces is it the single most important source. The Atlantic provinces rely on consumption taxes more than on income taxes, while Alberta derives the largest proportion of its income from royalty payments. Figure 3.3 shows that, although all provinces have received transfers from Ottawa, the "have-not" provinces rely more heavily on transfers than do the wealthier provinces. Table 3.2, which summarizes own-source revenues, reminds us of the significant differences among the underlying economic drivers

FIGURE 3.2: Evolution of Provincial Government Revenues since 1989

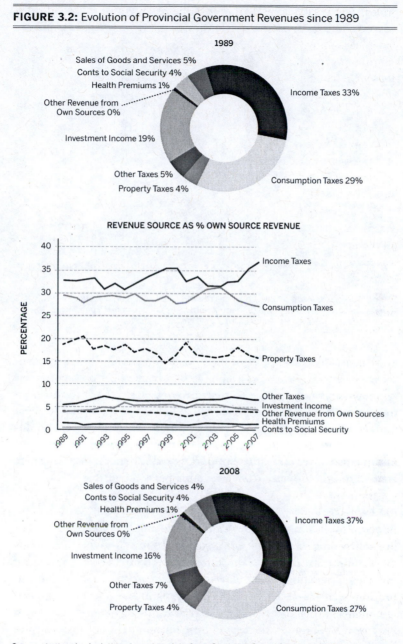

Source: Authors' calculations based on data from Statistics Canada, Table 385-0002: Federal, Provincial and Territorial General Government Revenue and Expenditures, for Fiscal Year Ending March 31, Annual (Dollars), CANSIM (database).

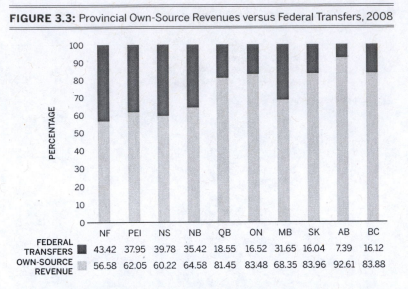

FIGURE 3.3: Provincial Own-Source Revenues versus Federal Transfers, 2008

	NF	PEI	NS	NB	QB	ON	MB	SK	AB	BC
FEDERAL TRANSFERS	43.42	37.95	39.78	35.42	18.55	16.52	31.65	16.04	7.39	16.12
OWN-SOURCE REVENUE	56.58	62.05	60.22	64.58	81.45	83.48	68.35	83.96	92.61	83.88

Source: Authors' calculations based on data from Statistics Canada, Table 385-0002: Federal, Provincial and Territorial General Government Revenue and Expenditures, for Fiscal Year Ending March 31, Annual (Dollars), *CANSIM (database).*

in each province. Manufacturing in Ontario and Québec, for example, affords these provinces a significant advantage in both corporate and personal taxes. All the Western provinces derive significant revenues from resource income (described as "investment income" in Table 3.2). Little wonder that proposals to impose national taxes with differential regional effects, such as a carbon tax, are met with resistance in some provinces and either support or indifference in others. There is no "typical" province from a revenue perspective.

EXPENDITURES

In 2008–09, federal and provincial governments spent about $300 billion on income security, health, and education. Although the provincial governments have constitutional authority over social programs, the federal government has played a significant role in designing and funding many of them. Through matching grants and block grants, the federal government has transferred funds to the provinces with varying restrictions on the use of these funds. Many restrictions were lifted as part of the 1995 federal budget so that, except for residency

TABLE 3.2: Sources of Provincial Own-Source Revenue (per capita and as a percentage of total own-source revenue averaged over 1989–2008)

PROVINCE	OWN-SOURCE REVENUE	INCOME TAXES[1]	INVESTMENT INCOME[2]	CONTRIBUTIONS TO SOCIAL SECURITY[3]	CONSUMPTION TAXES[4]	PROPERTY TAXES[5]	OTHER TAXES[6]	OTHER REVENUE FROM OWN SOURCES[7]	HEALTH PREMIUMS[8]	SALES OF GOODS AND SERVICES
NF	4224.3	1278.6	501.8	206.3	1683.8	14.0	288.6	16.6	0.0	234.3
	100.0	30.3	11.9	4.9	39.9	0.3	6.8	0.4	0.0	5.5
PEI	4423.7	1291.6	410.3	139.5	1686.2	350.8	178.0	7.2	0.0	359.1
	100.0	29.2	9.3	3.2	38.1	7.9	4.0	0.2	0.0	8.1
NS	3954.2	1477.0	361.1	167.4	1514.7	46.0	137.1	6.4	9.9	233.8
	100.0	37.4	9.1	4.2	38.3	1.2	3.5	0.2	0.2	5.9
NB	4467.7	1363.0	733.7	149.1	1499.5	367.5	153.9	15.8	0.0	184.8
	100.0	30.5	16.4	3.3	33.6	8.2	3.4	0.4	0.0	4.1
QC	5833.9	2462.8	386.8	263.0	1491.2	198.4	732.4	21.8	48.2	229.2
	100.0	42.2	6.6	4.5	25.6	3.4	12.6	0.4	0.8	3.9
ON	4918.0	2113.2	214.9	247.7	1561.6	158.0	409.6	15.8	18.7	178.6
	100.0	43.0	4.4	5.0	31.8	3.2	8.3	0.3	0.4	3.6
MB	5129.2	1659.6	963.5	141.2	1490.8	294.9	396.0	18.2	0.0	164.6
	100.0	32.4	18.8	2.8	29.1	5.7	7.7	0.4	0.0	3.2
SK	5884.8	1600.2	1528.6	156.6	1574.3	222.7	497.0	18.9	0.0	286.0
	100.0	27.2	26.0	2.7	26.8	3.8	8.4	0.3	0.0	4.9
AB	6582.2	1971.2	2588.0	201.2	764.4	306.3	285.4	21.2	223.2	221.1
	100.0	29.9	39.3	3.1	11.6	4.7	4.3	0.3	3.4	3.4
BC	5669.1	1659.0	1146.1	233.2	1501.9	514.9	158.2	31.6	256.9	167.2
	100.0	29.3	20.2	4.1	26.5	9.1	2.8	0.6	4.5	2.9

1   Included are personal, corporate, mining, and logging taxes as well as taxes on payments to non-residents and other income taxes.
2   This category includes natural resource royalties, remitted trading profits, interest income, and other investment income.
3   This category is primarily composed of contributions to workers and compensation boards and contributions to non-autonomous pension plans.
4   Included are general sales taxes, alcoholic beverage taxes, tobacco taxes, amusement taxes, gasoline and motive fuel taxes, custom duties, and remitted liquor and gaming profits.
5   Included are general property taxes, capital taxes, and other property-related taxes.
6   Included are payroll taxes, motor vehicle license fees, natural resource taxes and license fees, and miscellaneous taxes.
7   Included are fines and penalties, capital transfers from provincial sources, other donations, and miscellaneous revenue from other provincial sources.
8   Included are the premiums levied by some provinces and used specifically to finance their hospitalization, medical care, and drug insurance plans.

Source: Authors' calculations based on data from Statistics Canada, Table 385-0002: Federal, Provincial and Territorial General Government Revenue and Expenditures, for Fiscal Year Ending March 31, Annual (Dollars), *CANSIM (database).*

requirements, the provincial governments have complete control over what can be broadly described as social welfare programming.

Similarly, as suggested in Chapter 1, within the broad requirements of the Canada Health Act, the provinces are free to manage their health care budgets as they see fit. Of course, the limits of the Canada Health Act are periodically tested, but the point is that the federal government, even though it does not have the jurisdiction, nonetheless provides billions in support of health care. Even in education, where the federal presence is far less pronounced, the federal government has traditionally provided support for postsecondary education, first in the form of tax room and later in the form of unconditional grants. Further support is provided through research councils and grants to provide for capital projects. In short, the expenditure picture of the provinces is profoundly influenced by the role of the federal government, which was described in Chapter 1.

Discernible patterns in provincial spending have been established over the past several years. The main trends are the overall decline in debt service spending, the overall increase in spending on health care, and the relative stability of other spending priorities. Health care spending has been increasing for decades (see Figure 3.5). In 1933, only 3.7 per cent of total (provincial, municipal, and federal) government spending was aimed at health care; by 1965, after the introduction of universal hospital insurance (and on the eve of the introduction of universal medical care coverage), that proportion had increased to 10.7 per cent. By 2009, 19.3 per cent of all government spending was for health (Rosen, Wen, and Snoddon 2012, 13–14). The steady growth of health care spending was interrupted briefly during the mid-1990s, but continued after that and at a much faster pace than overall provincial spending. For example, between 1997–98 and 2003–04, the growth in health care spending in the provinces was 7.9 per cent annually, compared to a growth in overall provincial spending of 4.9 per cent (Landon et. al. 2006, 22).

Although education and social services make up approximately the same proportion of provincial spending as they did 20 years ago, both have grown in absolute terms. Between 2001 and 2009, for example, provincial spending on education and social benefits increased by approximately 50 per cent. Although the provinces are responsible for almost all education spending, social benefit spending is more complicated. In the first place, the costs are determined not by fixed dollar amounts but by the numbers of people who are eligible to receive support. Unless they wish to change the conditions under which individuals qualify, governments have no control over the costs of social programs. The risk to the provinces is mitigated because the federal government is a significant player. Through a series of programs, including employment insurance (EI) and the National Child Benefit Supplement (NCBS), the federal government contributes about 40 per cent of social benefit spending, not counting the Canada Pension Plan. The NCBS is the federal government's contribution to a joint National Child Benefit initiative, in which federal and provincial support payments to eligible families and individuals are combined into single payments (Treff and Ort 2010, 8:8). The federal government's role in social benefit spending, then, is far more extensive than the one it plays in education spending.

Unlike spending in program areas, spending on debt servicing has declined over the past 20 years, especially at the federal level, but it has not been a smooth reduction. Between 1989 and 1995, the overall (average) provincial debt expenditures increased by approximately 32 per cent, and the proportion of expenditures consumed by debt payments climbed from 14 per cent to 17.1 per cent. In contrast, between 1996 and 2009, the overall debt servicing expenditures of the provinces decreased by approximately 36 per cent, and the share of provincial spending devoted to debt servicing declined from 17 per cent in 1995–96 to 9.3 per cent in 2009, a reduction assisted by exceedingly low interest rates.

The reduction in provincial debt since 1995 has been uniform but not dramatic. Until 2008, a generally favourable economic environment increased economic activity and consequently improved debt to GDP ratios in almost all provinces. Along with the federal government, Alberta, Saskatchewan, Manitoba, Newfoundland and Labrador, and Nova Scotia experienced significant budget balance improvements and significant reductions in debt (Tapp 2010, 11). Alberta managed, for a brief period, to eliminate its debt altogether (see Figure 3.4). At the same time, most provincial governments took deliberate steps to improve their budget situations. In a process unlike those experienced in most European countries, these episodes of fiscal consolidation were achieved largely through spending reductions as opposed to revenue increases. Economists differ on the relative advantages of one versus the other, but, to the degree that a consensus exists, it favours spending reductions on the grounds that these are more likely to have positive macroeconomic effects, including the encouragement

FIGURE 3.4: Provincial Debt Levels (per capita), 1989, 1999, 2009

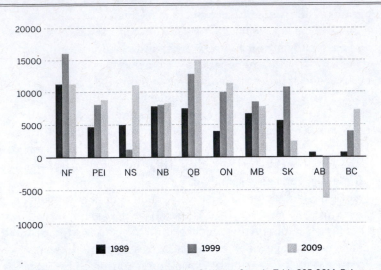

Source: Authors' calculations based on data from Statistics Canada, Table 385-0014: Balance Sheet of Federal, Provincial and Territorial General and Local Governments, Annual (Dollars), CANSIM (database), using E-STAT (distributor), last updated July 16, 2009; and Statistics Canada, Table 384–0002: Gross Domestic Product (GDP), Expenditure-Based, Provincial Economic Accounts, Annual (Dollars), CANSIM (database), using E-STAT (distributor), last updated on July 8, 2009.

of private consumption. But no two governments went about the task in the same way. For example, Alberta was much more aggressive than most in terms of spending reductions, focusing in particular on reducing expenditures in the areas of conservation, economic development, and social services (Boothe 2001). British Columbia increased taxes (and changed the tax base), much as Saskatchewan did, but also increased spending, in part to respond to significant population increases. Ontario cut both spending and taxes and allowed economic growth to make up the shortfall while Québec made much more modest spending cuts (Hale 2006, 395).

The pattern of public finance in the provinces is constantly shifting, even though budgeting is largely an incremental exercise in which governments normally make small adjustments to existing spending priorities and change their revenue picture only marginally each year. Over time, small changes add up to big ones, and, occasionally, severe shocks oblige governments to rethink the basics. No one person or group of people ever decided that income taxes would make

FIGURE 3.5: Expenditures as a Percentage of Total Cross-Provincial Expenditures, 1989–2008

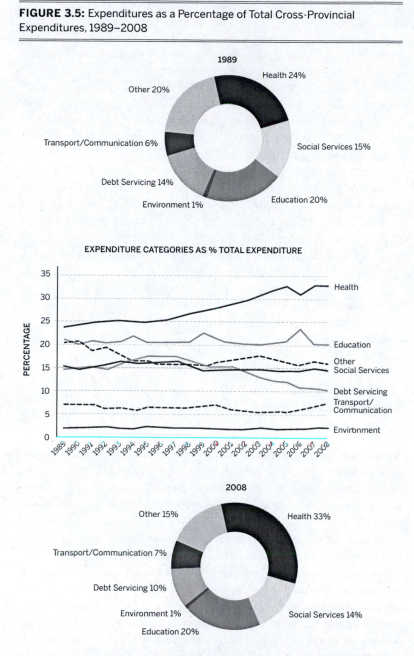

1989

Health 24%

Other 20%

Transport/Communication 6%

Social Services 15%

Debt Servicing 14%

Environment 1%

Education 20%

EXPENDITURE CATEGORIES AS % TOTAL EXPENDITURE

Health

Education

Other
Social Services

Debt Servicing
Transport/
Communication

Environment

2008

Other 15%

Health 33%

Transport/Communication 7%

Debt Servicing 10%

Social Services 14%

Environment 1%

Education 20%

Source: Authors' calculations based on data from Statistics Canada, Table 385-0002: Federal, Provincial and Territorial General Government Revenue and Expenditures, for Fiscal Year Ending March 31, Annual (Dollars), *CANSIM (database).*

up a large portion of public revenues, but the provinces have come to rely more and more on this source of revenue. Similarly, while local governments were large spenders relative to the provinces until World War II, since then they have become significantly smaller players. Decisions were made at each budget, but these decisions were not, by themselves, the driving force behind the massive shifts we have witnessed. They have been the product of shifts in ideas about what constitutes priorities, what fairness requires, where efficiency is to be found, and what combination of taxes and expenditures will reliably produce economic growth.

Each assessment of our fiscal health, whether provided by professional economists or people trying to balance their chequebooks, finds something to worry about. At the provincial level, where most of the spending is done, politicians worry about whether expenditure commitments can be sustained and how much they can count on federal transfers. Consumers of public goods such as education and health care worry about whether quality and equitable access can be maintained or improved. Business analysts and economists worry about the effects of spending and taxing on the business climate, specifically whether tax incentives will improve or higher rates of taxation will dampen the willingness to make new investments. Here are some of their worries about taxing and spending in the years ahead.

Taxing and Spending Challenges

THE PERSISTENT ISSUE OF PROVINCIAL GOVERNMENT SIZE

Attempts to compare the size of government in the provinces, both now and over time, are plagued by conceptual difficulties, including the need to consider certain obviously important sources of "expenditure," including tax relief ("tax expenditures") and regulatory burden. Government can look very large to those who have to contend with its requirements or very small to those whose needs go unmet. In addition, as we have seen, there are important technical and definitional questions regarding just what counts as "government." For example, should universities and public hospitals be included in definitions of government, or should government be defined more narrowly as those activities that governments directly manage? Decisions depend, to a large degree, on the purposes of the exercise. To facilitate comparison among the provinces, we use data that reflect a relatively broad, expenditure-based definition of government size.

In spite of these conceptual challenges, there are two points that can be made: first, government growth measured in terms of expenditures as a proportion of GDP has slowed considerably since the 1990s. Before then, Canada fit the pattern of an ever-expanding public sector, one that grew substantially during World War II and continued to grow from the 1950s until the early 1990s. Following the recession that began in 1990, governments reduced their transfer payments to both individuals and businesses, and they reduced spending in other areas as well. By 2003, real government size in Canada (the ratio of government expenditures to GDP) was 27.1 per cent, 3 per cent lower than it was in 1961 (Ferris and Winer 2007, 193).

Second, there is only weak evidence that long-term trends in government growth are the product of political manipulation. Governments are often accused of engaging in calculated spending in advance of elections, creating the so-called electoral budget cycle (Blais and Nadeau 1992), and research on the Canadian provinces suggests that all governments, regardless of political stripe, prefer to reduce taxes and make visible expenditures during election years. However, there is no evidence of partisanship on the revenue side (Kneebone and McKenzie 2001). How much of an effect do these political calculations have on the overall size of government? They might invite the conclusion that government is larger than it would be in the absence of an electoral budget cycle. There is evidence, however, for the idea that political competition obliges periodic reductions in spending, so, over the long run, political parties provide the level of spending that the political community desires (Ferris, Park, and Winer 2006). In other words, governments seek an equilibrium state of taxing and spending, one that represents, for a defined period, the consensus position on how big governments should be.

If there is a consensus based on public opinion, it has certainly changed since the 19th century, when the idea of the "night watchman state" allotted to government the role of protecting property rights and providing security. The welfare state of the 20th century was an entirely different construct, premised on the idea that the state has some responsibility for the equitable distribution of opportunities and, when necessary, the redistribution of income. Debate about the kind of state that Canadians want will take place increasingly at the provincial level because the provinces are the principal providers of welfare benefits and services. Also, the provinces' taxation and royalty policies are the ones most capable of either encouraging or disrupting economic growth.

Government size and the pace of government growth remain relevant, but it appears increasingly problematic to argue that there is a specific level of government size that is "best." Much depends on the composition of government spending and the effects of spending on overall economic productivity. Those who are wary about the growth of government have a specific worry that public spending could "crowd out" private investment and so distort productive investment. For example, government spending on privately provided public goods, such as a safe blood supply, might reduce the willingness of private actors to make voluntary contributions toward it. The evidence for this concern is weak (Andreoni 1993). On the other hand, strong evidence exists that certain types of government spending, on infrastructure, for example, induce private investment beyond what could have ordinarily been expected (Aschauer 1989).

Can transfers have a similarly positive effect? In Québec, day care has been publicly subsidized since 1997, with the cost set initially at five dollars a day. Research shows that these investments have had a significant positive impact on the participation of women in the workforce and on their earnings (Fortin 2011; Lefebvre and Merrigan 2008). For some observers, these results more than justify the public expenditure. Needless to say, these kinds of arguments need to be based on probative evidence and a consideration of other goals and alternative expenditure regimes. Not all programs can be expected to have beneficial or benign effects, and there is always the issue of opportunity costs to consider. (Opportunity cost is defined as the cost of any activity or program measure in terms of the value of the next best alternative—the one not chosen.) But the idea that government spending is, by definition, wasteful cannot be sustained on the evidence, even if it is conceded that government subsidies interfere with market allocation.

The question of too much or too little government is complicated in federal systems by the fiscal illusion that is created when taxes are not directly connected to expenditures. Fiscal illusion occurs when citizens are unaware of the total cost of providing a public good so are inclined to want more of it than is consistent with efficiency norms. Specifically, if provincial citizens consume high levels of provincially supplied services but pay relatively low levels of provincial taxes, they are encouraged to over-demand services and resist efforts to cut spending in accord with national austerity efforts (Wibbels 2000, 659). This gap between demand and supply occurs because transfers from the central government are not visible as taxation and are not directly connected to the provision of services. The natural inclination to consume services using someone else's money can complicate national adjustment policies when there is a pressing need to trim deficits, change the role of provincially owned enterprises, or reorganize financial systems on a province-by-province basis.

A general response to upward pressures on provincial budgets has been to look for productivity improvements in the delivery of services. Productivity has become a debate about how provincial governments might find different ways to accomplish policy goals, either by improving on existing delivery systems or by becoming less reliant on the coercive character of the state and more reliant on collaborative service provision. As this discussion gathers momentum, the question is not whether there is too much or too little government, but rather whether social welfare can be improved or enhanced with different policy instruments.

THE LOOMING ROLE OF HEALTH CARE SPENDING

The growth of public health care spending is a product of several converging influences. First, technology (embodied knowledge of all kinds) has provided us with new possibilities for improving and extending life. It is impossible to know what comes next, but improvement in pharmaceuticals is one area that promises to place significant upward pressure on costs.

Second, increases in income and improved insurance give us the apparent wherewithal to use the new technologies (Smith, Newhouse, and Freeland 2009). Our increasing wealth as a country means that we are in a position to afford more health spending than we have in the past. Improvements in labour productivity have helped generate wealth, and these improvements will continue, at least for the next five years. Of course, governments do not need to spend marginally available public dollars on health care, but it is useful to appreciate that the pattern of spending across OECD countries suggests that wealthier countries spend more on health than poorer ones. Part of the reason is that Canadians demand this kind of spending, even though they significantly underestimate the costs (Drummond 2012, 150).

Third, demographic changes suggest that the population as a whole will begin to consume public health care services in ever-greater quantities in the years ahead. The average Canadian is living longer, and the average age is increasing. The real question is whether longevity simply increases the average age at which citizens begin to need more expensive health care services or whether it means that more people will need more services for a longer time. There is no consensus on this issue.

Finally, more proximate causes of spending include changes in the demand for and supply of health care professionals. Compensation in the health care sector has increased faster than in the rest of the economy, while, at the same time, productivity growth has been slower. Demand for health care workers has grown relative to supply, creating a wage squeeze for provincial governments. This effect and the relatively high level of unionization and professional collective bargaining extant in the health care field have meant that those employed in the sector have more wage bargaining power than those employed elsewhere in the economy (Dodge and Dion 2010, 15).

These structural conditions do not determine health care spending; they set the stage for choices, and the fact is that, collectively, we are choosing more health care spending than we have in the past. In its 2010 budget, British Columbia indicated that 90 per cent of its new spending would be for health care; in Manitoba, 60 per cent of all new spending went to health care; and, in Alberta, the figure was 40 per cent. In Ontario, health care spending was eclipsed only by stimulus measures intended to shore up the recession-ridden provincial economy (Treff and Ort 2010, chap. 10). If it can be assumed that politicians are offering the package of policies demanded by the median voter, then the reason we are getting more health care spending is that we are demanding it. Of course, supply is important as well. Once decisions have been made to provide care in tertiary centres, for example, it requires an act of political will to change the nature of the care to make more efficient use of facilities. Increase the supply of doctors and, without other interventions, you can assume more tests and more prescriptions. In these scenarios, our first array of choices—who delivers health care where—sets up conditions for ongoing public spending that we might not have initially anticipated from a government policy and planning perspective.

Whatever the reasons for accelerated health care spending—and there are fingers pointing in all directions—provincial cabinet ministers watch in amazement as health departments gobble up an ever-greater share of the budget. They are naturally inclined to suspect that their own priorities are being sacrificed for what has become a singular obsession. They are not alone in their analysis. From former provincial finance ministers (McKinnon 2003, 229) to well-respected macroeconomists (Drummond 2012, chap. 5), the fear is that health spending is endangering other spending priorities and that, eventually, it will eat up the entire provincial budget. This fear has also been referred to as "crowding out," but, in this case, it is one spending priority that crowds out all others. The result is a kind of perfect storm in health spending. We are wealthier as a country and therefore more inclined to spend on health care. However, our labour productivity will eventually fall as a result of our aging population's lower participation rate, and this may make it more difficult to sustain the economic growth that health care funding requires.

So far, the data do not support the direst predictions. The assumption that larger spending shares for one purpose mean smaller shares for others omits two important considerations. First, a growth in revenues might permit spending on other programs to increase, even if not at the same rate as increases in health care spending. The share of the provincial budget used for health care might expand, but revenues may be robust enough that other areas can benefit as well. From 1989 until 2003 it appears that this was the case. Apart from a short period in the 1990s when health care spending continued to grow while other areas were in retreat, the pattern of mutual growth continued into the 21st century. If the "crowding out" hypothesis were to hold up, there should be a negative relationship between health care spending and spending in other program areas ("robbing Peter to pay Paul"). But a systematic analysis of spending patterns revealed no relationship (Landon et al. 2006).

The second reason that health has been able to grow without negative consequences for other priorities is the decline of debt service charges in all provinces. As deficits and debts have fallen so has this important part of provincial budgets. The fiscal dividend that has accompanied balanced budgets and lower interest rates has benefitted health much more than other spending areas (Landon et al. 2006, 133). How much longer can this go on?

In December 2011, the federal government announced that, although it would continue to fund the Canada Health Transfer (CHT) at a 6 per cent annual growth rate until 2016–17, after that, the CHT will grow in line with a three-year moving average of nominal GDP growth (with a minimum increase of 3 per cent per year guaranteed).

The CHT will be reviewed again in 2024, but, by then, provincial contributions to escalating health care spending will have grown substantially. With provincial GDP estimated to grow at a rate of 3.7 per cent annually between 2017 and 2024 and health spending estimated to grow at a 5.1 per cent rate, the provinces will soon bear the lion's share of the responsibility for reducing program spending at the pain of plunging deeper into debt (Matier 2012). This new reality should place even greater pressure on provincial governments to "bend the cost curve" (in other words, slow the rate at which health care costs increase).

DEPENDENCY ON RESOURCE REVENUES

Countries and regions that depend on natural resource revenues often end up with poor economic outcomes. There appears to be a strong tendency for politicians in resource-rich countries to extract resources at a rate that is more rapid than socially optimal and to spend the resulting revenues in ways that do not generate long-term growth. Public employment expands as the party in power consolidates its hold in anticipation of expanding revenues. Intense and bitter political conflict ensues. Long resource booms mitigate overextraction to some degree by providing the assurance of continued prosperity. In the absence of this assurance, however, politicians are inclined to discount the future and exploit the resource at a rate that is socially suboptimal. Economists have described this situation as the "resource curse"— the paradox of wealth leading to slow growth and political turmoil.

The resource curse is a concept developed to describe almost exclusively the development path of low-income countries with weak economies and troubled politics. Developed countries (as well as a few exceptional developing countries such as Indonesia and Botswana) appear to have largely escaped the resource curse thanks, it is argued, to mature political institutions including a strong commitment to the rule of law and a high-functioning bureaucracy (Robinson, Torvik, and Verdier 2006). Can Canadian provincial governments relax and not worry about the fact that much of their wealth depends on resource extraction?

Let us consider some of the reasons that relaxing may be premature. First, the classic "Dutch disease" phenomenon is always lurking in the background of any resource-based economy. Named after the adverse effects that offshore natural gas discoveries in the 1960s had on Dutch manufacturing, the key idea is that "boom" sectors can have negative effects on lagging sectors. One direct effect is the upward pressure that natural resource exploitation often places on the value of the local currency. For example, when the Canadian dollar appreciates because of increasing prices for natural resources, the result can be detrimental (or even devastating) for sectors such as manufacturing, whose products are priced in world markets. Intense competition for labour, brought on by the boom, can also have the effect of "choking off" other sectors. There is nothing automatic about these effects (see Corden 1984 for the complications), and much can be done to ameliorate them, but, for Canada as a whole, the uneven distribution of natural resources means that short-term shifts in employment and migration have to be managed to reduce long-term detrimental effects on the economy as a whole.

The provinces are responsible for managing natural resources, and they are entitled to the direct revenues. Section 109 of the Constitution Act, 1867 awarded the provinces the right to manage their natural resources, and this responsibility was clarified and strengthened in the Constitution Act, 1982. The purpose was to provide the provinces with an independent revenue base, and efforts by the federal government to tax resource industries have met with considerable provincial complaint. The federal government, in contrast, has relied much less than the provinces on natural resource revenues. The federal government's role in this arena has largely been the management of trade relations that accompany significant natural resource endowments. As long as prices and revenues are relatively stable, a reasonable synchronization of responsibilities can be achieved (Cairns 1992). But when international prices for commodities such as oil and gas increase rapidly, the table is set for the second problem associated with resource revenues—namely, the federal government's sudden interest in the distributive effects of significant resource rents. Other than Québec's periodic flirtation with separation, nothing has placed greater pressure on the federation than the federal government's 1980s National Energy Program (NEP), which was intended to increase federal revenues from resources from 10 to 20 per cent. The Western Provinces reacted with incredulity, followed by condemnation. The NEP fed into long-standing resentments about the ways in which the federal government had managed resources until their formal transfer to the provinces of Manitoba, Saskatchewan, and Alberta in 1930.

The third problem with resource revenues is the significant onus they place on provinces to use them to diversify their economies or at least to provide for adequate long-term incomes for future generations. For the provinces, the challenge has been to provide citizens with some of the immediate benefits of these revenues while investing the remainder in the diversification of the local economy. Meeting this challenge has occasioned a balancing act in which government officials in resource-rich provinces try to limit consumption spending while they endeavour to predict a future they do not control. Volatility in resource prices obliges finance departments to impose discipline at times when it appears none is required.

In the case of Alberta, resource revenues from non-renewable resources contributed what would later be seen as a relatively modest $280 million per year just before 1974. Even at that, it was enough to fund, on average, 28 per cent of the province's spending. By the end of 1981, after the OPEC price shock, $2.3 billion came to the province from this source (an almost tenfold increase), and it supported twice as much of a rapidly expanding expenditure budget. Acknowledging the need to prepare for the long term, the provincial government established the Alberta Heritage Savings Trust Fund, supplied it with a $1.5 billion investment in 1976, and promised to contribute 30 per cent of future resource revenues. A large surplus quickly accumulated in the fund, but, by the 1980s, the original commitment had to be abandoned. Program spending had increased rapidly and oil prices had plummeted. Volatility was not something the Alberta government was ready for, and the province went from a net surplus to a position of deficit and accumulated debt. Efforts to deal with that debt focused on spending, as we have mentioned. But persuading politicians to remain on a steady fiscal course when resource revenues suddenly recovered proved to be a persistent problem (Kneebone 2006).

Saskatchewan experienced the same sort of budgetary challenge when finance officials assumed in 2009 that potash prices would continue to maintain extraordinarily high levels. Potash royalties of about $1.9 billion were expected to make up 20 per cent of total government revenues that year. When prices fell precipitously, the original budget had to be revised radically and only $100 million of potash revenues remained in the budget forecast. The vulnerability of governments to price shocks (positive and negative) has not discouraged critics from arguing in favour of changes to royalty regimes so that a greater share of revenues remains either to pay current bills or to contribute to future operational and infrastructure spending in an effort to achieve greater intergenerational equity. In 2007, the

Alberta government proposed a significant increase in royalty payments from the oil and gas industry. In 2010, those increases were reversed in the face of threats of investment withdrawal on the part of oil and gas companies.

The final general problem of resource revenues is the revenue imbalance they create across the provinces. This imbalance is largely a problem for national governments that are obliged to assume responsibility for introducing some equity in the revenues of the provinces. But equalizing all provinces based on the soaring revenues of a few is a daunting fiscal task. Should resource revenues be treated the same as any others? The resource-dependent provinces insist otherwise, arguing that, even as their revenues increase, they should still be eligible for equalization (assuming they would otherwise qualify) because resource revenues are non-renewable and, as such, should be invested in the province's future. Besides, if increases in resource revenues mean dollar-for-dollar decreases in equalization payments, there is no incentive to develop the resources.

In 2005, the federal government addressed these concerns by signing the Atlantic Accord with Nova Scotia and Newfoundland and Labrador to compensate these provinces for 100 per cent of lost revenue via the equalization formula. Other resource-dependent provinces, like Saskatchewan, began demanding the same treatment, while Ontario questioned the wisdom of increasing equalization payments at all. In 2006 an Expert Panel on Equalization and Territorial Formula Financing, created by Prime Minister Paul Martin, recommended a comprehensive set of changes intended to achieve a new balance in the overall approach. Among other things, the panel suggested equalizing 50 per cent of resource revenues, eliminating side deals (like the Atlantic Accord), and increasing funding to the equalization program itself.

Changes are bound to spark negative reactions from some, positive reactions from others. In some parts of the world, the uneven distribution of resource revenues leads to civil war. In Canada, we fight our battles in the political arena. But no one should draw from that the comfortable conclusion that satisfactory outcomes are always available. Provincial leaders are well aware of their own electoral support base, and they often have little incentive to compromise. Imposed solutions create bitterness and almost always trigger demands for renegotiation. Canada may have escaped the conventional resource curse, but unevenly distributed resource revenues continue to place pressure on a political system already made fragile by ethnic and linguistic division.

THE QUESTION OF VERTICAL IMBALANCE

As noted at the outset of this chapter, with the exception of the equalization policy, the Canadian constitution is largely silent on the matter of financial transfers between different orders of government. The reality is that the Fathers of Confederation did not expect the provinces to require much more fiscal capacity than they were originally given. They considered that intergovernmental fiscal relations would end once issues of taxing authority had been determined and the federal government had made initial transfers to allow provincial governments to offer equal services to citizens. Things have worked out very differently.

Without question, policy areas largely or exclusively under the responsibility of provincial governments—health, education, and social assistance, in particular—have grown substantially in terms of citizen expectations over the past 50 years. Nor is there much disagreement that the federal government is well positioned to introduce a strong element of equity into the lives of Canadians (regardless of where they live) by providing provinces with the capacity to offer services at levels that cost provincial governments roughly the same amounts. That leaves two vexing questions: how much should the federal government transfer to the provinces, and how should these transfers be accomplished? The provinces disagree among themselves on both of these questions, but the major disagreements are between the provinces and the federal government.

The answer to the first question, the amount that should be transferred, raises the question of how much vertical imbalance actually exists. Led by Québec, provincial governments have argued that the taxing powers of the federal government are far in excess of its needs relative to federal areas of responsibility. Superficially, this argument is correct. The federal government routinely collects more funds than the provinces and engages in several different transfers (Treff and Ort 2010, appendix B). For some, the mere existence of transfers is evidence of a fiscal gap. Of course, if that were true, the federal government could end the gap simply by ending the transfers, leaving the federal government in perpetual surplus and the provinces in perpetual deficit.

This logic suggests a second approach to fiscal imbalance, one in which imbalance between revenues and expenditures is understood to be the result of a mismatch between constitutionally assigned areas of jurisdiction and access to tax fields. The report of Québec's Séguin

Commission (2002) adopted this second interpretation, although it did allow that there is no longer much difference in the tax fields assigned to the different orders of government. The problem is partly historical: "the existing occupation of taxation fields by the two orders of government puts the federal government at an advantage" (Séguin 2002, 53). Put another way, inertia and the grip of the status quo favour those who have occupied lucrative tax areas for some time.

However persuasive the historical argument, in most federal states, constitutionally recognized subnational governments can rarely achieve economies of scale in tax collection and seldom raise revenues consistent with their expenditure requirements (Oates 1972). As long as the country, as a whole, is the relevant reference point (the "national community"), there will be an onus on federal governments to provide a measure of equity in provincial spending capacity (Banting and Boadway 2004). Beyond that, federal governments are also typically concerned to avoid the inefficient migration of people and investment. For their part, the provinces can only engage in a limited amount of tax and expenditure competition before imperilling their own budgets. For these reasons, the federal government possesses a unique capacity to affect provincial budgets by making unilateral determinations regarding the scale of and conditions for transfers. The provinces do not enjoy a similar advantage because, of course, they are seldom, if ever, transferring money to the federal order of government. Both governments, however, are limited by the presumptive capacity of taxpayers to assume the burden of funding programs, no matter who pays for and manages them. Thus, some have argued that the optimal solution to vertical fiscal imbalance is the achievement of a transfer regime that minimizes the efficiency cost of taxation in the federation as a whole (Boadway and Tremblay 2005).

The current dispute over vertical fiscal imbalance was framed by the 1995 federal budget, in which the federal minister of finance announced that existing funding programs would be rolled into a new Canada Health and Social Transfer (CHST) and that the cash portion of the program (about 20 per cent of the total) would be significantly reduced over succeeding years. During those years, the federal government's financial position improved substantially while the provinces' situations deteriorated. The provinces maintained that, whatever argument existed for reducing transfers to achieve a balanced budget, the federal government was not justified in cutting transfers more than it cut its own program expenses (Lazar St-Hilaire, and Tremblay 2004).

Debate followed, and the federal government made the case that the provinces had adequate room to increase taxes if that was their preferred means of dealing with budgetary pressures.

So is there a vertical fiscal imbalance? The safest answer seems to be "yes." It is safe because the task of finding a perfect balance between revenues and responsibilities rests on so many short-term and long-term fiscal considerations that, at any given time, the most neutral of observers will find some suggestions for improvement. At the moment, the federal government has undisturbed access to the most lucrative sources of revenue, and it has the greatest capacity to absorb debt obligations. The provinces, on the other hand, have been successful in reducing their deficits (at least until 2008) by cutting program expenditures and enjoying the benefits of GDP growth. Their economic positions are more precarious, however. As a whole, they have had less success than the federal government in reducing their debt levels, and they remain vulnerable to economic downturns.

The provinces have responded to their position by extracting agreements from the federal government to provide program transfers (the Canada Health Transfer and the Canada Social Transfer) for extended periods, thereby allowing them to manage their economies without fear of unilateral federal withdrawal. The CHT, for example, was established in 2004 and is guaranteed until 2014. Equalization formulas have not been as stable, even though, as stated above, the concept of equalization was embedded in the Constitution Act, 1982. Certain provinces, particularly British Columbia and Saskatchewan, initially, but now Newfoundland and Labrador as well, have shifted back and forth over the years between being eligible or not eligible for transfers, from being "have-not" to "have" provinces. And these flips often depended on the treatment of resource revenues in transfer calculations. The entire equalization project became increasingly politicized after 2004 as the opaque formula withstood assaults not just from the resource-rich but also from the suddenly poor provinces, such as Ontario whose demand for "fairness" and eligibility for equalization payments put the entire system in doubt (Lecours and Béland 2010). Boessenkool (2010) suggests that this situation could be improved if the federal government were to transfer "permanently" a revenue source, such as the GST, to the provinces. Whether harmonization could be guaranteed following such a move is an open question, but this kind of reform would have the benefit of obliging provinces to use own-source revenues to fund program changes, which in turn would promote a more responsible political culture (Richards 2008).

What is positive about these suggestions, and about the current state of debate, is that neither the federal government nor the provincial governments are willing to risk the federation to insist on their positions. With some remarkable exceptions, most provincial politicians have focused on obtaining a measure of financial security from the federal government while still insisting on the existence of a structural imbalance. The federal government, having once balanced its books on the backs of the provinces, seems to have adopted a much more analytic perspective on imbalance—a mixture of economic and political calculation—designed to foster a measure of mutual respect and even independence. The occasional failure to achieve this result should not be read as a fundamental deficiency in the public finances of the country.

THE CHALLENGE OF DEBT MANAGEMENT

In the aftermath of the 2008 recession, governments spent vast amounts to promote a Keynesian-inspired recovery. The resulting levels of indebtedness were seen as deeply alarming in some quarters, setting off a predictable demand for fiscal restraint and balanced budgets. Almost all Canadian provinces had achieved the previously elusive goal of a balanced budget by 2008, but all but a minority found themselves back in deficit positions in the years that followed. Deficits have been largest in Ontario and debt levels highest (about 30 per cent of GDP) in Québec and the Atlantic provinces. Some of this new indebtedness arises because of the cyclical effects of deficit spending, but the OECD estimates that, in Canada as a whole, the structural deficit is about 1.6 per cent of GDP due to spending increases going into the recession (Guillemette 2010). All of this structural deficit is located at the provincial level, especially in provinces such as Québec and Ontario. A structural deficit means that, in these provinces, the economy cannot be expected to sustain current spending levels, even when the recessionary environment has receded and productivity has improved. That reality has recently prompted an unprecedented review of government spending in Ontario with a call for "strong fiscal action" via a root-and-branch reform of provincial public services (Drummond 2012)

Disagreements over the extent to which governments can and should act to achieve fiscal stabilization meant that not all governments reacted to the 2008 recession in the same way, although a remarkable level of coordination among OECD countries staved off financial collapse. Now what? For some governments, the road to continued recovery lies in a rapid return to the balanced budgets enjoyed over the past 10 years. The federal government picked the target date 2014 (subsequently revised), and embarked on a policy of retrenchment led by job losses in the public service. Some of the provinces have followed suit. In Saskatchewan, for example, the government's 2010 budget announced a reduction in the size of the public service by 15 per cent over four years. The Ontario government aimed at a more modest 5 per cent reduction in its 2009 budget, a cutback that translated into 3,400 jobs lost in a public service of approximately 68,000.

Under these conditions, what will be the long-term trend in public sector employment and government growth? Many economists see a periodic reduction in the size of the public service and a reconsideration of entitlement programs as a pro-growth strategy (a pro-*economic*-growth strategy, that is). On the other hand, using cutbacks for the specific purpose of returning to periods of surplus is a risky strategy. By far the easiest way to deal with deficits and debt is to grow the economy. Spending reductions in the mid to late 1990s certainly helped balance provincial budgets, but economic growth played by far the biggest role. So reductions in government spending need to be timed so they do not choke off growth. Put another way, it is not invariably bad practice to run deficits if they sustain recoveries. Eventually, of course, investment responds positively to signals of fiscal prudence. The question is when to retrench and by how much?

It is obvious that some provinces are in a better situation than others to reduce debt service payments. And while it is not so obvious, it is also important to acknowledge that reductions in spending and improvements in debt-to-GDP ratios cannot be counted on to last. No provincial government has succeeded in isolating itself from economic downturns or from global shocks. Cyclical economic changes—witness the 2008 recession—have a way of inducing deficit spending and challenging governments to rethink the services they can afford to provide. In short, expenditure budgets are constantly being reviewed and efficiencies constantly being sought. The relative persistence of health care increases and entitlement program spending belies a constant concern on the part of provincial finance ministers to find savings and reduce commitments. In many cases, these commitments consist of transfers to third parties—universities, health regions, and school boards—that do not carry the primary political responsibility to justify expenditure choices.

Until the recession of 2008, provincial debt had been on the decline, and, in Alberta at least, it had been ostensibly eliminated. The recession meant a reduction in revenues and a sudden expansion in demand for fiscal intervention that placed all provinces in a more precarious state and gave rise to the natural concern that, collectively, the provinces might slip back into a situation in which deficit financing became normal and debts were allowed to accumulate. Many observers, particularly those working in a public-choice framework, suspect governments of seeking to deliver gifts of public finance while someone else—future generations or other governments—pays for them. Citizen-voters, they reason, share the same inclination. If given the chance, they would gladly acquiesce in a situation in which someone else covered their debts. It is possible for politicians to give expression to this inclination by accumulating debts that will constrain the actions of future politicians but allow present-day incumbents relative freedom to indulge their own policy preferences. Put in a more positive light, it is possible to adopt an "equilibrium" approach to public finance and argue that, over a "long-time horizon budget," properly managed deficits can reduce the excess burden of taxation. This kind of "intertemporal optimization" approach is reassuring only as long as tax rates are smoothed out and the debt-to-GDP ratio comes down. For too many governments on too many occasions, neither situation has occurred.

For example, during a 20-year period from fiscal year 1969–70 to 1989–90, the federal government was particularly lax in its approach to its deficit. In the latter 10 years of that period, the federal government allowed its debt-to-GDP ratio to increase by 27 per cent (Kneebone 1994, 155). Many provinces—Saskatchewan, Alberta, Manitoba, and Nova Scotia—did not do much better, but some provinces actually reduced their debt-to-GDP ratio during the same period. True, the provinces have some incentive to allow debts to grow. In a monetary union, there is always a presumption that, if one member of the union builds high debt levels, the central government will eventually bail that member out rather than allow its demise to affect the entire financial system. If the federal government were to monetize the debt of deadbeat provinces by printing money, everyone, not just the delinquents, would absorb the inflationary costs.

So far, that has not happened. Although some provinces have come close, on occasion, to being unable to meet their financial obligations, they have, by and large, kept their debt levels in hand. The major reason that debt levels have not become unmanageable is that provinces must pay a "default premium" to lenders since they cannot monetize their debt by devaluing the currency. This default premium is registered in the interest rates on provincial bonds. Bond-rating agencies provide a clear indication of the size of that premium, which in turn is an economic barometer of provincial fiscal health.

An alternative to relying on the signals provided by bond agencies is for governments to provide their own signals. Adopting fiscal rules such as a balanced budget requirement is an example. According to the International Monetary Fund (IMF), by early 2009, 80 countries had national or supranational fiscal rules. By contrast, only 7 countries had fiscal rules in 1990. The rapid expansion of these rules occurred first in Europe and Latin America, but many low-income countries have adopted them by being signatories to supranational agreements. Originally, countries adopted single rules, but now multiple fiscal rules are the norm (IMF 2009). Among Canadian provinces, by 2010, eight had legislation requiring that their budgets be balanced, seven had placed legal limits on debt obligations, and five had special requirements for increasing taxes. The first rules were adopted in the 1990s and focused on spending restraint; the second generation of rules, adopted only a few years later, targeted deficits and balanced budgets (Tapp 2010). In their assessment of the Western Canadian provinces, Simpson and Wesley (2012, 308) conclude that balanced budget legislation was "neither strong enough to restrain expenditure growth to revenue growth during the good times, nor was it adequate to prevent governments from running deficits during the bad times."

This legislation is almost entirely political in motivation. It signals a government's commitment to publicly endorsed standards of fiscal prudence, but following rules does not automatically produce sound policy or even the anticipated fiscal outcomes. None of the major goals of macroeconomic policy—distributive justice, stabilization (low inflation), and allocative efficiency—are readily served by these kinds of measures, and no credible macroeconomic theory requires an annual balanced budget. On the contrary, good fiscal policy needs a substantial measure of flexibility to meet unexpected developments in a measured fashion, and most OECD countries have given themselves the opportunity to balance budgets over a business cycle. Without flexibility, self-imposed rules have the tendency to induce bad behaviour, including efforts to redefine what constitutes a deficit and to shield certain expenditures from being counted. In short, this type of legislation requires politicians to make promises that they find difficult to keep.

The Canadian provinces provide ample illustrations. In the face of impending deficits after 2008, three governments—Alberta, Saskatchewan, and the Yukon—drew down "rainy day funds" to avoid being labelled as being in deficit positions. Three other provinces— Québec, Manitoba, and British Columbia—amended their legislation to provide themselves with more time to meet their targets, while Nova Scotia simply repealed its prohibition against tabling a deficit budget (Tapp 2010, 15). The federal government has declined to adopt fiscal rules, but, had it done so, it would be in a much better position than the provinces to comply with these rules. Part of the problem for the provinces is the lack of contingency plans and the absence of credible long-term spending projections. Provincial politicians have taken the oath of fiscal discipline, but they have very little protection against forced renunciation in the face of sudden drops in revenues or unanticipated long-term expenditures.

The precarious position of provincial finances is illustrated by the inability of most provincial governments to predict accurately where they will end the fiscal year (Busby and Robson 2010). Most provinces—the exceptions are Québec and New Brunswick—routinely over- or underestimate revenues so that their budget projections at the beginning of the fiscal year are seldom realized in the public accounts by the end. On the expenditure side, Manitoba and Prince Edward Island do the best job of actually spending the budgeted amount. The rest of the provinces often spend more than originally projected. Over time, spending overruns add up to billions of dollars, further imperilling efforts to balance budgets. Revenue surprises, positive or negative, are sometimes too large for governments to address through in-year adjustments; at other times, they provide the temptation to spend windfalls. In short, provincial budgeting is a precarious affair, and fiscal consolidation a perilous political task. In the past 20 years, the provinces have shown that they are capable of rescuing their bottom lines when forced to do so. The bad news is that there is no way of anticipating when that might be or of rapidly adjusting budgets when doing so is necessary.

Conclusion

Taxing and spending instruments are among the most powerful means modern states have to change their long-term direction and the living conditions of their citizens. Canadians tend to make demands of their provincial governments that, at least in most realms, are remarkably similar. It is safe to presume that virtually everyone wants a sound health care system that anticipates problems and responds equitably and efficiently. Similarly, most provincial residents are prepared to pay taxes to obtain an education system that equips students to participate and thrive in a competitive world. Most residents prefer to drive on roads that are paved and to consume water that is free of contaminants. And so on.

These sociopolitical realities push provincial governments toward solutions that bear a strong resemblance to one another. For example, all provincial governments have been spending proportionately more on health care in the past decade than in previous years. Local demographics force spending patterns to diverge somewhat, but there are strong pressures toward convergence. Provincial governments pay close attention to one another, often deliberately adopting successful innovations from other jurisdictions, and they measure their progress against province-wide standards. The federal government, for its part, has embraced (sometimes with reluctance, sometimes with enthusiasm) its responsibility to render provincial governments equally capable in attending to the needs of their citizens.

On the other hand, there is no doubt that the provinces remain very different from one another in their taxing and spending choices and in their overall fiscal performance. The median voter in Québec may demand a package of goods and services from government that roughly matches the package demanded by the median voter in British Columbia, but differences exist in the interpretations of what constitutes providing "a sound health care system" or "good schools" and in the relative priority of one provision over the other. Even more important, the provinces do not share the same revenue opportunities. The increasing freedom to expand their tax bases does not make them equal, either in terms of the number of resident corporate head offices in their cities or in their oil and gas reserves. Divergence in revenue amounts and sources has not changed much during the past 20 years. The provinces are not moving as a group, or in a single direction, when it comes to tax sources. Each province pursues its own revenue strategy, with resource-dependent provinces—including Québec, given its reliance on hydroelectric exports—constructing revenue regimes quite different from those of the other provinces.

On the expenditure side, the provinces are less dispersed than they were 20 years ago. Demand for public services does not differ radically across the country, and the federal government's transfer payments seem to have contributed to convergence rather than the other way around. With fewer and fewer restraints placed on how provincial governments can spend their transfers, some imagined a world in which the provinces would pursue their own unique (or perhaps politically driven) agendas. Data from the 1970s, the 1980s, and the early 1990s suggested otherwise (Atkinson and Bierling 1998), and since 1995, convergence in health and social spending has continued. But total spending has not converged; the provinces remain rather different from one another in terms of total per capita spending.

The forces for convergence or divergence in provincial taxing and spending are all subject to political calculus and competition. In each province, the political dynamic generates unique solutions beyond those required by different economic circumstances. The provincial cultures are themselves historical residues of experience of the choices of previous governments. They cannot be erased from the minds of voters or expunged from the calculations of provincial politicians. Some provincial choices seem obvious; others are influenced by ideological differences among the political parties and even by the personal chemistry of political leaders (or their lack of it). There is no danger that the provinces will end up as homogeneous entities with little fiscal personality. Each budget presents them with the opportunity to assert their distinctiveness even as they face the same global and national forces that press them together.

There is an abiding tension in the Canadian union. On the one hand, there are strong sentiments in favour of developing national living standards and measuring progress against them. According to this view, the national community matters, and equity is a prominent value. Against this perspective is the idea that the provinces should be allowed or even encouraged to develop distinctive fiscal regimes based on unique advantages and local preferences. The provincial community becomes the focal point of innovation and distinctiveness. The country is moving in this latter direction. Is it sustainable? As provincial premiers begin to quarrel with one another over fiscal policy, special subsidies, monetary targets, and pipeline access, there is reason to worry that political fissures will expand to threaten Canada's very existence. Occasional divisive eruptions are a warning that subterranean trends are at work, placing stress on the federation. One way to track these trends is by paying attention to taxing and spending patterns. As much as they reveal the distinctiveness of the provinces, they also point us in the direction of emerging political and economic problems. No one can predict the future, but the topics covered in this chapter go to the heart of our collective capacity to realize both local and national aspirations.

CHAPTER FOUR

The Provincial Regulatory State

Introduction

So far in this volume, the focus has been on how provincial governments contribute to public policy objectives by taxing, spending, and investing. Although those roles are significant, in that provincial activities in these areas directly or indirectly contribute more than 30 per cent of national economic activity in any given year, they are just the tip of the iceberg of how provincial governments affect our lives. Some assert that, in the 21st century, the state will have its greatest effect through its use of legislation and regulation (Majone 1994). Most of the activities we engage in on a daily basis are governed by a mix of "hard" and "soft" law that is established by provincial legislation or regulation or sanctioned by devolved authorities, such as municipalities, regulatory agencies, or self-governing professions or organizations.

The emergence of the provincial regulatory state is partly the result of increased interactions in our economy and society, all of which fall in the domain of provincial authority, and partly in response to the diminished expectations that taxing, spending, direct employment, investment, government ownership, or direct program delivery can meet the needs of the economy and society. In many jurisdictions, the default assumption is that individuals are the best ones to make decisions about their production, consumption, savings, investments, and personal, social, and cultural choices, but, to be effective, they need a common set of known rules, the oft-sought "level playing field" that doesn't advantage some at the expense of others.

In many ways, regulation is the quintessential example of government choosing to steer rather than to row, and it does so through the new application of old tools of persuasion (Osborne and Gaebler 1992; Salamon 2002). This chapter discusses the nature of governance through legislation and regulation, the scale and scope of the provincial regulatory state, several ways that provinces have acted as experimental laboratories for regulatory innovation, and an array of challenges and opportunities facing those interested in both the study and administration of legislation and regulation.

The Concept of Regulation

Although a large body of scholarship is devoted to the consideration of the tools of government, for the purposes of this analysis, we can lump the options into three categories of tools: command and control systems, incentives and disincentives, and regulation.

States initially were conceived of and operated as command and control structures. Although the command and control system remains in direct public programming (such as welfare, hospitals, and schools in Canada) and in state-owned and -directed corporations (such as the many provincial utilities), governments are concerned that, in some instances, the model is inflexible, costly, cumbersome, and inefficient. In the place of command and control systems, most provinces have moved to use complex legislative, regulatory, and fiscal structures to redirect individual action to conform to public goals. All provinces use their fiscal powers to change the incentives for individual action, subsidizing desired actions (such as saving for retirement) and taxing actions that are undesirable (such as smoking). As a result, a blended state-market approach has evolved in most provinces. One area that most scholars think is increasingly important is regulation. Majone (1994) argues that regulation now forms the new borders between the state, the economy, and citizens—and is the primary battleground for ideas on how the economy and society should be run.

Several scholars assert that regulation has become the preferred policy tool for many governments, prompting claims that we now live in the age of the "regulatory state." There are at least three textbook definitions of regulation that offer concentric circles of ever-widening scope. First, regulation, in the narrowest sense, involves government promulgating rules, which are accompanied by mechanisms for monitoring and enforcement. A somewhat larger definition incorporates any direct state interventions in the economy, which would include both rules and other incentive structures put into place. Then, at its widest, the definition of regulation could encompass all the mechanisms of social control or influence affecting all aspects of behaviour from whatever source, intentional or not, which opens the field to all impacts of commission or omission. The difficulty is that these textbook definitions are both too loosely focused (by including both actions and inaction and collateral effects) and too tightly centred on the state. British scholar Julia Black (2002, 20) argues that one could perhaps more constructively investigate regulation as the "sustained and focused attempt to alter the behavior of others according to defined standards or purposes with the intention of producing a broadly identified outcome or outcomes, which may involve mechanisms of standard-setting, information-gathering and behavior modification." Black's decentred definition adds particular value as it captures the changing nature of regulation, which has recently expanded as its definitions, actors, forms, domain, and instruments have evolved. This decentring has flowed from the way our world is becoming more complex, fragmented, and interdependent and from the reality that the distinction between public and private matters is increasingly blurred. In such a world, regulation is often co-produced, not formally sanctioned by the state, and is seldom confined to any specific territory. Decentred systems tend to be hybrid creations of government and non-governmental actors (Phillips 2007). One example might be the regulatory system for new agri-food products. In Canada, research targets reflect a blend of commercial, scholarly, and public interests, and researchers draw on capital from commodity check-off organizations, technology firms, national research councils, and federal and provincial intramural research programs. Each of these funding sources uses its own framework to assess for merit and risk (e.g., commodity groups look at the economic effect on producers, multinationals have their own scientific and ethics boards and risk management strategies, national research councils have ethics guidelines and leveraging and commercialization goals, and the public agencies have specific decision grids). Until a new agri-food technology is proposed for unconfined release into the environment, safety is the exclusive responsibility of the research establishment—with the caveat that unauthorized releases are subject to both regulatory and civil remedies. At the point when a firm has something it seeks to commercialize, the formal regulatory risk assessment system goes into action, drawing on a set of international principles, practices, and processes such as are embodied in Good Laboratory Practice, public and industry standards, standard operating procedures (SOPs), and other codified sets of rules. The actual risk assessment of any candidate technology or product is undertaken in a collaborative way, with proponents and regulators negotiating the structure and specifics of the assessment, the firms producing the regulatory evidence, and the regulators, at times supplemented with outside expertise, undertaking the evaluation. If a product is then approved for release, any unintended risks are managed jointly by the owner of the product, the regulator, and the users, all in the context of general tort law and of the statutory and regulatory obligations placed on the owner. In essence, no stage of the process is exclusively in the hands of a single actor—all of the steps are negotiated and managed in the context of the overarching goals and interests of public health and safety and commercial and economic success (Phillips 2007).

Within any regulatory system, wherever its borders are drawn, we can examine regulations in two main alternative ways (Majone 1994). The normative view (espoused predominantly in the United States and by many right-of-centre governments in Canada) asserts that public regulation is justified only when the market or individual citizens are incapable of producing a social optimum (what is often called a "Pareto optimum"). Regulatory action is thus justified only when there is some sort of "market failure": a monopoly; the creation of externalities, e.g., the secondary or "spillover" production of benefits to society for which companies are inadequately rewarded or the creation of detriments, such as pollution, for which they are inadequately punished; the provision of incomplete or asymmetric information, e.g., not informing the consumer of potential safety hazards; or the consumption of public goods, such as satellite television broadcasts or search and rescue services, without adequate payment. This narrow view of regulation suggests that the system operates in the best interests of the greatest number, using some majoritarian or utilitarian method of development. The contrasting, positive theory, formulated by economist George Stigler (1971), suggests that self-serving individuals and groups can capture a regulatory system and forgo the public interest (defined as the protection and benefit of the public at large or some significant subclass). Instead of acting in the interests of the general public, then, those in control of the regulatory system design and operate it primarily for the benefit of some small, privileged subgroup in society. In this context, Anne Krueger's (1974) theory of rent seeking posits that firms seek to influence governments to construct favourable regulatory structures, or companies engage directly in constructing voluntary regulatory systems to reduce competition and generate market power that can be exploited. One can see examples in the regulatory system in Canada that conform to each of these perspectives.

Regulatory actions can also be seen as an integral part of the fiscal system that underpins the Canadian federation. Posner (1971) asserts that a significant part of the regulatory effort in many advanced industrial economies really acts as a form of taxation and income redistribution. In effect, the rules and their enforcement have substantial fiscal implications. Consequently, regulation can be seen as one aspect of the federal-provincial fiscal superstructure. Tiebout (1956) posited a pure theory of local expenditure, whereby it makes economic sense for local expenditures to vary to meet the different local interests and then to let citizens move to where the local costs and benefits best match their preferences. In effect, local or provincial governments should be able to tailor their offerings of policies, programs, and regulations to suit local needs and interests. Citizens who do not value the array of public goods or regulations on offer in any region are able to effectively "vote with their feet" by moving to other regions that offer a more attractive mix of policies. This theory offers a strong theoretical rationale for diversity in regulatory practice at the local and provincial level, and it somewhat offsets the general preference of business and policy advisors to seek interprovincial or international regulatory coordination or harmonization in an effort to "level the playing field" for firms and sectors conducting business in multiple jurisdictions or seeking to compete through trade. Moreover, as will be discussed in some detail, subsidiarity of regulatory authority in Canada has facilitated significant innovation in regulatory practice that might not have emerged if there were only a single, central regulatory authority.

Conceptually, analysis of regulatory systems can take several routes. First, many scholars and practitioners focus on the processes of developing and managing regulations. This approach generally puts the greatest emphasis on efficiency. Second, some analysts and practitioners are more concerned about the relative impact of specific regulations—are they justified, and do they offer returns adequate to justify their costs? This approach tends to have a normative framing, looking for efficacy and balance in the system. Third, central agencies, politicians, industry, and many regulators have been especially concerned in recent years about the interconnectivity of regulations. They examine the effects of interrelated regulations on different actors in the same jurisdiction and on similar actors in competing or complementary jurisdictions, for example. These analyses are often part of an effort to further the coordination and harmonization of regulation, which has varied widely in pace and scope in recent years. The internationalization of good regulatory practices through the proselytizing efforts of a few key developed nations and the collaborative processes of the OECD has led both to more coordination, i.e., to a gradual narrowing of differences between systems based on voluntary international codes of practice, and to harmonization, i.e., the standardization of regulation into identical forms (Davies 2002). Canada's provinces have been especially engaged in this third approach to regulation in an effort to ensure they can generate optimal economic and social benefits in their jurisdiction.

Legislation and Regulation in Canadian Provinces

Provinces draw their legislative and regulatory powers from the constitutional division of powers. As previously noted, the Canadian federation assigns through the Constitution Act, 1867 (formerly known as the British North America Act, 1867), powers to the federal government, to the provinces, or jointly to both orders of government. The federal government has authority over national priorities (see sections 91 and 92[1] of the Constitution Act, which related to defence, banking, foreign affairs, and many other national-level fields). Thus, the federal government regulates international and national trade and commerce, unemployment insurance, the postal service, defence, navigation and shipping, fisheries, quarantine, banking, weights and measures, bankruptcy, patents, copyrights, Indians and reserves, citizenship, marriage and divorce, criminal law, penitentiaries, and the works connecting provinces—those beyond the boundaries of one province and those within a province but to the advantage of Canada or more than one province. Provinces, in contrast, were assigned matters of a local nature, including education, labour markets, and business regulation (see especially sections 92, 92A, and 93 of the Constitution Act). Consequently, they have most of the authorities that affect our daily lives, including responsibility for municipalities, education, natural resources, the formalization of marriage, the protection of property and civil rights, the administration of civil and criminal justice, the incorporation of companies, the management and sale of public lands, the oversight of prisons and hospitals, and all matters of a merely local or private nature. Joint provincial-federal responsibilities are detailed in sections 94A and 95 of the Constitution Act and relate to pensions, agriculture, and immigration.

The actual scale and scope of activity is significant. On average, provinces have passed and are enforcing and implementing more than 500 acts each, which then generate something in the range of 900 to 3,000 specific regulations depending on the province. Table 4.1 shows the diversity of provincial legislative effort and offers some indication of the relative scale and direction of this effort. It is important to note that there is significant diversity among provinces as to the nature of this effort; some provinces (e.g., Alberta) legislate more than regulate while other provinces have more regulations than legislation. A somewhat dated study by Jones and Graf (2001) suggests also that provinces have been differentially engaged in regulatory reform—they reported that Alberta reduced the number of effective regulations almost by half between 1975 and 1999 while the Ontario and federal governments added 30 per cent and 53 per cent more regulations, respectively, over the same period.

Given the division of powers between the federal and provincial governments, it is inevitable that our lives are fundamentally affected by provincial rule making from sunup to sundown and from cradle to grave. As we wake in the morning and blearily look at the clock, the price and terms for the electricity used to power the clock are undoubtedly regulated by provincial statute, and, in some jurisdictions, the time on the clock is set by provincial fiat (i.e., Newfoundland's half-hour offset, Saskatchewan's year-long adherence to CST, and each province's determination of the start and end of daylight saving time). The homes we wake in were built according to standards set in provincial or municipal building codes by provincially regulated trades and general contractors, assessed by local or provincial inspectors, and sometimes protected by provincially mandated or facilitated warranties. Many of the foods we eat for breakfast—or for any meal of the day—were produced by farmers working within provincially administered marketing

TABLE 4.1 The Federal and Provincial Legislative and Regulatory Footprint

	LEGISLATION (DECEMBER 2011)	REGULATIONS PASSED IN 1999	PAGES OF REGULATIONS PROMULGATED IN 1999	TOTAL REGULATIONS IN FORCE IN 1999	PERCENTAGE CHANGE IN REGULATIONS IN FORCE, 1975 TO 1999
Canada	4305	616	2730	2925	+53%
NL	2292	110	588	—	—
PE	765	51	177	—	—
NS	1930	144	714	—	—
NB	1350	71	814	—	—
QC	3256	331	5408	—	—
ON	2375	637	1490	1868	+30%
MB	2192	183	1825	—	—
SK	1303	155	897	—	—
AB	2058	291	1153	979	−48%
BC	1906	471	987	2262	−8%
YT	1864	67	52	—	—
NT	876	104	411	—	—

Sources: The CanLII databases of the Federation of Law Societies of Canada, http://www.canlii.org/en/; Jones and Graf (2001); various provincial government websites that list legislation.

structures (e.g., the provincial marketing boards for eggs, milk, butter, pork, chickens, turkeys, and vegetables). Then these foods were transported and delivered to a local store (whose hours of operation and public health and safety rules are provincially mandated). The transportation system used for food delivery is also provincially regulated (especially commercial trucking). To get to work, you might walk, bike, drive, bus, or use the light rail—the rights and obligations of both users and suppliers are laid out in highway traffic, licensing, and municipal codes. Once at work, most workers are governed by labour standards, occupational health and safety regulations, and workers' compensation rules, as well as by a provincially administered trade union or a provincially mandated, self-governing professional association, such as those for doctors, lawyers, engineers, nurses, architects, accountants, agrologists, policemen, and teachers, to name but a few. Moreover, the structure and operation of the firms that employ us are, for the most part, provincially incorporated, regulated, and governed. As we contemplate our duties, our benefits, our hours of work and terms of employment, the subtle hand of government guides and directs our choices. Once work is done and we contemplate our leisure, provincial laws and regulations define who can access what activities (e.g., bars, live entertainment, movies), at what time, and in what place. These and many more rules, which are often quite subtle, govern almost every activity we might consider. Over the course of our lives, provincial rules are even more significant, as they define our rights to public services from the moment of birth (e.g., at the hand of a licensed midwife at home or in a hospital with an accredited specialist). Throughout our adolescence, we use the education system, and provinces define the curriculum, how it should be delivered and accessed, and the minimum standards for progression and completion. We rely on provincial regulation in the context of economic, social, and criminal justice and in terms of our ability to access quality-controlled supplementary services and support as we age and require additional care. Ultimately, our deaths, the disposal of our bodies, the wrap-up of our affairs, and the dispersal of our estates are mediated by provincial rules.

Until recently, the constitutional division of authorities translated largely into watertight compartments for the respective competencies. According to the 1937 "Labour Conventions case" (*Attorney General of Canada v. Attorney-General of Ontario*, 1937), although only the federal executive is empowered to enter into international treaties, the federal government cannot legislate to implement treaties in areas that fall within provincial jurisdictions (Barnett 2008). Other federations, such as Australia, empower their federal authorities to legislate to implement treaties, even if the subject matter falls outside federal jurisdiction (Eid 2001). A recent Supreme Court of Canada decision—*Mavis Baker v. Canada (Minister of Citizenship)*, 1999—has opened the possibility that international instruments might be used as powerful interpretative guides to domestic statutory construction even though they have not been implemented by our lawmakers in provincial or federal statute—whether this opens up provincial jurisdiction to federal engagement is yet to be seen (Norman 2012).

Key Areas of Provincial Regulatory Innovation

The current structure of the federal-provincial system is a source of both tension and innovation. This is especially true in the regulatory realm, where provinces have unique areas of authority but there are significant opportunities for rules and systems to interlock and over-lap. In the face of that complexity, governments and citizens have developed a range of top-down, bottom-up, and collective efforts to create innovative regulatory policies.

In the first instance, governments everywhere are learning from each other about new and better ways to develop, manage, review, and renew legislation and regulation. The first move along this line came in the 1980s, as conservative governments in the UK, US, Australia, New Zealand, and Canada came to power on platforms of reducing the role of government, including by reducing regulatory red tape. In Canada, Erik Nielsen, the deputy prime minister in the Mulroney Conservative government in the spring of 1986, developed a federal regulatory reform strategy that, for the first time, called for all new regulations to be subject to economic and social cost analysis and committed the government to greater public involvement in the regulatory process. To demonstrate its commitment, the federal government later that year created the Ministry of State for Privatization and Regulatory Affairs, which worked with the Office of Privatization and Regulatory Affairs to promote the government's regulatory objectives. One early result was that the average time-frame for regulatory approval decreased to three from nine months (TBS 1997). The main focus in the 1986–91 period was to review and amend federal telecommunications, transportation, and environmental regulations, all of which had knock-on effects on the provinces. After this time, the federal government moved authority for regulatory reform to the Treasury Board Secretariat and put a new plan into place that commits the government to annual regulatory plans, regulatory impact analysis (RIA) statements for all new regulations, public consultation and information delivery on all draft regulations, and amendments and review of all regulatory efforts over set periods (statutes every 10 years and regulations and regulatory programs every 7 years) (TBS 1997). The 2012 federal budget added several elements to regulatory policy, introducing a "one-for-one" rule requiring agencies not add to the "burden" of regulations, especially for small and medium-sized firms. In support of those principles, the federal government has borrowed a burden calculator from Alberta and has indicated it may introduce some form of "burden credits" that can be banked or traded among regulatory agencies. It is too early to assess how these developments will affect the regulatory system in Canada.

One result of the general efforts to govern more effectively through regulation is that leading regulatory innovators in Canada, the US, Australia, the UK, and New Zealand worked with other member states at the OECD to develop best practices on regulatory impact assessment. The current best practices posit that effective regulation requires these things: a political commitment to RIA; the careful allocation of responsibilities for RIA program elements; the use of a consistent but flexible analytical method; the application and targeting of RIA to existing as well as new regulations; the development of strategies for data collection; the integration of RIA with general policymaking as early as possible in the process; extensive public involvement, which necessitates communicating RIA results effectively; and continuous training for regulators (OECD 1997). Although the provinces may not have been the leaders in regulatory reform, they were responsive. In the first instance, conservative provincial governments, and a few left-of-centre governments in the late 1980s and into the 1990s all emulated the federal processes of reviewing existing regulations and then establishing more structured processes for regulatory action. These efforts have been stylized as initiatives in support of regulatory reform, red tape reduction, smart regulation, better regulation, or regulatory excellence, to name but a few (David Redmond and Associates 2011). The Saskatchewan effort at regulatory reform is representative of other provinces' efforts. In the first term of the Grant Devine Conservative government, there was a program to reduce and revise the regulatory burden on firms in the province. Although this program reduced the number and size of regulations, little changed in terms of the effects of regulations. In 1995, the Romanow government formalized that effort with a Regulations Act, which committed the government to reduce provincial regulations by 25 per cent within 10 years. The government reported that, during the mandate of the so-called "Regulatory Reform Initiative," 98 per cent of the province's 945 regulations were reviewed and the total net reduction in regulations was 28 per cent by 2004–05, the last year of the initiative (David Redmond and Associates 2011). What is less clear is what effect this type of technical reform had on the impact and reach of the rules.

In response to the difficulty of readily identifying the impact of regulatory reform, both the federal and many provincial governments have attempted to sharpen their focus on the goals, administration, and impact of regulations in specific areas. This changed focus led to two specific approaches: 1) institutional and administrative reform

that offered one-stop service for federal, provincial, and often municipal regulations and 2) federal-provincial and interprovincial agreements to coordinate or harmonize regulations in an effort to remove
impediments to economic mobility within the federation.

The one-stop model has been around in various shapes and sizes
for the better part of 25 years. Often, the leading innovator using this
model is a province that creates a program, service organization, or
set of service centres to provide a single window into the regulatory
process for incorporating and operating a business in the province.
Although these initiatives have a range of names—BC's Small Business
Lens, Alberta's Business Link, and the joint federal-provincial programs such as Canada Business Ontario and the Canada–Provincial
Business Service Centres in the rest of the provinces—they generally
offer the same basic access to business forms and program applications
and advice, and these are delivered either face to face in major centres
or via telephone, fax-back systems, or the Internet. The information
offered usually addresses how to register a business and how to obtain
all the necessary operating and zoning permits, financing, marketing,
technology, and skills programming for supporting and growing a
business. Also on offer are the forms and rules related to labour markets, the environment, public health and safety, and taxation, among
many others. Although one might quibble about who thought up the
ideas behind many programs and services on offer, the provinces were
directly involved in their development and implementation and, consequently, influenced both their nature and number and the structures
used to offer them. In short, the one-stop model has been a form of
competitive innovation, with diffusion initially between the two orders
of government and then, more generally, among the provinces.

A second approach to streamlining and making more effective regulation has involved intergovernmental negotiation. In the 1980s and
early 1990s, provinces began to suspect that their local rules and processes were fragmenting the Canadian labour, capital, product, and service markets (some asserted the economy was becoming Balkanized),
at the very time that the national government was opening up trade
links through the Canada–United States Free Trade Agreement (1987),
the North American Free Trade Agreement (1994), and the "Uruguay
Round" of the General Agreement on Tariffs and Trade, which yielded
the World Trade Organization (WTO) Agreement in 1995. Policy
actors asserted that the largely disconnected provincial regulatory
systems in some ways made it easier for foreign companies to trade

in Canada than for domestic firms to trade interprovincially. A range of efforts to rebalance international and interprovincial trade regulation ensued, led respectively by the federal government and then by provinces that were neighbours and sought to work out mutually beneficial agreements. Shortly after NAFTA came into force, the federal and provincial governments negotiated what became the Agreement on Internal Trade (AIT), a binding agreement to govern interprovincial commerce. The agreement laid out a set of guiding principles (non-discrimination among Canadian persons; right of entry and exit; no obstacles to interprovincial trade, except when justified by legitimate objectives; and reconciliation and transparency), and it directly addressed regulatory issues in 11 specific policy areas, including procurement, investment, labour mobility, consumer-related measures and standards, agricultural and food products, alcoholic beverages, natural resource processing, energy, communications, transportation, and environmental protection. To add teeth to the agreement, the signatories created a permanent secretariat and a dispute resolution process for governments, individuals, and the private sector (ITS n.d.).

As discussed in Chapter 1, on top of this agreement, several neighbouring provinces have negotiated bilateral or multilateral agreements that address specific irritants or opportunities between the provinces. In 2007, a new Ontario-Québec Trade and Cooperation Agreement (2011) was created that incorporated aspirational economic development goals (e.g., innovation corridors, joint tourism marketing, multimodal transportation, a high-speed rail link, and coordinated green development) and that addressed several specific regulatory issues (e.g., common notice and transparency rules related to matters affecting bilateral trade; mutual recognition of labour qualifications for professionals and tradespeople; and harmonized rules for financial services, transportation, procurement, trade in agricultural and food products, and the environment). Concurrently, the provinces of Nova Scotia, New Brunswick, and PEI pursued a Maritime Economic Cooperation Agreement, which enshrines in provincial statute many of the same goals of the other agreements but which has a particular focus on economic advancement through labour and product mobility and consistent regulatory systems. But, in spite of lofty goals, the local view is that the "wind has gone out of the sails" for achieving gains from greater economic integration via deregulation, particularly in the area of agri-food trade (Robinson 2005). Most recently, after more than a decade of discussion among Western premiers about the potential to strengthen the Western Canadian economy through a greater liberalization of markets, BC and Alberta, both with right-of-centre governments, signed in 2006 the Trade, Investment and Labour Mobility Agreement (TILMA) to reduce impediments to the free flow of people, investment, and products through the mutual recognition and reduction of barriers to market access. The premiers in Saskatchewan and Manitoba, both leaders of NDP governments, declined to participate. In 2010, with a new right-of-centre government in Saskatchewan, TILMA was extended to incorporate Saskatchewan and renamed the New West Partnership Trade Agreement (NWPTA 2009).

Provincial governments have also been at the forefront of regulatory innovations in several key areas, such as labour, the environment, agri-food trade, and financial regulation.

One of the earliest and most pervasive and influential areas of government regulation relates to the workplace. Although the constitutional division of powers suggests that the provinces are the appropriate locus for labour legislation and regulation, there has been a healthy contest between the two orders of government over who will do what first. The first move came at the federal level when the Macdonald government responded to the Toronto Typographical Union strike with the first federal Trade Unions Act in 1872. Although that innovation was only slowly taken up and formalized—Saskatchewan, for instance, only passed a provincial trade union act in the 1940s with the election of the social democratic Cooperative Commonwealth Federation (CCF) government—the provinces branched out and added key parts to what we now regard as the critical underpinnings for the labour market. Ontario, for example, became the first province to introduce a state social insurance plan with the Workmen's Compensation Act in 1914. Before this innovation, the only recourse for employees injured on the job was to sue their employers for damages. A provincial Royal Commission recommended a no-fault, mandatory insurance scheme that was adopted by the province (Ontario Workplace Tribunals Library 2009). Another innovation, the Occupational Health Act that Saskatchewan passed in 1972, is considered the first legislation in North America that makes workplace health and safety the joint responsibility of management and workers. The legislation enshrined workers' rights to know about hazards in the workplace, to participate in health and safety issues through workplace committees, and to refuse unsafe work. These provincial innovations are now commonplace policy across Canada and in much of the developed world.

The environment is another area of significant regulatory innovation. In the past generation, governments have markedly increased their assessment and management of the environmental effects of industrial developments, be they agri-food enterprises, mines, forest operations, manufacturing plants, roads, rails, pipelines, airports, or water diversions. The general rule has been that what happens in a province gets regulated within that province. That position changes when the activity falls within federal jurisdiction or when the development has impacts that cross provincial boundaries (e.g., air and water discharges) or impinges on an international boundary (such as water flows) or on federally regulated coastal waters. In the same way that the general approach to regulation is becoming more rigorous and structured, environmental regulation is being more formally structured. Now a major focus of governments, this form of regulation has as its general intent optimizing development, subject to certain irreducible standards of public health, safety, and environmental integrity.

One major challenge in the field of environmental regulation is that some of the larger developments can, at times, trigger the oversight of both federal and provincial regulators. One of the biggest reviews in Canada ever was the assessment of seven different uranium-mining proposals in Saskatchewan in 1991, which required action by both the province and the federal government. The package included the mining of nine ore bodies, the construction of one mill, the design of two tailings management facilities, and the expansion of associated transportation infrastructure. A major innovation from that process was the use of a single review panel jointly mandated by the federal and provincial governments. Using a single assessment to address the legislative and regulatory needs of both governments made it possible to eliminate duplication and reduce the costs and time required. The joint review was also the first to include the consideration of regional cumulative impacts resulting from the development of several projects within the same timeframe and geographic area. By reviewing several projects under a single mandate, the panel was able to consider the cumulative environmental and socio-economic effects of all of the proposed developments, which offered it an opportunity to consider options to reduce the overall impact of the developments by combining some aspects of the operations. One specific outcome was the decision to custom-mill ore from several mines at a limited number of sites, thereby reducing the number of mills and tailings management facilities to be built and decommissioned (CEAA 1997). This practice of joint review was not widely adopted until recently. With the passing of the Canadian Environmental Protection Act (S.C. 1992, c. 37), a series of federal agreements with individual provinces were negotiated to coordinate joint reviews—in short, to implement practically what has come to be known as the "one project–one assessment" approach. The practice until recently was for federal authorities to limit the scope of a federal assessment to include only aspects of a project that fell under federal jurisdiction; all aspects that were provincial responsibilities were removed from any federal assessment. As a result, a development would usually be reviewed comprehensively and thoroughly at the provincial level, but the federal agency would do a less rigorous screening, relying instead on the provincial assessment as part of its review. A recent court case in BC triggered a change, providing for a more integrated review; this is now managed through a policy entitled the "Use of Federal-Provincial Cooperation Mechanisms in EIAs pursuant to the Canadian Environmental Assessment Act" (CEAA 2010). In a related manner, provinces have begun to try to co-regulate natural resources, such as wetlands, grasslands and forests, watersheds, inland fisheries, and various other place-based flora and fauna with First Nations, Inuit, and Métis and sometimes with non-Aboriginal interest groups, such as Ducks Unlimited. There are undoubtedly real-world examples of shared management in most provinces. Two well-documented examples are the effort of the Québec and federal governments to co-manage salmon in the Restigouche River with the Listuguj Mi'gmaq (Native Nations Institute 2010) and the forestry co-management agreement involving the province of Saskatchewan, the Meadow Lake Tribal Council, and Mistik Management Ltd. (Orb 2008).

Provinces and the federal government have also competed and collaborated to assess and develop performance-based regulation. Traditional prescriptive regulation tells operators exactly what they must do to comply with the law while performance- or goal-based regulation identifies outcomes that operators must achieve but allows them to choose how to do so. As far back as the early sixties, the federal government experimented with performance-based requirements in the building code—in 1965, Part 9 of the National Building Code was published with a set of functional requirements but without any specific technical requirements (Oleszkiewicz 1994). This approach has diffused into several areas, such as environmental and operational safety for oil and gas drilling, both onshore and offshore, and it is particularly useful when the proper approaches to managing risk effectively are too diverse (site-specific, for example) to be defined fully in regulations (Conference Board of Canada 2004). In those cases, defining the required outcomes and leaving it up to operators to figure out how to comply with these goals often works more effectively.

Cooperation between individual provinces and the federal government has also begun to facilitate greater interprovincial trade in some agri-food products. For example, a recent Interprovincial Meat Trade Pilot Project, which includes federal, provincial, and territorial governments, created a series of experiments to investigate barriers and to better position provincially regulated processed meat as a safe, high-quality product in other markets in Canada (CFIA 2011).

Although one might get the impression that all is sweetness and light in regulatory matters between the provinces and the federal government and that common sense drives effort, there remain some hard files that have seen little movement. The single largest issue now facing Canada, and most advanced industrial economies, is the effective and efficient regulation of financial markets. Given the constitutional division of powers, the stock exchanges and many financial institutions—excluding chartered banks and a few federally chartered trust and insurance companies—are governed by provincial rules. Although the exchanges are supervised by provincial securities commissions, they are essentially self-regulating, which causes some concern for the federal government. Provinces have not been keen to give up or share this authority, as most provincial officials and ministers believe that doing so would reduce their ability to influence and encourage locally useful innovations in local capital markets while others are concerned that national regulation might lead to consolidation and loss of access to the markets themselves. In the past, several provinces have used this flexibility to support innovative financial structures, such as the *caisses populaires* in Québec that are networked through the Desjardins Group, which owns and also operates a securities brokerage and a venture capital firm. Other examples include the provincial credit unions outside of Québec, ATB Financial (a creation of the Alberta Treasury Branch), and various local savings and loan institutions. Moreover, several provinces have benefitted by developing local stock exchanges; at the peak of this development, there were exchanges in Vancouver, Calgary, Winnipeg, Toronto, and Montreal (the Halifax exchange has long since ceased independent operations). In 1999, the four key stock exchanges (not including Winnipeg, which was invited in later) restructured to become more specialized in an effort to increase their competitive abilities. The Vancouver and Alberta stock exchanges formed the National Junior Equities Market (the Vancouver Stock Exchange or TSX-V), which took over Canadian Dealing Network activities from the Toronto exchange (then the TSE). Toronto was renamed the TSX and became responsible for trading all Senior Canadian Equities (assuming some activity from the Montreal Stock Exchange, MSE). The MSE now concentrates on trading futures and options (which are no longer traded on the TSX) (Grant 2012).

The reorganization of provincial exchanges is at the root of two important developments. First, the consolidation of junior equities in Vancouver gave Canada the base, ultimately, to become the single largest market for trading in venture-based and established mining stocks. In 2011, the TSX and TSX-V were home to 58 per cent of the world's public mining companies, and issuers listed on these two markets were involved in raising 60 per cent of the world's mining equity capital. Over the previous decade, those two exchanges were involved in more than 80 per cent of the mining equity raised globally (Hanick, Vernon, and Brown 2012). Second, the TSX has recently become a takeover target of the London Stock Exchange (LSE), as the leading global markets attempt to bridge across time zones and leading national economies. (By 2007, the LSE had already acquired Borsa Italiana and partnered with the NASDAQ in the United States while the NYSE had merged with Euronext; in 2012, NYSE Euronext had a deal pending to merge with Deutsche Börse, but this merger was scrapped after the EU offered strong opposition.)

The global financial crisis that started in 2008 represented a tipping point in financial regulation. Though, over the past 45 years, most of the studies by independent analysts favoured a Canadian securities regulator, little progress was made (Pan 2009). In 2008, the global financial meltdown, brought on because of ineffective financial regulation in the United States and the EU, re-energized the federal government. It appointed an expert panel on securities regulation, which, in 2009, pointed to concerns that the fragmented structure of the financial regulatory landscape (with up to 13 jurisdictions involved in some decisions) could slow responses to global capital market events—the provincial regulation of the capital market may simply be at the wrong level. Moreover, the diffusion of authorities unevenly allocates resources between policy development, supervision, and enforcement, which leads to inefficient and undesirable differences. On the basis of this set of concerns, the final report of the expert panel recommended the establishment of a single Canadian securities regulator to administer a single securities act for Canada. The federal government accepted the recommendation, set up a Canadian Securities Transition Office to lead the effort, and appointed an advisory committee of participating provinces and territories—which included all provinces and territories except Alberta, Manitoba, and Québec (CSTO 2011). Given the incomplete support of the provinces, the federal government referred its draft legislation to the Supreme Court of Canada for a ruling on whether the matter was within the legislative authority of Parliament. In late December 2011, the Court ruled that the federal government's attempts to unify securities regulation in Canada were unconstitutional (Supreme Court of Canada 2011). And so the debate continues.

Perhaps the most promising aspect of regulation in Canada is that the debates and disputes in one field seldom spill over and derail or slow efforts in other policy areas. Given that these policy areas are largely populated by highly skilled experts with common world views, common vocabularies and concepts, and common assessments regarding what constitutes good regulation, policymakers are often able to overcome the sometimes heated political discourse that dominates other aspects of federal-provincial politics in Canada.

Issues and Challenges

Legislation and regulation, especially at the provincial level, reflect the battle lines in Canadian society. Rules assign rights and duties, they limit or empower action, and, as asserted by Posner (1971), they effectively tax and redistribute. The challenges facing all regulators, including Canadian regulators, can be categorized into questions of efficiency and efficacy. Although regulations can and often do substitute for other government measures, they are not always the most efficient way of addressing problems. Similarly, though regulatory systems have undertaken efforts to become much more accountable, responsible, and transparent, fundamental theoretical and practical challenges face the system in coming years.

Federal and provincial legislative and regulatory processes have become much more structured and purposeful in recent years. Stigler's

(1971) concern that the positive approach to regulation would increase rent-seeking opportunities (i.e., enhance the chances that some groups could manipulate the economic environment to ensure their own advantage) is now fully recognized in both the literature and in the management of Canadian government regulatory systems—at least within traditional areas of regulation. Recently, there has been significant government effort in Canada and globally to review and restructure regulations that are outdated or that are judged to generate more costs than benefits. Interventions in agri-food marketing (especially the use of quotas), in transportation and telecommunications, in resource industries, and in various other goods and services areas have been revised, coordinated, or harmonized to enhance competition and reduce economic inefficiency. The challenge is that, while traditional regulatory capture is being managed, difficulties have arisen due to the use of regulation in a wide range of new areas or due to the privatization of regulatory power. Much of the current theory assumes that only producers have an incentive to seek "rents" or economic advantages. Perdikis and Kerr (1999) assert that consumers are now actively rent seeking but that our rules, processes, and institutions are not designed to counteract this pressure. Consumers are increasingly attempting to assert their preferences not only through what Hirschman (1970) called exit, voice, and loyalty but also through demands on governments and firms to enact potentially discriminatory and economically inefficient legislative and regulatory provisions. This consumer advocacy can be a particular problem at the provincial level, where relationships between regulators and the regulated are often close and personal. Our regulatory systems are not well structured to handle these pressures. The result can, at times, be discriminatory policies that might generate consumer benefits but at the expense of owners of capital or labour. At times, regulations may generate opportunities for businesses to rent-seek in the wake of market imperfections. Consumer-initiated regulations might very well meet the "legitimate objectives" test embedded in most trade agreements, but they still can be discriminatory and inefficient (Smyth, Phillips, and Kerr 2009; Smyth, Kerr, and Phillips 2011). A greater concern might arise if dominant firms and industries take onto themselves the role of regulating to meet these new consumer preferences—there is a real possibility that, if the state devolves authority and fails to oversee the implementation of voluntary regulation, firms will use their new power to collude and act in an anticompetitive way. Political scientist Robert Gilpin (2001) has suggested that, in the extreme, we risk ending up with a neo-medieval system in which we are overgoverned by a complex web of vested interests, creating regulation that is analogous to the guild structure of the Middle Ages.

A second and equally problematic issue is that public policy systems, in Canada and abroad, appear to exhibit a collective inability to develop and manage decision-making processes for complex problems. Most regulatory effort assumes clear causal links, with specific ends addressed by specific regulatory measures. Although many problems are like this, we are discovering that some problems are more complex and interconnected. Both at the level of the individual decision maker in the market and at the level where public servants develop and deliver effective public policies in the fields of health care, welfare, education, the economy, justice, and trade, among others, it is increasingly difficult to find explicit cause-and-effect relationships. There are significant feedback loops that can translate simple solutions into perverse outcomes. Some are concerned that these types of problems have grown exponentially in recent years, but theory and practice related to complex decision making is lagging (Phillips 2007). Although more responsive and sophisticated regulatory structures may seem like obvious solutions to this challenge, they could also become part of the problem itself if they add to the complexity of the system.

In any modern economy and society, effective governance requires the facility to develop, adapt, and adopt new ideas and organizational structures. Ultimately, this process involves the identification, assembly, and use of disparate types of information and knowledge through a wide range of social governing systems. Legislation and regulation tends to be too formal, too slow, and too inflexible to meet many needs in this world. Instead of direct regulation, we are seeing a rise in co-regulation, partnerships, and self-regulation, all of which engage new groups with new interests in new ways.

Recent theoretical work suggests that our problems may be deeper than simply getting the architecture right. Modern and experimental behavioural theories challenge our faith in the rationality of those tasked with decision making. Experiments in both personal and economic decision making (e.g., Kahneman and Tversky 1979; Smith 1976, 1982) suggest that individuals make decisions based on their starting frames and an array of heuristics (general rules) that only occasionally deliver results consistent with the predictions of rational-actor, public-choice models. Many difficult policy problems are characterized by multiple interacting parameters, outcomes of unknown probability, and nonlinear relationships among the interested parties. Current decision theory assumes that the rules of rational cognition can be applied to a clearly defined, probabilistic set of choices and outcomes. These assumptions are used to identify optimal or likely policy outcomes. Recent advances in theory and analysis challenge this narrow, somewhat deterministic approach. The field of behavioural psychology has done groundbreaking research into the role of frames and heuristics in individual decision making. This emerging field operates from the perspective that an individual's cognitive processes are not necessarily ordered in a strictly rational way—in other words, processes that engage well-intentioned and intelligent people may not yield predictable outcomes. The best of intentions could lead to the worst of outcomes. This problem could become greater as the policy system engages a greater diversity of actors with widely different backgrounds and expectations. A fuller and better understanding of decision theory and practice is needed to construct more effective regulatory regimes. This challenges policy analysts to frame their analyses of decision making more carefully and administrators to disentangle actors and events and to audit and assess the impacts of specific legislative or regulatory actions.

Conclusion

The interplay between federal and provincial regulatory authorities illuminates the diverse theoretical approaches to the study of regulation. There is evidence of both normative and positive approaches to regulation and of strategic rent seeking, competitive rule making, and administrative and policy innovation consistent with the Tiebout (1956) thesis about the efficacy of local and regional administration. Throughout, the underlying tension between the provincial and the federal systems remains—central governments seek to advance a regulatory agenda of coordination and harmonization while provincial governments rebuff efforts that stifle their authority to address local concerns with innovative solutions.

In the context of the evidence offered in this chapter, one can see the normative approach permeating much of the policy innovation at the provincial level, as provincial governments individually and sequentially have addressed public good and other market failures by advancing legislation and regulation to redress asymmetric information and bargaining power in labour, capital, and commercial markets and to protect and sustain human health and the natural environment. Nevertheless, there is significant evidence that many of the specific legislative and regulatory measures related to labour markets, agri-food marketing, and the financial markets offer real opportunities for rent-seeking and anticompetitive behaviours. The introduction of regulatory impact assessment, new policies and processes to assess the relative costs and benefits of specific regulations, and substantial federal-provincial coordination are all attempts to limit the potential for economically destructive rent seeking on the basis of regulations.

Similarly, the federal-provincial regulatory landscape is an obvious place to look for tensions between the normative approach to regulation—which tends to support central government action to enact universally applied, harmonized regulations throughout a nation—and an approach based on the Tiebout thesis, which argues that federal-provincial and interprovincial diversity enables a better match between local goals and local means. Moreover, there is significant evidence that provincial experimentation with regulations in a wide range of fields has led to substantive innovation. The development of much of our labour policy, the unique global capacity of Canada for raising capital to back global mining ventures, and innovative approaches to managing the environment all are inextricably linked to the authoritative role of provinces in these fields. Although one cannot say with any certainty that the central government would not otherwise have happened on these approaches, there is no reason to suppose that they would have. Thus, the Canadian experience lends strong support to the Tiebout thesis.

Both in Canada and across the global market economy, the regulatory world is a microcosm of the multilevel and multifunctional nature of governing. This is especially true in the Canadian federation, with strong governments at the federal and provincial level and an increasingly competent local order of government. It is likely that Canada and its provinces will continue to find innovative solutions to existing and emerging Canadian problems, but these governments may also find ways to contribute to global economic and social development by innovating and diffusing new regulatory models to other jurisdictions. In some ways, the regulatory landscape symbolizes the quintessential Canadian approach of moderation and professionalism. Although the provincial regulatory state is, at times, a source of friction, it is frequently a source of innovation and compromise that helps to address the challenges of a dynamic economy and society.

CHAPTER FIVE

Civil Society, Policy Networks, and the Production of Expertise

Introduction

The future of public policy and public administration in the provinces will be guided by several emerging trends prompting governments at all levels to modernize and adapt to new social, political, and economic realities. As has been discussed in previous chapters, government has traditionally been defined by hierarchal top-down structures and a technocratic, expert-driven bureaucracy, with conflict occurring between the state and external actors (other jurisdictions, civil society). Through its institutions, the state manages many delimited and decomposable problems using established linear planning and implementation processes. However, the modern policymaking process does not always lend itself to classic public administration approaches to problem handling because many modern social, ecological, economic, and technological problems are characterized by complexity and ambiguity surrounding social goals. As a result, problem-solving activities involve an increasingly diverse set of actors with governments having to steer policy activities through multilevel interorganizational negotiations (Rhodes 1996) and from within new information and communication environments (Margetts 2009).

This chapter takes a systematic look at the complex and modern relationship between those involved in policy governance, both state and non-state actors, and the production of policy expertise in the provinces. The decentralized nature of Canada's federal polity and new trends in network governance and information communication technologies have altered provincial governance policy advice systems significantly. Provincial policy analysts have traditionally played a dominant role in policy formulation, implementation, and fiscal allocation processes; however, in modern policy settings, policy knowledge and innovation come from a variety of different sources with collaborative, multilevel policymaking activities being common. As Kettl (2000) observes, in the past, much government power and authority grew from expertise; however, the increased availability of information and new information communication technologies (ITCs) have shifted government influence away from this monopolistic position (McGuire 2000). As a result, provincial policy networks increasingly operate as key knowledge production agents, playing an active role in problem definition, policy design, and program implementation. Across Canada, the variable interests within these provincial policy networks go a long ways toward explaining why similar access to information has resulted in divergent policy choices.

Provincial policy networks vary across Canada, with different regional priorities influencing the nature of network organization. Each policy network's reception to new ideas will be filtered through both an institutional and historical context shaped by political elites, the region's economic base, advocacy coalitions, public values, and policy capacity (Dunn 2006b; Wiseman 1996). Ideational structures have a significant effect on policy network organization, provincial or otherwise. For example, in the eighties and nineties, both the diffusion of neo-liberal ideas associated with public management reform and the pressures on the provincial public services to downsize, cut programming, and restructure service delivery had very different impacts across the provinces. Although all the provinces introduced major expenditure reductions, the discourse surrounding these activities was influenced by different normative assumptions that were emblematic of provincial cultures and related to views about federalism and the role of government. In Alberta and Ontario, ideas associated with neo-liberalism were typically embedded in partisan discussions surrounding the size of government and laissez-faire economics. Alternatively, conversations concerning the appropriate reform agenda in Québec focused more on modernization and the renewal of the public service. Although the political mood of Alberta and Ontario produced strong support for neo-liberal ideas and provided political elites with the opportunity to legitimize some policy options while ignoring others, public views in Québec supported a major role for the public sector in policy development (Clark 2002). In sum, the transfer of policy ideas into the provinces is shaped by both the legacy of each province's distinct culture and the policy environment in which decisions are negotiated.

We begin this chapter with a discussion of five key concepts, which we then use to examine policy knowledge production in the provinces. These five concepts are civil society, the policy analysis movement, collaborative policymaking, the network society, and the digital state. We then consider several key trends and associated challenges facing the provinces' capacity to produce innovative policy ideas and to develop public service expertise. First is the impact of information communication technologies on government. Second, we examine policy analytic capacity and the provincial government's supply of policy advice. Third, the trend toward greater public engagement and stakeholder participation is considered, a trend that has significantly altered provincial political cultures and decision-making processes. Finally, we discuss the emerging virtual civil society and examine some future trends associated with second-generation web technologies and post-Internet policy activity.

Key Concepts

CIVIL SOCIETY

Individuals engage collectively in a wide range of associations and communities that help to define and mobilize their values, interests, and practices. These organizations are defined in several ways, but all exert authority in the civic domain. They are variously labelled the third sector, not-for-profit organizations, voluntary organizations, interest or pressure groups, civil society organizations (CSOs), or non-governmental organizations (NGOs). However these civil authorities are labelled, they span our lives, from cradle to grave.

The concept of civil society is a good starting point for the study of these actors. A working definition of this concept from the Centre for Civil Society of the London School of Economics is illustrative:

> Civil society refers to the arena of uncoerced collective action around
> shared interests, purposes and values. In theory, its institutional
> forms are distinct from those of the state, family and market, though

in practice, the boundaries between state, civil society, family and market are often complex, blurred and negotiated. Civil society commonly embraces a diversity of spaces, actors and institutional forms, varying in their degree of formality, autonomy and power. Civil societies are often populated by organisations such as registered charities, development non-governmental organisations, community groups, women's organisations, faith-based organisations, professional associations, trade unions, self-help groups, social movements, business associations, coalitions and advocacy groups. (Kaldor, Anheier, and Glasius 2004)

Civil society actors are inextricably involved in policy development, variously leading, following, or feeling alienated as they attempt to fit into and drive the policy system. One can see that the opportunities for engagement will vary depending on whether the system is dealing with simple or highly technical matters and whether the issues under review are uniquely placed within the competence of a single order of government or under the jurisdiction of multiple levels and regions (Teisman 2000).

Civil society produces key elements that make our economy and society work. The collective or civil sector relies on informal kinships to effect what might be called "reasonable" reciprocity (Benáček 2005). Their instruments of power are far less structured than those of the state (with its coercive administrative institutions) or of the market (which uses money, capital, and contracts). Civil society actors rely on culture, moral codes, natural law, and social cohesion to achieve consensual, often ethically based exchanges and action.

Both at the small group size and in the integrated whole, civil society actors develop norms and conventions that create social space and provide the foundation for governing both intra-organizational activities and external efforts. All of these organizations exhibit shared attitudes and make claims upon other groups in society for the establishment, maintenance, or enhancement of forms of behaviour that conform to their shared attitudes (Truman 1951). To succeed, each inevitably needs to identify some unifying norms, values, beliefs, or assumptions; to develop a common language; to choose an acknowledged set of methodologies or practices; to identify and mobilize members and partners; to define goals or targets; and, ultimately, to develop a set of governing rules that will manage the relationships in the organization.

Beyond the two traditional authorities of family and religion, Canadians belong to an array of civil society structures that reflect the complexity of their condition as modern social beings. Ethnic groups, schools, trades, and workplaces offer structure and identity, while our social and leisure pursuits offer meaning and purpose. There are tens of thousands of groups, charities, and organizations devoted to extending our values, pursuing our interests, and sustaining specific practices.

THE POLICY ANALYSIS MOVEMENT

Civil society actors play a growing role in policy governance and in the production of expertise and policy ideas because, in our society, there is no single source of idea production but rather a marketplace of information, some of it novel and some of it traditional. Crossing the increasingly porous boundary between state and civil society, provincial policy analysts work with structured analytical tools and techniques to provide decision makers with quality advice and optimized solutions to public problems. Public executives and government ministers use this information to inform solution selection using rational analysis in the context of political feasibility, democratic expectations, and provincial priorities. Consequently, the skill sets of policy analysts are the very foundation of a government's capacity to achieve its intended actions. The influence of the policy analysis movement in Canada and shifting procedural norms, such as those related to collaborative policymaking and to network governance, have significantly altered the knowledge bases of provincial policy analysts.

Today the origins of novel information are increasingly diverse. Information emerges not just from within the context of empirical research but also from public enthusiasm, political preferences, historical norms, and shifting democratic expectations. With the aid of new interactive, collaborative technologies, the Internet and the web have fundamentally altered the means by which policy actors participate in policymaking activities; all of governments' traditional civil society partners and stakeholders are going online (Margetts 2009). As second-generation web technologies continue to grow in popularity, governments increasingly experiment with various social media campaigns that are supported by extensive electronic-government (e-government) architecture. Although the applications of digital governing tools remain in the early stages of development, there is growing evidence that this trend will have significant implications for politics, public administration, and civil society, namely, that the density of online communication networks will provide greater access to information, more opportunities to engage in public debate, and an enhanced capacity to undertake collective action.

The policy analysis movement refers to the personnel and resources (authority, analytic method, and knowledge) used to produce policy analysis. The legacy of the policy analysis movement dates back to the late 1960s and early 1970s, when an influential group of intellectuals began to accumulate bureaucratic skills and, increasingly, to connect analytically grounded knowledge (e.g., impact assessment, cost-benefit analysis, comparative analysis, gender-based analysis) with policy-making. As Michael Mintrom (2007) explains, the "use of the term [policy analysis] is intended to imply a deliberate effort on the part of many people to reconceive the role of government in society and renegotiate aspects of the relationships that exists between individuals, collectives, and governments" (145). Although not all policy analysts share the same sense of purpose, there is a general recognition that modern policy analysis does more than simply supply advice to decision makers, and that it also plays a role in encouraging democratic engagement and supporting transparency and accountability.

Early conceptualization of policy analysis typically cast its purpose as primarily advisory, with professional public servants informing the decision-making processes of the elected (Lindblom 1958; Wildavsky 1979). Today, however, the purposes of policy analysis are highly varied, ranging from providing advice to determining optimal implementation processes, evaluating programs, and, most important here, identifying possible solutions to public problems (Bardach 2000; Spicker 2006; Yanow 1999). Although the post–World War II policy enterprise did enjoy some success in developing programs that improved societal well-being, there were just as many policy experiments that failed to produce good advice. As deLeon and Vogenbeck (2007) suggest, the earlier policy analytical approaches (cost analysis and system analysis) often tried to solve problems without fully appreciating how the social and political conditions surrounding the policy shaped the alternatives selected and the courses of action taken.

The modern policy analysis movement is critical of the classic technocratic approach, and, as a result, the search for precise solutions increasingly was replaced by the recognition that the often unquantifiable impacts of ideology, values, and belief systems were inherent in all formal analysis and must be taken into account in both policy formulation and implementation (deLeon 1997). Thus, although contemporary policy analysis is produced both inside and outside government and continues to apply rigorous analytic methodologies to optimize policy outcomes, more and more analysts are aware that public problem solving is also shaped by historical and political circumstances (Bevir and Rhodes 2001; Howlett and Lindquist 2007). In this context, policy analysis is as much about idea generation, sectoral expertise, and serving various publics as it is about "speaking truth to power" (deLeon and Vogenbeck 2007).

The supply of policy analysis in Canada is abundant with a diverse number of producers creating a large marketplace for policy advice within civil society. Numerous think tanks and research institutes produce policy analysis with a range of disciplinary and interdisciplinary perspectives available. National, regional, and provincial policy research institutes produce research, commentary, and analysis and circulate their conclusions in such publications as *Policy Options / Options politiques* (Institute for Research on Public Policy [IRPP]) and *Window on the West* (Canada West Foundation), all freely available online. In addition, there are several influential national journals, such as *Canadian Public Policy* and *Canadian Public Administration,* that focus on key national, regional, and provincial policy problems. Conferences offered by a variety of policy-based institutions provide opportunities for direct exchange, as does membership in policy-based organizations (Brooks 2007).

Training professional policy analysts in Canada has also become increasingly popular, with several universities offering professional graduate programs in public policy and public administration. These programs are generally theoretically informed and evidence based, and graduates have the capacity to apply a variety of models and analytical techniques to specific policy problems and issues. As a discipline, policy studies has developed a growing body of knowledge related to the policy process, and it continues to move forward collectively in the production of various analytical approaches. As a result, both federal and provincial governments are increasingly populated with professionally trained policy analysts who tend to possess generalized knowledge of the policy process and of methods of policy analysis (Brooks 2007). In addition, a variety of professional associations exist, with organizations such as the Canadian Evaluation Society providing specialized professional development workshops across the country through provincial chapters. As the policy analysis movement continues to grow, so too will the analytical precision available to address policy problems; however, this evolution will force the discipline to adjust constantly to shifting public preferences and new forms of governance arrangements (deLeon and Vogenbeck 2007).

COLLABORATIVE POLICYMAKING

As governments increasingly adopt collaborative approaches to policy design and implementation, steering policy processes has become crucial to modern governance. In almost every policy area, networks of state and non-state actors are engaged in policy development processes. Collaborative policymaking is a process by which consensus-driven dialogue is initiated by a public institution to craft solutions to public problems. The goal of collaborative policymaking is to identify options that serve mutual interests. Provincial collaborative projects are increasingly common as governments adopt a wide range of consultation activities in order to improve the public's perceptions of governmental accountability, transparency, and responsiveness to civil society needs. This new governance trend advances management approaches based on negotiation and persuasion, as opposed to the command and control practices associated with traditional public administration (Salamon 2002).

The long-established system of Canadian government is vertical in its architecture, with the executive holding the lion's share of decision-making power and the ministries structured as hierarchal systems with power and authority flowing from top to bottom. Within the conventional model, accountability travels up the ladder of power until it eventually reaches the minister's office, with legislative boundaries in place to demarcate accountability based on the functions of government and the roles of public servants. In recent years, however, there has been a departure from this model as new approaches to public administration, as well as changing political cultures and demands for increased access and transparency, have shifted the organizational boundaries of government and the policymaking process (Kettl 2002). As Savoie (2004) describes, the "result is that the organizational space once occupied by politicians and public servants has been opened up to outsiders or has become shared territory within government" (2). As a result, governments have developed several different collaborative policy tools to gather public inputs and create greater opportunities for democratic participation.

THE NETWORK SOCIETY

The network society is the sociological description of how social relations are increasingly structured around networked forms of organization that accommodate information exchange in the post-Internet era. One of the key bases for this organizational repositioning is the accommodation of information. For the first time in human history, mass amounts of information may be collected, stored, and searched using networked technologies. The network society has become one of the most popular metaphors to describe how these changes in social organization and economic structures have been triggered by new information communication technologies (ICTs) and associated processes of mass information production. Governments have had to adjust to these new social and economic realities, which have had significant implications for classical organizational structures.

Traditional problem-solving structures of government are based on two forms of political organization: hierarchies and markets. Political organization is a social structural process that distributes power through access to resources and participation in decision making; in a market organizational structure, the logic ordering this distribution is based on the aggregation of one-to-one relationships (exchange) while, in a hierarchical organizational structure, it is premised on one-to-many relationships (control). As an ideal type, a market form of organization assumes that relationships among actors are episodic and serve to facilitate exchange between self-interested players. Alternatively, a hierarchal form of organization is based on top-down power structures in which authority flows down to subordinates. Although both types of political organization continue to characterize governance, a third organizational form has become increasingly popular for explaining how policy preferences driven by society are changing problem-solving approaches: network organization. A network organizational structure uses a logic premised on many-to-many relationships in which influence replaces or supplements classic exchange-and-control approaches. As a result, governments increasingly engage in various network activities, in some cases creating and managing networks and in other instances becoming part of established network arrangements to negotiate settlements.

Policy network analysis has been a popular scholarly pursuit in Canada and has an established body of literature that defines policy networks as sector-based constellations of interests with different stakeholders conferred with varying degrees of influence in the decision-making process (Atkinson and Coleman 1989; Coleman and Skogstad 1990). Traditionally, network structures were thought to evolve over time with institutionalized relationships producing various network types. For example, some networks are organized around loosely knit affiliations among global policy institutes and advocacy coalitions, which have minimal access to decision makers, while others are organized around privileged access to centres of power. There are numerous examples of national policy networks in Canada; almost every policy sector is characterized by a diverse set of interests seeking to influence policy development (Boase 1996; Coleman, Skogstad, and Atkinson 1996; Howlett and Rayner 1995). Policy networks and the outcomes that policy actors are able to achieve are influenced by numerous factors, including state involvement, the social structures that characterize the networked relationships among the state and other actors, and the network's receptiveness to new ideas and actors (Hajer and Wagenaar 2003; Howlett 2002; Montpetit 2003).

Compared to federal policy networks, those at the provincial level are relatively understudied; however, numerous types of provincial policy networks exist in Canada, with knowledge transfer, coordination, collaboration, regulation, and provincial advocacy being among their most common goals. Knowledge transfer policy networks are designed to organize, create, identify, and distribute knowledge to improve policy outcomes, and they are often managed by public sector organizations to facilitate policy development processes. For example, the Alcohol Policy Network, governed by Public Health Ontario, focuses on various aspects of healthy alcohol policy and includes over 600 individuals and organizations engaged in ongoing dialogues on research, prevention, and services. A second type of provincial policy network is a structured coordination network, such as the Alberta Public Libraries Electronic Network, which is managed by the Alberta Library, funded by Alberta Municipal Affairs, and designed to maximize information resource sharing and promote public access to information through electronic options (Alberta Municipal Affairs 2009). Third, collaboration policy networks feature various partners working toward a shared policy or program goal. An example is the Saskatchewan Parks and Recreation Association, a non-profit umbrella organization representing over 400 communities and partners with a mandate to promote healthy, active communities through parks and sport. A fourth type is the regulatory policy network, such as British Columbia's forestry policy network. These networks are typically characterized by closed historical collaboration between industry and provincial governments (Howlett and Rayner 1995). A fifth type is the provincial advocacy network that features a lead organization connecting network members who advocate for policy changes and share policy preferences. From the Nova Scotia Cultural Action Network, which is dedicated to research and lobbying to develop the province's creative economy in Nova Scotia, to the Ontario Coalition Against Poverty, which promotes the interests of the poor and homeless, provincial advocacy networks are prevalent in Canada.

As policy development processes are increasingly organized around networked social structures, administrative strategies focused on network governance have become more important to modern public administrators seeking to coordinate a group of stakeholders through a set of explicit actions. The three most commonly discussed types of network governance are citizen engagement, policy formulation, and policy implementation. First, network governance is a popular strategy for addressing civil society's demands for greater transparency and accountability, as it may be used to open decision-making processes to more representative citizen participation. Governing control in this type of setting is focused on legitimacy to ensure that government can continue to affect behaviour and shape preferences. Second, network governance may be used to manage the policy formulation process by coordinating relationships among policy actors and by directing the selection of policy alternatives. Third, network governance is used in implementation processes when the focus is on network performance and the application of substantive policy instruments to achieve a desired outcome. The effect is that governments no longer hold a monopoly over implementation but instead manage how the process occurs.

Policy networks are key sites of idea production, so they are populated with various experts, key stakeholders, government officials, and advocacy groups. Historically, in Canada, the public service has been a closed system with limited public participation and democratic engagement. Today, increased access to participation in the policy processes and the ubiquity of information have created a plurality of expertise, with ideas coming from a wide variety of sources, including think tanks (Abelson 2007; Lindquist 1993), consultants (Spears 2007), academics (Borins 2003; Cohn 2007), and advocacy groups (Stritch 2007). In other words, civil society actors are now directly interacting with the provincial state in the production of knowledge and policy ideas, as information communication technologies expand engagement online and provide new opportunities for policy learning.

DIGITAL GOVERNMENT

Using information communication technologies (ICTs), the Internet, and the World Wide Web (the web) to improve communication and service delivery between government and civil society is a key aspect of modernization in the public sector. E-government serves several functions including service delivery, information provisioning, and information collection, while purposes include expanding communication and information sharing both internally (vertically and horizontally) and externally (between government and the public). Interest in e-governance has grown significantly and will continue to expand in the future as the social dimensions of Web 2.0 technologies further pressure government to enlarge communication pathways between governments and citizens.

Chadwick (2006) suggests that there are two dominant approaches to e-government: managerial and e-government as democratization. The managerial orientation is a new public management approach; it focuses on the customer and is largely concerned with effective service delivery and cost reduction. Alternatively, the e-government-as-democratization orientation, which also focuses on citizens, uses digital technologies as a means to enhance communication and interaction with the public. According to Chadwick (2006), these two orientations represent one of the main tensions in the development and implementation of e-government agendas because decision makers must ask whether "it is about better government or better democracy?" (184).

Every provincial government in Canada hosts a website and provides services online; however, there are significant provincial variations in e-government capacity. In addition, there are differences in Internet usage among provincial populations, with 65.3 per cent of Newfoundland and Labrador residents having home Internet access compared to 83 per cent of British Columbia residents (Statistics Canada 2010). Public sector websites expand pathways of communication for a government and its various clients, facilitate new governing strategies to manage informational resources, and support information exchange among autonomous units. Provincial governments provide an extensive amount of online content, including ministerial reports, policy analyses, research papers, and other related policy information. Indeed, Canadian citizens used e-government in 2009 mainly to search for government information, with 57.6 per cent of Canadians using electronic channels for this task (Statistics Canada 2010).

The impact of the Internet and the web on governments and the publics they serve has been profound. As all levels of government seek to reap the benefits of information technologies and web-based communication technologies, most past initiatives have overwhelmingly adopted a managerial orientation. For example, Hyson's (2009) study of how 10 provincial and territorial ombudsman offices used e-government technology found a strong convergence on the managerial orientation, with most website designs focused on information dissemination and electronic service delivery. As a result, both the federal and provincial governments have become very proficient at website development and electronic service delivery while e-government agendas adopting a more democratic orientation have been less common. In other words, many provincial e-government agendas remain more focused on automation than democratization. Still, digital trends emerging from Web 2.0 and social networking sites will eventually compel the public sector to use web technologies that promote collaboration and networked interaction. Although enhanced democratic engagement is an expected outcome of digital government (Dixon 2010), current evidence of substantive change remains limited to anecdotal evidence and ad hoc experimentation.

In the future, digital government and second-generation web technologies will significantly alter how policy ideas are developed and shared. In its original 1990s incarnation, the web (Web 1.0) was predominantly a *publishing* medium with users accessing static content created by professional developers. However, during the 21st century, the web began to evolve into a true *communication* medium characterized by interactive user-created media content (Manovich 2009). Second-generation web technologies (or what is commonly referred to as Web 2.0) promote peer-produced user content, participatory information sharing, and online collaboration. The emergence of social collaborative technologies such as social networking sites (SNS), blogs, and wikis has spawned numerous virtual communities including Facebook, LinkedIn, Myspace, and Wikipedia, all of which facilitate interaction between individuals with similar experiences and interests. In addition, Internet phones and the provision of mobile support for web connectivity allow users to be connected to their online world constantly. In Canada, though some government agencies and departments are already experimenting with collaborative media, many others remain wedded to the early web model of one-way communication.

Nonetheless, examples of an incremental transition are emerging as early adopters experiment with and demonstrate the democratic potential of Web 2.0 technologies. Several experimenters do stand out. Take for example Calgary's Mayor Naheed Nenshi, who used Web 2.0 technologies to garner electoral support and to encourage voter participation when he ran successfully for mayoral office in 2010. Nenshi's online elections campaign included such platforms as a website, Facebook, YouTube, and Twitter, in addition to a crowd-sourcing exercise that saw campaign volunteers translate Nenshi's platform video and brochures into 23 different languages. Another example is Saskatchewan Premier Brad Wall, who regularly uses Twitter to engage the public, respond to civil society demands, and set policy agenda. For instance, in response to a social media campaign, he directed the Saskatchewan Ministry of Health to look into the case of Violet Revet, a three-year-old girl suffering from a rare disease. Similarly, in response to an individual citizen on a local radio show, Premier Wall tweeted his support for launching a line of motorcycle license plates for veterans.

Despite the excitement surrounding e-government as democratization, there remain numerous challenges to public sector implementation. The organizational culture of governments is risk averse, and, without a basic set of best practices on managing risk, support for social media use may be undermined by traditional administrative propensities to control the message. Furthermore, there are several information, privacy, and official languages concerns (Fyfe and Crookall 2010), which are further exacerbated by many of the Westminster structures described in Chapter 2. Thus, although the popularity of social media for political purposes and the use of blogs and Twitter for providing political commentary are standardized features of the modern democratic landscape, politicians and bureaucrats often resist the levels of collaborative capacity that e-government as democratization demands.

Issues and Challenges

Several recent trends have shifted provincial governments' informational priorities, and, although the purposes of policy analysis and program innovation remain the same, changes in the processes through which information is collected and shared have had profound effects on policy learning and expertise.

DIGITAL GOVERNMENT

The Internet and the web have significantly altered how society communicates, how services are delivered, how information is shared, and how government is organized. As Dutil et al. (2008, 78) describe it, e-government "has brought with it a rhetorical flourish of promises to reinvent the business model of government on the one hand and to redesign the institutional conduct of democracy on the other." As the use of e-government as a managerial approach intermingles with modernization agendas that push e-government toward a more democratic orientation, the shift from e-government to e-governance will produce new tensions both between centralization and decentralization and between policy ambition and policy responsibility.

Every province has developed e-government capacity, with many jurisdictions delivering services, communicating with stakeholders, and gathering public input through electronic channels. Beyond the various functional applications of ICTs, several social outcomes associated with a wired society must be considered, as these will create new tension within the federation. First are widespread expectations among Canadians that services should be provided online and should be integrated across all levels of government. Second is the increasing competition to attract online users' attention, which suggests that governments must possess the technical and organizational capacity to compete online. Third, because of the emergence of second-generation web technologies and the participatory potential of social media, future government agendas concerning public engagement will also inevitably shift.

Citizen-centred service delivery is a key policy priority across Canada with most levels of government developing digitized service transformation strategies to improve public sector effectiveness and efficiency. Citizen-centred service refers to the delivery of services from a citizen perspective so that services are integrated across governments, e.g., one-stop service, and multiple service channels are provided, e.g., face-to-face, telephone, and Internet service (Kernaghan 2005). As Canadians become increasingly sophisticated users of online services, the activities of service-delivery agencies must become increasingly integrated across federal, provincial, territorial, and municipal governments. Despite sharing the goal of providing integrated services and one-stop, single-window delivery (as discussed in Chapter 4), the provinces have divergent ideas on how to structure and govern service delivery. For example, Service New Brunswick, which is a Crown corporation, was the first Canadian multiservice public sector agency to provide all direct public services on behalf of the government. Alternately, Service Nova Scotia and Municipal Relations was created as an individual ministry in 2005, and Service BC was established as a division in the Ministry of Labour and Citizens' Services (Roy and Langford 2008).

Governments expend considerable public resources to provide citizens with information online. Using the web to disseminate information and inform the public has expanded governments' potential capacity to provide information and to affect behaviour in network settings. Currently, however, governmental presence on the web remains quite passive, as the public has no obligation to either seek out information or to respond to online initiatives. Consequently, government websites must attract public attention to exercise influence effectively and shape policy debate. Information is a standard policy instrument that refers to governments' "attempts at influencing people through the transfer of knowledge, the communication of reasoned argument, and persuasion" (Vedung 2007, 33). Internally, governments are expected to integrate informational holdings across departments, jurisdictions, and other institutional boundaries; however, the processes involved with coordinating and sharing data are confounded by both technical and social problems. Technical challenges come from diverse information technology systems and applications while social challenges arise from diverse populations and organizational mandates. There are also several administrative challenges, such as ensuring privacy and security while providing service delivery through multiple channels (in person, over the telephone, by the post, and through the Internet). Websites operate as the external face of e-government, and, unlike internal-facing e-government (with its program-specific functions and organizational integration mandates), the external face of the state cannot be managed directly.

The provincial governments' capacity to attract the attention of information users is significantly less than that of the federal government. Take for example public health information, which is the sixth-largest body of informational content on the web (Ayers and Kronenfeld 2007). The provisioning of online health information has been shown to improve health care decision making and patient outcomes (Harrison and Lee 2006). Although constitutional responsibility for the administration and delivery of public health services in Canada is shared between the federal and provincial governments (as opposed to health care itself, which is a provincial jurisdiction), the purposes of public health policy and associated programs are to promote health, prevent disease, and prolong life across the entire population. The federal state's involvement in identifying large-scale priorities and supporting public health goals is critical to successful policy implementation at all levels, as it is through such centralized leadership that the public health policy domain gains its symbolic presence as a national issue (Steffen 2005). Equally important, however, are provincial and territorial governments and regional health authorities, all of which share responsibility in managing and delivering the complex networks of local health services (Marchildon 2006). Yet Marchildon and McNutt (2007) found that provincial governments were noticeably underrepresented in a web crawl of influential public health websites, meaning that consumers of public health information are more likely to locate and utilize federal information.

Beyond informational provisioning and service delivery, the provincial governments are also experimenting with e-consultations to enrich traditional democratic arrangements. Online consultations have become popular collaborative policymaking tools among the provinces, which typically use such processes to expand public engagement and renew democratic governance. Recent examples include New Brunswick's 2010 e-consultation on the creation of a new centre of excellence for children and youth who have complex needs and Manitoba's 2011 online consultation on the use of cap and trade as a mechanism to reduce the province's greenhouse gas emissions. The nature of the typical provincial e-consultation process tends to be fairly uniform: input is gathered using questionnaires or workbooks that ask participants to provide opinion or comments on the policy issues being considered. The problem with most, if not all, of these online consultations is the lack of government commitment to value the feedback and incorporate citizens' voices into policy development (McNutt 2009). Despite these provincial experiments in the electronic engagement of citizens, only 2.5 per cent of Canadians have actually provided an opinion in an e-consultation process (Statistics Canada 2010).

Governments are not the only providers of information online; they compete with a variety of sources for users' attention. For example, civil society organizations such as research institutes and think tanks have been shown to have a significant influence online, and these provide a wide variety of policy-related information. As active participants in the policy analysis movement, such organizations encourage public dialogue on numerous federal, regional, and provincial policy issues, providing various types of analysis and promoting diverse dialogues (McNutt and Marchildon 2009). Social networking has also added a new dimension to policy discourses by diversifying the types of media available: bloggers provide alternatives to journalists, interest organizations use Twitter to post action alerts, and advocacy groups use Facebook to attract members, for example.

Social media applications have also become popular in the public sector. Governments around the world use social media technologies to enhance democratic engagement, inform citizens, collaborate internally, and strengthen existing partnerships with civil society actors (Dixon 2010; Osimo 2008). Examples from Canada are not difficult to find. In 2010, as part of Canada's National Anti-Drug Strategy, Health Canada created the "DrugsNot4Me" Facebook fan page to launch a major youth drug prevention campaign. Federal blogs are used by the Office of the Privacy Commissioner of Canada, the National Gallery of Canada, the Canadian Museum of Nature, and Canada Business while Natural Resources has produced a suite of informational YouTube videos providing educational material and promoting sustainable development.

Provincial governments are also turning to social media tools to improve policy outcomes with several provinces producing social media guidelines and various provinces experimenting with different platforms. The purpose of social media guidelines varies across the country. Alberta and British Columbia, for example, treat social media as a communication tool, Nova Scotia views it as an interactive instrument, and Saskatchewan and Manitoba approach it from a service delivery perspective (Deschamps 2012). In terms of social media use, the provinces of Alberta, British Columbia, Manitoba, Nova Scotia, and Prince Edward Island all host dedicated YouTube channels providing various videos featuring new legislation, existing programs, and key speeches. In addition, all five provinces have Twitter accounts that they use to market public events and Facebook accounts featuring public dialogue on various policy issues and recent government announcements. In other provinces, individual organizations are experimenting with different platforms for different purposes. For example, each summer, the Saskatchewan Ministry of Tourism,

Parks, Culture and Sport hires a Saskatchewanderer, a student who travels across Saskatchewan showcasing the province through blogs, tweets, Facebook entries, and traditional media.

Interestingly, Canadian cities are among the most common users of social media applications: every national capital except Québec City hosted Facebook and Twitter accounts and produced content for YouTube in 2012. For example, the City of Toronto hosts a Facebook page focused on historical sites in the city to raise public awareness, engage the community in dialogue, and answer specific questions. The City of Edmonton is using multiple social media services. It hosts several different Facebook and Twitter accounts, provides content on YouTube, and has created various blogs, which all serve to connect local government with citizens and provide information.

Overall, information communication technologies have significantly altered the marketplace of policy ideas. The sheer volume of information available creates significant competition for users' attention. Although information is critical in both governing and the policymaking process, the extraordinary increase in the creation and dissemination of information may cause shifts in the traditional drivers of issue saliency. The policy analysis industry is increasingly using electronic channels to market its research and analysis, and advocacy groups and Internet organizations are using social media to get their messages out.

POLICY ANALYTICAL CAPACITY

It is well established that the supply of policy analysis will impact advice systems, interjurisdictional learning, and policy and program outcomes. As discussed in Chapter 2, much of the public service's credibility in the democratic policymaking process is premised on its expertise, on its ability to provide good advice, in other words, on its ability to enhance the government's policy capacity. Policy capacity is "the intellectual dimension of governance, that is, the capacity of the system to think through the challenges it faces" (Bakvis 2000, 73). In recent years, policy capacity at both the national and subnational levels has diminished due to outsourcing, restructuring, and downsizing (Howlett and Lindquist 2004). Traditionally, policy capacity was characterized by a professionalized bureaucracy, advisory boards, policy units within departments, and commissions, all of which provided rational policy analysis and advice (Rasmussen 1999). Today, policy capacity is multidimensional and is thought to include policy analytical capacity, governing capacity, and citizen engagement, all of which shape the legitimacies of decision-making processes and democratic institutions (Canadian Policy Research Networks 2009).

Policy analytical capacity has been a major focus of the modern policy analysis movement in Canada, which encourages the application of a contextualized lens to policy analysis and rejects pure traditionalist methods in favour of evidence-informed approaches that move beyond statistical data analysis and analytical evidence to include evidence from citizens and stakeholders as well as from practice (Howlett and Lindquist 2007). Although "evidence-based policy" analysis draws exclusively on hard facts using scientific data (e.g., data on health or the environment), quantitative analysis, and social science methods (e.g., cost-benefit analysis or network analysis), "evidence-informed" analysis is based on studying hard facts within a given social, political, cultural, or economic context. In the case of evidence-informed policy analysis, normative assumptions (about how things *should* be) are used to interrupt data and ensure that the realities surrounding a proposed program or policy are taken into account.

All provincial policy analysts work with structured analytical tools and techniques to provide decision makers with quality advice and optimized solutions to public problems. Public executives and government ministers use this advice to inform solution selection using rational analysis in the context of political feasibility, democratic expectations, and provincial priorities. Their skill sets are the very foundation of a government's capacity to achieve its intended actions. Historically, provincial policy analysis has been considered a technocratic enterprise that employs an army of professional bureaucrats devoted to the preservation of established order. Today, however, policy analysts are increasingly aware of values, political contexts, and professional ethics, an awareness that shifts the nature of advice toward evidence-informed analytical work (Radin 2000). One of the key drivers behind this shift is to ensure that policy analysis not only includes efficiency and effectiveness assessment but also considers the key democratic matters that will also influence problem definition and solution selection. The core assumption is that improved policy analytical capacity among analysts will improve the overall policy capacity of government, which, in turn, will directly impact the nature of idea production and knowledge sharing.

Policy analytical capacity refers to the government's ability to produce or collect information that may be used in policy formulation and decision-making processes (MacRae 1991). Right across

Canada, the policy analytical capacity of governments is in trouble, and many policy analysts lack the capability to produce evidentiary policy analysis (Howlett 2009b). Research suggests that this is particularly true in the provinces where serious policy analytical deficits undermine the capability of provincial public services to learn and innovate (McArthur 2007; Howlett and Newman 2010). Recent profiles of subnational policy analysts suggest that those based in the provinces tend to be "process-oriented troubleshooters" who are "relatively inexperienced and untrained in formal policy analysis or analytical techniques" (Howlett 2009a, 65). Although subnational analysts are typically young, mobile, and well educated, they often lack substantive knowledge in the sector in which they work and, as a result, "tend to bring only process-related knowledge to the table" (Howlett and Newman 2010, 133). To combat this trend, many provinces have created strategies to address the policy analytical deficit through new recruitment practices and enhancing their professional development training.

For example, in 2000, Ontario established the Policy Innovation and Leadership initiative designed to shore up lost policy capacity. It focuses on innovation, strategic thinking, collaboration, creating greater research capacity, promoting organizational learning, and cross-ministry coordination. The key motivation behind the initiative was the province's recognition that the policy function was relatively underdeveloped and unable to meet the complexities of the modern political and economic environment. Activities in the program include the creation of a policy network, the development of a toolkit, new modes of information sharing, and various policy learning events. Similarly, in 2007, Nova Scotia developed the Policy Excellence Initiative to strengthen the policy capacity of the public service (Nova Scotia 2007). British Columbia took a different approach and established the Knowledge and Information Services branch with a mandate to promote best practices in privacy and information sharing, improve evidence-informed decision making, and develop effective information management. The branch collaborates with other government departments and the public in conducting four core functions: managing legislative and regulatory changes and the governments' strategic privacy policy; developing, maintaining, and communicating the government's information management and information sharing policies; guiding information practices; and providing evidence-informed decision support. In addition to these specific initiatives there are also several cabinet-level activities taking place in Alberta, Manitoba, and Newfoundland and Labrador (Howlett and Joshi-Koop 2011).

The public sector is also using social media tools to enhance the capacity of knowledgeable individuals and organizations both inside and outside government to collaborate and *co-produce value and meaning* in policy formulation processes. For example, in 2008, to help create an information-sharing environment, the Government of Canada launched the GCpedia, an internal wiki used by those working from a computer on a government network to share information and collaborate. On the social networking site LinkedIn, members can connect to organizations such as the Institute of Public Administration of Canada or the Canadian Evaluation Society (including many of its provincial chapters) and follow discussions, post questions, and generally engage in policy conversations. The nation's top bureaucrat, Privy Council Clerk Wayne Wouters, is a significant champion of the use of social media in the federal government, arguing that social media presents new opportunities for public engagement, for governments and citizens to co-produce value, and for governments to enlist citizens in the design or delivery of government services.

Policy analysis is a key resource in the policymaking process because it allows those with a common interest in a policy area to share ideas, develop criticisms, pressure governments, articulate interests, and understand the implications and contours of a policy topic. Trends toward consultation, collaborative policymaking, and network management have significantly altered provincial decision-making processes, and the previous commitment to the rigour of evidence-based policy analysis is now being challenged by a greater emphasis on political relevance and civil society inputs.

POLICY NETWORKS

To combat the loss of public sector expertise, governments began to rely on various network arrangements to replace lost knowledge. Engagement in policy networks provides governments with the opportunity to create new relationships and strengthen established ties, while also facilitating policy learning through information exchange. Despite the clear advantages of policy networks, such governance arrangements do redistribute power in decision-making processes and can have significant implications for the Westminster system (Montpetit 2005). Although the nature of relationships in policy networks varies significantly, there is a cross-sectoral tendency toward networks that incorporate participants from various intergovernmental organizations, from civil society (both the private and not-for-profit sectors), and, in some cases, from outside the nation. Despite such similarities each network is also conditioned by institutional inputs, historic contexts, and the connections between administrative agencies and policy interests.

Canada's decentralized federal system is ideally suited to the development of intergovernmental networks, as discussed in Chapter 1. In policy systems having relatively undeveloped networks, governance arrangements will continue to be authoritative. However, most Canadian policy sectors have witnessed the entrance of new actors, largely as a result of collaborative policymaking activities. Two of the key new players in both provincial and federal networks are Aboriginal governments and cities. Aboriginal participation in provincial policy networks is influential in a range of sectors such as forestry (Hoberg and Morawski 1997; McGregor 2011), urban policy (Peters 2005); land management (Wellstead and Rayner 2009), coastal management (Wiber et al. 2010), and health systems (Quantz and Thurston 2006), to name but a few. Municipalities are also active in provincial policymaking processes. Rural communities, for example, host various local policy networks concerned with economic development, planning, and sustainability while urban agendas often intersect with provincial priorities in environment sustainability, settlement, economic development, and population well-being (Burch 2010; Raphael et al. 2001). In addition, the number of direct relationships between cities and the federal government has also grown, especially in such sectors as homelessness and infrastructure, and provincial jurisdiction over cities is frequently circumvented by federal funding initiatives (Slack and Bird 2007). The expansion of the number and type of actors participating in provincial policy networks has challenged many traditional power relationships as new actors bring new ideas and new understandings of policy problems to the table. These networked arrangements facilitate extensive policy learning and innovation among federal, provincial, and local policy actors.

Policy development in the provinces is not, however, limited to domestic policy settings; the internationalization of provincial policy networks has altered knowledge production, policy development, and governing priorities. Internationalization refers to the process of non-domestic policy actors and institutions affecting the conditions for domestic governance. As authority is redistributed and the scope and scale of social problems are redefined, the capacity of centralized, top-down institutions to respond directly to governance challenges has declined. Although federalism and regionalism have always shaped the creation and dissemination of policy innovation in the provinces, the introduction into the mix of international organizations such as the Organisation for Economic Co-operation and Development, the World Health Organization, and the United Nations is new. The provincial role in the formulation of foreign trade policy, for example, has grown considerably, as federal commitments to expanding global markets and North American economic integration encroach on provincial jurisdiction (Skogstad 2002).

The provinces' responses to foreign policy decisions vary considerably, both nationally and regionally. In the West, for instance, British Columbia's interest in softwood lumber, Alberta's interest in energy, and Saskatchewan's interest in potash all motivate provincial actors to engage in global policy network activity in those sectors (Kukucha 2004, 2005, 2008). In contrast, Québec's foreign relations have been shaped by the province's sovereignist aspirations, which have promoted discourses focused on protecting the province's distinct cultural and linguistic heritage (Bélanger 2002). Provincial level involvement and influence in foreign policy activities, however, is uneven: British Columbia, Alberta, Québec, and Ontario all possess the capacity to engage in such diplomatic activity, but smaller provinces often lack the resources and expertise necessary to engage in such conversations (de Boer 2002).

Policy think tanks and research institutes are also significant brokers of policy ideas in the provinces and are active participants in provincial policy networks (Lindquist 1993; Stone 2007). As both creators and disseminators of policy-relevant information, such organizations supply various types of facts, research and analysis (including academic papers), policy evaluations, performance reviews, policy analysis, and program evaluations. The nature of policy think tanks varies, with many regionally based organizations focused explicitly on local issues and problems. For example the Canada West Foundation publishes information of importance to Western Canadians while the Mowat Centre for Policy Innovation is focused on Ontario, and the Atlantic Institute for Market Studies works on issue of concern to Atlantic Canadians. National think tanks also commonly target provincial policy areas. Canadian Policy Research Networks, C.D. Howe, and the IRPP all publish policy-relevant information concerning the viability, efficiency, and effectiveness of provincial policy and programming initiatives. Think tanks, especially those that are research based and nonpartisan, serve an important function in policy learning in networks, supplementing the province's policy capacity and providing expert policy advice to decision makers while still shaping public debate (Abelson 2007).

Although policy networks produce innovation, the purposeful creation of a network can also be an innovation in and of itself. It is well established in public administration literature that networks promote processes of learning and idea generation (Borgatti and Cross 2003). In Canada, networks are commonly used to share policy knowledge, and numerous national, regional, and provincial organizations are involved in network-based exchanges. For example, the federal emphasis on provincial and regional economic development has promoted the establishment of many regional policy networks whose expertise is drawn from local industry, universities, and other research institutions that share a common knowledge base. Often, Ottawa supplies both policy direction and funding to support regional areas of specialization and expertise, a course of action that results in very different policy focuses and uneven research and development capacities.

Idea production, information sharing, and collaborations are all key network activities in which policy learning takes place through various forms of network exchange. Networks with access to a diverse supply of information will increase policy capacity because network members will share experiences and knowledge. However, recent evidence suggests that, within provincial governments, interjurisdictional learning may be limited. For example, Howlett and Joshi-Koop (2011, 91) found that provincial environmental policy analysts rarely engaged in routine communication with other civil society actors or other government employees, and when they do, they "fail to routinely use information from these sources in policy development and formulation." Although many commentators believe that lost policy capacity at both the provincial and federal levels could be partially addressed through collaborative arrangements, the ability to benefit from such network activities depends on levels of provincial expertise, government support for policy learning, and the enthusiasm or reluctance of provincial governments (and their employees) to share power.

VIRTUAL CIVIL SOCIETY

There is extensive evidence suggesting that social media are changing advocacy and how civil society organizes for action. There are numerous examples of social media being used to mobilize people around a specific cause; however, the tactics employed to achieve these outcomes are varied and are often beyond the control of any one organization. There are several fundamental differences between traditional civil society and virtual civil society. First, there has been the emergence of "flash activists" who use social media to mobilize the masses and promote issue awareness. These activists use an arsenal of social media tools including Twitter, blogs, and Facebook. Second, social media have radically increased the influence of free-agent activists, ones not connected to organizations but rather to causes. To build trust, governments using social media must treat the technology as participatory, enabling people to create as well as consume media (Lai and Turban 2008; Reynolds 2010; Russo et al. 2008). The cumulative result is that provincial governments must learn to operate in the context of the social web.

The social web refers to the socialization or interaction of people using web-based social software, including the entire suite of social media tools. These second-generation web technologies support participatory user-contributed content that may be used to create buzz, collaborate, share information, or socially organize. Whether it is the "Twitter Revolution" during the 2009 Iranian elections, the viral Facebook campaign during the 2011 popular uprising in Egypt, or social media's role in the UK riots, civil society is using the Internet to disseminate information and garner support for a cause. In many cases, bloggers and citizen journalists were key drivers behind these initiatives. These individuals use various social media platforms (blogs, Facebook, Twitter, and so forth) to communicate with mass publics, alert their networks to important events, and engage interested users in joining the conversation.

Governments cannot simply rely on their organizational websites to engage civil society—they must be proactive. There are numerous opportunities for governments to engage different civil society groups and online social movements. In the Web 2.0 era, listening is as important as talking. Tapping into collective intelligence and learning what people are saying and doing provides governments with crucial resources they can use in coordinating networks, policy learning, and idea production. Timing is key when a cause or issue goes viral

(Bradley 2010). Knowing their audience and maintaining a presence in the social web will allow governments to join in different conversations strategically, create buzz purposefully, and, in some cases, engage in corrective blogging. Building loyalty through meaningful engagement requires governments to develop an ongoing dialogue with the public, one that fosters both collaboration and conversation. Despite some experimentation by the post-Internet public sector, the use of web technologies to enhance communication between government, stakeholders, and citizens remains limited.

Despite the slow rate at which Canadian governments have adopted social media, the general public's use has expanded rapidly. International trends suggest that provincial governments will have to develop sophisticated digital strategies that integrate web, social media, and mobile technologies to keep pace with emerging expectations surrounding "smart government." In terms of advocacy, social media applications are extremely popular among activists and interest groups who use digital tools to organize, communicate, and advocate preferred policy alternatives (Langlois et al. 2009). Similarly, non-profit organizations use social media tools to improve organizational effectiveness, increase community presence, serve clients, elicit donations, and market events (Briones et al. 2011; Kanter and Fine 2010). In sum, numerous civil society organizations use social media to organize and market local events and advance their political or social agendas, while public intellectuals, political pundits, and citizen journalists host blogs or Twitter accounts using these tools to promote policy dialogues with attentive online publics (Murthy 2011).

For those that question the implication of social media on governments and civil society, consider that the public take-up rate of social media has been one of the faster growing communication trends in history. Facebook was launched in February 2004, and, by December of that year, had attracted close to 1 million active users. Seven years later, the number of active users had grown to more than 750 million. In a single month, 30 million plus pieces of content (e.g., hyperlinks, blog posts, new stories) are shared by Facebook users, with the average user creating 90 pieces of content per month. Between 2009 and 2011, active users accessing Facebook through their mobile devices grew from 65 million to 250 million while minutes spent on Facebook worldwide grew from 6 billion to 23 billion. Social networking sites are a platform for both active communication among users and passive observation of social news (Burke, Marlow, and Lento 2010).

The influence of the Internet in general, and the interactive, collaborative potential of Web 2.0 technologies in particular, will continue to create both opportunities and tensions for governments. From an organizational context, social media provides many opportunities to maximize impacts and improve effectiveness and efficiency (DiStaso, McCorkindale, and Wright 2011; Malita 2011; Miller 2009). From a social context, emerging evidence suggests that social media fosters social inclusion, encourages stakeholder participation, and advances democratic dialogue (Tondeur et al. 2011). Finally, from the public engagement context, social media tools offer new opportunities for collaboration, consultation, public education, transparency, and accountability (Dixon 2010; Eggers 2005). Despite the seemingly positive benefits, there are also negative implications associated with new digital tools. Social media benefits are variable across populations; the perennial digital divide between people who have effective access to digital and information technology and those who do not persists into the Web 2.0 era (Cotton 2009; Pfeil et al. 2009; Watling 2011). In addition, there are new manifestations of old problems, such as privacy and security, and solving them is a major priority in the information technology sector because social media sites are prone to various types of cyber threats (Boyd 2008; Leitch and Warren 2009).

As civil society moves online, governments must expand their social media capacity and embrace tools that facilitate interactive and participatory uses of digital technology. A growing body of exploratory research suggests that Web 2.0 technologies are fundamentally changing how people socialize, communicate, shop, participate in public affairs, and learn—and that these changes will have consequences for society, politics, and the economy (Thomas and Sheth 2011). Consequently, keeping pace with new web technologies will be critical to governments committed to knowledge-based economies that simultaneously foster innovation and promote social cohesion.

Conclusion

Networked arrangements in both society and in policymaking have significantly catalyzed knowledge production and policy expertise. Information communication technologies, lost policy capacity and the popularity of networked governance arrangements all influence knowledge production activities at the provincial level. Although the purposes of policy analysis and program innovation remain the same in the provinces, the processes associated with the production of ideas have changed. Previous commitments to rigorous, evidence-based policy analysis are diluted by a greater emphasis on political relevance and civil society support. In addition, losses in the provincial governments' capacity to conduct policy analysis internally, combined with the effects of the Internet, have changed where ideas come from and lessened the impact of government-sponsored information (Margetts 2009). As Donald J. Savoie (2003) observes,

> governments have less control over who knows what and when and a new networking model is emerging which does not conform to the old command and control departmental model. Boundaries within government, between departments, and between governments and outside groups and citizens are less clear than they were thirty years ago. In brief, the internet is opening up government everywhere to scrutiny on a scale never seen before. (22)

Each of these trends influences the production of policy ideas and the types of political analysis undertaken by the provincial state. Within the context of the networked society, new information communication technologies, and collaborative policymaking, governments are changing how they work in modern policy settings.

In all of the Canadian provinces, representative democracy and traditional executive power arrangements promote hierarchal governing structures. These governing arrangements are, however, being challenged by multilevel policy networks in which power is distributed. The transfer of policy ideas among provincial policy actors does create patterns of policy response in many sectors, as numerous scholars comparing provincial policy developments have demonstrated (Imbeau et al. 2000; Dunn 2006b). If future governance arrangements are to overcome the tensions between centralization and decentralization, hierarchies and networks will have to become mutually supportive. In the long term, the relationship development potential of social media will affect politics, government coordination, and citizen engagement. When social media is combined with network governance and collaborative policymaking, the emerging conflict between evidence-based and informed policymaking will inevitably lead toward a policy process focused more on normative interests and value-based decision making.

Unfortunately, scholars and practitioners have only recently become actively engaged in rigorous examinations of social media applications and of the capacity of digital tools to serve government priorities. Because of both the Internet's potential for supporting online political mobilization and the changing nature of activism, governments face a serious digital learning curve. From the creation of social media metrics for measuring government performance to the development of strategies to increase dialogue with civil society using social collaborative technologies, the transition to Government 2.0 will be characterized by both opportunities and barriers. Developing a research base on how governments might adopt digital tools to improve internal organizational processes, such as the sharing of information or collaborating across ministries or jurisdiction, will provide much needed advice on enhancing policy capacity. Although it is still unclear how second-generation web technologies will affect government, it is clear that their effects on civil society will influence public sector engagement processes and long-term policy capacity.

Conclusion

This book investigates the growing importance and complexity of provincial policymaking in Canada. Far from being inferior or less worthy of study than its federal counterparts, provincial public policies directly shape the lives of citizens, notably through the provision of education and health care services, the allocation of social welfare benefits, the implementation of economic and environmental regulations, and the development of policy expertise. The provinces are major sites of policy innovation in an era when globalization, the advent of a "network society," and pressures from Québec nationalism, Aboriginal governments, and large cities have helped promote forms of decentralization and networked governance that typically increase the role of provinces in policy debates and issues. To these factors, we must add the institutional logic of Canadian federalism.

Provinces both compete and collaborate with one another and with the federal government in what remains one of the most decentralized federal systems in the developed world. This decentralization is especially striking in fiscal matters, in which provinces enjoy considerably more autonomy, on average, than their counterparts in, for example, Australia, Mexico, or the United States. Yet this comparatively high level of fiscal autonomy coexists with a "fiscal imbalance" between Ottawa and the provinces, as well as with substantial levels of diversity in taxation and expenditure patterns among the provinces.

Each of the provinces draws on a different economic base, and each one has created a complex patchwork of taxation policies intended to both raise revenue and encourage economic growth. Each province has a different demographic profile, and each one has experimented with different policies in areas as diverse as pharmaceutical plans, day care, rent control, and university tuition. At the same time, all provincial governments are spending more on health care than ever before, and all have committed to reducing corporate taxes. The provinces pay close attention to one another's overall fiscal regime, and they seek to avoid damaging comparisons. Finally, all the provinces rely on the federal government for a considerable measure of their funding, for monetary policy, for environmental regulations, and for trade negotiations. Developments on these fronts often compel at least some of the provinces to join forces with one another. In short, the unique character and history of each province propels it down a particular policy path, but not so far that any province—including Québec or Alberta—can ignore what neighbouring provinces are doing or how the federal government is interpreting national priorities.

When discussing the role of the provincial civil services in governance and public policy, we have emphasized the diversity of provincial landscapes, which are shaped by distinct socio-economic environments, political cultures, and institutional legacies. Yet despite their enduring importance, provincial bureaucracies, like their federal counterpart, rely increasingly on broader policy networks to generate the expertise and knowledge they need to enact, implement, and evaluate policies that tackle a growing number of complex economic, environmental, and social challenges. From think tanks to academic policy analysts, a growing number of actors interact to produce expertise and knowledge, which is disseminated through new information and communication technologies. Finally, provinces play a central role in the field of policy regulation, where they face numerous challenges related to the governance of a complex, decentred society. Although a challenge to traditional modes of political, social, and bureaucratic regulation, the direct involvement of civil society actors in policymaking has the potential to improve both participation and governance in our multifaceted and multilevel political order, and the provinces have become the central hub of policy development and innovation in our polity.

Several key themes have emerged in this analysis of provincial public policy in Canada. First, this book stresses the enduring tensions between convergence and divergence among provinces within our federal system. Despite the fact that key differences among provinces in terms of size, political culture, fiscal autonomy, and access to resource revenues remain strong, powerful patterns of interprovincial policy diffusion have favoured clear forms of policy convergence, which have been taking place within both the organizational apparatus of the provincial state and in concrete policy areas, in terms of institutional, spending, and regulatory patterns. Clear cases of how provincial policies and governing structures have converged are related to distinct diffusion patterns, showing how innovative ideas have spread across the country, and these patterns have emerged in all provinces.

Second, our book suggests that the relationship between centralization and decentralization remains crucial to understanding provincial governance and public policy in Canada. Clearly, in recent decades, the dominant policy trend in Canada has been decentralization, a situation that has primarily benefitted the provinces. Yet the federal government remains a central policy actor in Canada, and, largely through its enduring fiscal and spending power, Ottawa remains a key partner of the provinces in at least some core policy areas. Moreover, the quest for policy autonomy on the part of large cities and First Nations, Métis, and Inuit peoples has created decentralizing pressures that may not benefit provinces in the long run. To a certain extent, the growing role of civil society actors and policy networks in policy development is another form of decentralization that has less to do with territory than with social organization and with the increasingly blurred boundaries between the provincial state and the rest of society. Considering all this, we see that decentralization remains a key issue in Canada, in particular as it relates to the changing interactions between different levels of governments and different segments of civil society.

Third, as with governments and policymakers at other levels, provincial governments are dealing with the well-documented tension between policy ambition and capacity. In fiscal policy, for instance, provinces face the tension between the need to improve services and regulations, on one hand, and, on the other, pressures from citizens and businesses to maintain competitive tax rates in a more global and competitive economic environment. Regarding the issue of intergovernmentalism, greater cooperation among levels of government in issues ranging from health care to environmental policy seems necessary, but the limitations of existing intergovernmental institutions are obstacles to better territorial governance in Canada. On the bright side, we see forms of policy adaptation that stress the capacity of the provincial state to adapt to new challenges and seize new opportunities, both in terms of public administration and partnerships with policy actors aimed at enhancing policy governance in Canada.

Considering these three factors and the growing policy importance of provinces, we should do everything we can to increase our knowledge of governance and policy development in Canada's provinces. This emphasis on the provinces does not mean that we have to neglect other levels of government. In fact, as suggested in this book, the federal government remains a crucial actor in important policy areas; it plays an enduring role, for example, in fiscal redistribution, among other things. As for municipalities, although they remain creatures of the provincial governments, new challenges concerning issues such as the environment, transportation, and immigration have led to calls for an extension of municipal powers in Canada. This reality reinforces the push for multilevel governance in Canada, for a structure in which provinces are more central policy players than ever. Considering this logic, the study of provincial policymaking and of the role of the provinces in governance seems to be lagging behind. Although Canada is one of the world leaders in the study of comparative federalism, much more should be done to improve our systematic and comparative understanding of public policy and governance in the provinces. It is hoped that this concise book will help bring about more of this scholarship, which is necessary to inform policy governance in Canada's federal system and network society.

Our agenda for future research can be divided into five main issues. First, there is a clear need for more comparative research about the changing policy roles of substate governments in economically developed federations such as Australia, Belgium, Canada, Switzerland, and the United States. This type of research should focus not only on federalism but also on how substate governments redefine their policy activities in our new economic, social, and environmental world. Comparing the policy roles of substate entities in different federal countries is probably the best way to avoid transforming the international scholarship on federations into a simple comparison of how central governments operate within constitutional constraints. Comparisons between Canadian provinces and devolved entities such as Scotland and Wales in the United Kingdom are also relevant.[1]

Second, we need more systematic knowledge about the provincial civil services and, more important for this book, about the relationship between the public service and the other forces involved in policymaking, notably the executive, the legislature, and civil society actors. Future research could stress the democratic role of the provincial civil services and their redefinition in the context of the broader engagement of civil society in policymaking. This analysis should also assess potential differences between the 10 provinces in terms of public administration and policy governance. For example, do smaller, less populated provinces operate and develop policy very differently than the larger provinces because of their size? Overall, we need to stress variations in administrative capacity related to factors ranging from the size of the province to the nature of its civil society, party system, and political culture.

Third, it is imperative to explore the differences and similarities between the provinces in fiscal matters by systematically comparing their development over time so that we can explain divergence and convergence among them. This type of analysis is especially crucial to debunk myths about provincial fiscal policy, such as the claim that health care spending necessarily "crowds out" other forms of expenditures—it may in some provinces but not in others.

Fourth, regarding policy regulation, we need more empirical studies about the effectiveness of provincial regulatory policies, especially regarding how provinces interact with other regulatory actors, such as the federal government. In the literature on provincial public policy, the focus is more on spending programs than on regulatory ones, which explains why the need for new research on the provincial state as a regulator is so pressing. Efforts to introduce smarter regulations or to reduce the overall regulatory burden are topics that should command our attention as governments seek to achieve efficiencies and preserve public goals without burdening the private sector.

Finally, regarding civil society and the production of policy knowledge, there is an undeniable need for more research about the growing policy implications of consultants, interest groups, professional associations, policy analysts, and think thanks in provincial policymaking. In a world characterized by the development of complex

---

1 For instance, on the issue of the relationship between substate nationalism and social policy, scholars have systematically compared Québec (Canada) with Flanders (Belgium) and Scotland (United Kingdom): Béland and Lecours 2008.

expert networks, we should place provincial policymaking in its broad environment, and doing this means considering not only the setting in which governance takes place but also the contexts of civil society and knowledge production, all of which is shaped by technological as well as social, economic, and political changes.

In addition to these five points, future research on governance and public policy in Canada should include the three territories, as they compare with provinces, in terms of governance structures and networks as well as fiscal resources and policy challenges. Although our short book excluded territories to focus exclusively on the provinces, comparing them with territories could help improve our understanding of governance and public policy in Canada. Sparsely populated, possessing a unique constitutional status, and relying extensively on federal funding, the territories are both resource rich and crucial for national security and for the well-being of thousands of Inuit and First Nation citizens. Considering all this, students of provincial governance and public policy could contribute to developing a more systematic research agenda that would bring in the three territories.

Overall, we need to frame more systematic comparisons between provinces and, when relevant, territories, so we can generate data that may feed cross-provincial and cross-territorial policy learning, knowledge that spreads across Canada, from coast to coast and north to south. Although studying one province at the time is entirely legitimate and necessary, more methodical comparative scholarship, both qualitative and quantitative, is required to advance research on provincial governance and public policy in our country. When combined with the international approach mentioned previously, this type of research could enhance scholarly knowledge while providing better data and analysis to inform citizens and policymakers, who could draw comparative lessons aimed at improving policy and governance in their substate jurisdiction and, perhaps, at the federal level, as Ottawa could learn from the provinces and vice versa.[2]

Considering the challenges facing us in areas such as education, the environment, immigration, population aging, and research and innovation, as well as health care reform, provinces are likely to keep becoming increasingly central to a growing number of policy and governance issues. In this context, taking provinces seriously as policy

---

2 On lesson drawing in policy research, see Rose 1991.

actors and comparing them in a more systematic way is essential. Because provincial governments are so important as policy actors, we need to increase our knowledge about them to inform public debates and policy issues in which they should remain essential for the years and the decades to come. As civil society actors are now crucial policy players in the provinces and beyond, the knowledge generated should help not only government officials but also citizens and the organizations they belong to make sense of our changing governance and policy world. In other words, it is because public policy is not only about civil servants and elected officials that ordinary citizens and civil society organizations should care about how policies are made with, and within, our 10 provinces.

References

Abele, Frances, and Michael J. Prince. 2003. "Counsel for Canadian Federalism: Aboriginal Governments and the Council of the Federation." *Constructive and Co-operative Federalism?* Council of the Federation Series 11. Kingston, ON: Institute of Intergovernmental Relations. http://www.queensu.ca/iigr/WorkingPapers/CouncilFederation/FedEN.html.

Abele, Frances, and Michael J. Prince. 2006. "Four Pathways to Aboriginal Self-Government in Canada." *American Review of Canadian Studies* 36 (4): 568–95. http://dx.doi.org/10.1080/02722010609481408.

Abelson, Donald. 2007. "Any Ideas? Think Tanks and Policy Analysis in Canada." In *Policy Analysis in Canada: The State of the Art*, ed. L. Dobuzinskis, M. Howlett, and D. Laycock, 551–73. Toronto: University of Toronto Press.

Aberbach, Joel D., Robert Putnam, and Bert Rockman. 1981. *Bureaucrats and Politicians in Western Democracies*. Cambridge, MA: Harvard University Press.

Adam, Marc-Antoine. 2005. "The Creation of the Council of the Federation." 2005 Special Series on the Interdependence of Democracy Initiatives and Federalism Initiatives. Working Paper, Institute of Intergovernmental Relations, School of Policy Studies, Queen's University, Kingston, ON, http://www.queensu.ca/iigr/WorkingPapers/Interdependence.html.

Agranoff, Robert. 2004. "Autonomy, Devolution and Intergovernmental Relations." *Regional & Federal Studies* 14 (1): 26–65. http://dx.doi.org/10.1080/13597560042000245160.

Ahmed, Habib, and Stephen M. Miller. 2000. "Crowding Out and Crowding In Effects of the Components of Government Expenditure." *Contemporary Economic Policy* 18 (1): 124–33. http://dx.doi.org/10.1111/j.1465-7287.2000.tb00011.x.

Alberta. 2007. *Policy Capacity: Strengthening the Public Service's Support to Elected Officials*. Edmonton: Government of Alberta (Mimeo).

Alberta Municipal Affairs. 2009. *Provincial Resource Sharing Network Policy for Alberta Public Library Boards*. Edmonton: Government of Alberta. http://www.mclboard.com/images/prsnp.pdf (accessed September 11, 2012).

Andreoni, James. 1993. "An Experimental Test of the Public Goods Crowding Out Hypothesis." *American Economic Review* 83 (5): 1317–27.

Aschauer, David Allan. 1989. "Is Public Expenditure Productive?" *Journal of Monetary Economics* 23 (2): 177–200. http://dx.doi. org/10.1016/0304-3932(89)90047-0.

Atkinson, Michael M., and Gerald Bierling. 1998. "Is There Convergence in Provincial Spending Priorities?" *Canadian Public Policy* 24 (1): 71–88. http:// dx.doi.org/10.2307/3551730.

Atkinson, Michael M., and William D. Coleman. 1989. "Strong States and Weak States: Sectoral Policy Networks in Advanced Capitalist Economies." *British Journal of Political Science* 19 (1): 47–67.

Atkinson, Michael M., and William D. Coleman. 1992. "Policy Networks, Policy Communities and the Problems of Governance." *Governance: An International Journal of Policy, Administration and Institutions* 5 (2): 154–80. http://dx.doi. org/10.1111/j.1468-0491.1992.tb00034.x.

Aucoin, Peter, and Herman Bakvis. 1993. "Consolidating Cabinet Portfolios: Australian Lessons for Canada." Paper presented at meeting of Canadian Political Science Association, Ottawa.

Ayers, Stephanie, and Jennie Kronenfeld. 2007. "Chronic Illness and Health-Seeking Information on the Internet." *Health: An Interdisciplinary Journal for the Social Study of Health, Illness and Medicine* 11 (3): 327–47. http://dx.doi.org/10.1177/1363459307077547. Medline:17606698

Baglay, Sasha. 2012. "Provincial Nominee Programs: A Note on Policy Implications and Future Research Needs." *Journal of International Migration and Integration* 13 (1): 121–41. http://dx.doi.org/10.1007/s12134-011-0190-8.

Bakvis, Herman. 2000. "Rebuilding Policy Capacity in the Era of the Fiscal Dividend: A Report from Canada." *Governance: An International Journal of Policy, Administration and Institutions* 13 (1): 71–103. http://dx.doi. org/10.1111/0952-1895.00124.

Banting, Keith. 2006. "Social Citizenship and Federalism: Is a Federal Welfare State a Contradiction in Terms?" In *Territory, Democracy and Justice: Regionalization and Federalism in Western Democracies*, ed. S.C. Greer, 44–66. New York: Palgrave Macmillan.

Banting, Keith, and Robin Boadway. 2004. "Defining the Sharing Community: The Federal Role in Health Care." In *Money, Politics and Health Care: Reconstructing the Federal-Provincial Partnership*, ed. Harvey Lazar and Francis St-Hilaire, 1–78. Montreal: Institute for Research on Public Policy.

Banting, Keith, and Richard Simeon, eds. 1983. *And No One Cheered: Federalism, Democracy and the Constitution Act.* Toronto: Methuen.

Bardach, Eugene. 2000. *A Practical Guide for Policy Analysis: The Eightfold Path to More Effective Problem Solving.* New York: Chatham House Publishers.

Barnett, Laura. 2008. *Canada's Approach to the Treaty-Making Process.* Background Paper No. PRB 08–45-E. Ottawa: Library of Parliament, Legal and Legislative Affairs Division.

Baskoy, Tuna, Bryan Evans, and John Shields. 2011. "Assessing Policy Capacity in Canada's Public Services: Perspectives of Deputy and Assistant Deputy Ministers." *Canadian Public Administration* 54 (2): 212–34. http://dx.doi.org/10.1111/j.1754-7121.2011.00171.x.

Béland, Daniel, and André Lecours. 2006. "Sub-state Nationalism and the Welfare State: Québec and Canadian Federalism." *Nations and Nationalism* 12 (1): 77–96. http://dx.doi.org/10.1111/j.1469-8129.2006.00231.x.

Béland, Daniel, and André Lecours. 2007. "Federalism, Nationalism and Social Policy Decentralization in Canada and Belgium." *Regional & Federal Studies* 17 (4): 405–19. http://dx.doi.org/10.1080/13597560701712643.

Béland, Daniel, and André Lecours. 2008. *Nationalism and Social Policy: The Politics of Territorial Solidarity.* Oxford: Oxford University Press.

Bélanger, Louis. 2002. "The Domestic Politics of Quebec's Quest for External Distinctiveness." *American Review of Canadian Studies* 32 (2): 195–214. http://dx.doi.org/10.1080/02722010209481080.

Benáček, Vladimír. 2005. "Three Dimensions of Modern Social Governance: Markets, Hierarchies and Kinships." In *Democratic Governance in the CEECs*, ed. A. Rosenbaum and J. Nemec, 407–28. Bratislava: NISPAcee Publications. http://www1.ceses.cuni.cz/benacek/3D-Apro5-full_version.pdf.

Bernier, Luc, Keith Brownsey, and Michael Howlett. 2005. *Executive Styles in Canada: Cabinet Structures and Leadership Practices in Canadian Government.* Toronto: University of Toronto Press/Institute of Public Administration of Canada.

Berry, William D., and David Lowery. 1984. "The Growing Cost of Government: A Test of Two Explanations." *Social Science Quarterly* 65 (3): 735–49.

Bevir, Mark, and R.A.W. Rhodes. 2001. "Decentering Tradition: Interpreting British Government." *Administration & Society* 33 (2): 107–32. http://dx.doi.org/10.1177/00953990122019703.

Black, Julia. 2002. *Critical Reflections on Regulation.* CARR Discussion Paper 4. London, UK: Centre for Analysis of Risk and Regulation, London School of Economics. http://eprints.lse.ac.uk/35985/ (accessed December 20, 2012).

Blagrave, Patrick. 2005. "An Analysis of the Impact of the Harmonized Sales Tax on Provincial Revenues in Atlantic Canada." *Canadian Public Policy* 31 (3): 319–31. http://dx.doi.org/10.2307/3552444.

Blais, André, and Richard Nadeau. 1992. "The Electoral Budget Cycle." *Public Choice* 74: 389–403.

Boadway, Robin. 2003. *Options for Fiscal Federalism.* Ottawa: Royal Commission on Renewing and Strengthening our Place in Canada.

Boadway, Robin. 2011. "Rethinking Tax-Transfer Policy for 20th Century Canada." *In New Directions for Intelligent Government in Canada: Papers in Honour of Ian Stewart*, ed. Fred Gorbet and Andrew Sharpe, 163–203. Ottawa: Centre for the Study of Living Standards.

Boadway, Robin, and Jean-François Tremblay. 2005. *A Theory of Vertical Fiscal Imbalance*. Queen's Economic Department Working Paper No. 1072. Kingston, ON: Department of Economics, Queen's University. http://qed.econ.queensu.ca/working_papers/papers/qed_wp_1072.pdf.

Boase, Joan Price. 1996. "Institutions, Institutionalized Networks and Policy Choices: Health Policy in the U.S. and Canada." *Governance: An International Journal of Policy, Administration and Institutions* 9 (3): 287–310. http://dx.doi.org/10.1111/j.1468-0491.1996.tb00244.x.

Boessenkool, Kenneth. 2010. "Fixing the Fiscal Imbalance: Turning GST Revenues over to the Provinces in Exchange for Lower Transfers." *The School of Public Research Papers* 3 (10): 1–22.

Bolleyer, Nicole. 2009. *Intergovernmental Cooperation: Rational Choices in Federal Systems and Beyond*. Oxford: Oxford University Press.

Boothe, Paul. 2001. "Slaying the Deficit Dragon." In *Deficit Reduction in the Far West*, ed. Paul Boothe and Bradford Reid, 135–64. Edmonton: University of Alberta Press.

Borgatti, Stephen P., and Rob Cross. 2003. "A Relational View of Information Seeking and Learning in Social Networks." *Management Science* 49 (4): 432–45. http://dx.doi.org/10.1287/mnsc.49.4.432.14428.

Borins, Sandford. 1986. *Investments in Failure: Five Government Corporations that Cost the Taxpayer Billions*. Toronto: Methuen.

Borins, Sandford. 2001. "Public Management Innovation: Towards a Global Perspective." *American Review of Public Administration* 31 (1): 5–21. http://dx.doi.org/10.1177/02750740122064802.

Borins, Sandford. 2003. "From Research to Practice: A Survey of Public Administration Scholars in Canada." *Canadian Public Administration* 46 (2): 243–56. http://dx.doi.org/10.1111/j.1754-7121.2003.tb00914.x.

Bourgault, Jacques. 2004. "Quebec's Role in Canadian Federal-Provincial Relations." In *Canada: The State of the Federation 2002—Reconsidering the Institutions of Canadian Federalism*, ed. J.P. Meekison, M. Telford, and H. Lazar, 341–76. Montreal and Kingston, ON: McGill-Queen's University Press for the Institute of Intergovernmental Relations.

Boychuk, Gerard W. 2006. "Slouching toward the Bottom? Provincial Social Assistance Provision in Canada, 1980–2000." In *Racing to the Bottom? Provincial Interdependence in the Canadian Federation*, ed. Kathryn Harrison, 157–92. Vancouver: University of British Columbia Press.

Boyd, Danah. 2008. "Facebook's Privacy Trainwreck: Exposure, Invasion, and Social Convergence." *Convergence: The International Journal of*

Research into New Media Technologies 14 (1): 13–20. http://dx.doi.
org/10.1177/1354856507084416.

Bradley, Phil. 2010. "Be Where the Conversations Are: The Critical Importance
of Social Media." *Business Information Review* 27 (4): 248–52. http://dx.doi.
org/10.1177/0266382110390976.

Briones, Rowena L., Beth Kuch, Brooke Fisher Liu, and Jin Yan. 2011. "Keeping
up with the Digital Age: How the American Red Cross Used Social Media to
Build Relationships." *Public Relations Review* 37 (1): 37–43. http://dx.doi.
org/10.1016/j.pubrev.2010.12.006.

Brooks, Stephen. 1989. *Public Policy in Canada: An Introduction.* Toronto:
McClelland and Stewart.

Brooks, Stephen. 2007. "The Policy Analysis Profession in Canada." In *Policy
Analysis in Canada: The State of the Art,* ed. L. Dobuzinskis, M. Howlett, and
D. Laycock, 21–47. Toronto: University of Toronto Press.

Brownsey, Keith, and Michael Howlett, eds. 2001. *Provincial State in Canada: Politics
in the Provinces and Territories.* Toronto: University of Toronto Press.

Burch, Sarah. 2010. "In Pursuit of Resilient, Low Carbon Communities: An
Examination of Barriers to Action in Three Canadian Cities." *Energy Policy* 38
(12): 7575–85.

Burke, Moira, Cameron Marlow, and Thomas Lento. 2010. "Social Network
Activity and Social Well-Being." In *Proceedings of the 2010 ACM Conference
on Human Factors in Computing Systems,* 1909–12. New York: ACM.

Busby, Colin, and William B. P. Robson. 2010. *Target Practice Needed: Canada's
2010 Fiscal Accountability Rankings.* Toronto: C.D. Howe Institute.

Cairns, Alan. 2000. *Citizens Plus: Aboriginal Peoples and the Canadian State.*
Vancouver: University of British Columbia Press.

Cameron, David, and R. Simeon. 2002. "Intergovernmental Relations in Canada:
The Emergence of Collaborative Federalism." *Publius: The Journal of
Federalism* 32 (2): 49–72. http://dx.doi.org/10.1093/oxfordjournals.pubjof.
a004947.

Cameron, David R., and Graham White. 2000. *Cycling into Saigon: The
Conservative Transition in Ontario.* Vancouver, BC: UBC Press.

Canadian Policy Research Networks. 2009. *The Future of Policy Capacity in
Canada: Roundtable Report.* Ottawa: Canadian Policy Research Networks.

Carroll, Barbara Wake, and Ruth J. E. Jones. 2000. "The Road to Innovation,
Convergence or Inertia: Devolution in Housing Policy in Canada." *Canadian
Public Policy* 26 (3): 277–93. http://dx.doi.org/10.2307/3552401.

CEAA (Canadian Environmental Assessment Agency). 1997. *Report of the
Joint Federal-Provincial Panel on Uranium Mining Developments in
Northern Saskatchewan (Cumulative Observations).* Ottawa: CEAA.
http://ceaa.gc.ca/default.asp?lang=En&n=A0159CFA-1.

CEAA (Canadian Environmental Assessment Agency). 2010. *Operational Policy Statement: Use of Federal-Provincial Cooperation Mechanisms in Environmental Assessments Pursuant to the Canadian Environmental Assessment Act*. Ottawa: CEAA. http://publications.gc.ca/collections/collection_2012/ec/En106-89-2011-eng.pdf.

CFIA (Canadian Food Inspection Agency). 2011. "Questions and Answers: Federal/Provincial/Territorial Interprovincial Meat Trade Pilot Project." Website of the Canadian Food Inspection Agency. http://www.inspection.gc.ca/english/fssa/meavia/interprov/queste.shtml (accessed December 10, 2012).

Chadwick, Andrew. 2006. *Internet Politics: States, Citizens, and New Communication Technologies*. New York: Oxford University Press.

Chandler, Marsha. 1982. "State Enterprise and Partisanship in Provincial Politics." *Canadian Journal of Political Science* 15 (04): 711–40. http://dx.doi.org/10.1017/S0008423900052021.

CICS (Canada Intergovernmental Conference Secretariat). 2004. *First Ministers' Conferences, 1906–2004*. Ottawa: Canadian Intergovernmental Conference Secretariat.

Clark, David. 2002. "Neoliberalism and Public Service Reform: Canada in Comparative Perspective." *Canadian Journal of Political Science* 35 (04): 771–93. http://dx.doi.org/10.1017/S0008423902778438.

Clark, Ian D., and Harry Swain. 2005. "Distinguishing the Real from the Surreal in Management Reform: Suggestions for Beleaguered Administrators in the Government of Canada." *Canadian Public Administration* 48 (4): 453–76. http://dx.doi.org/10.1111/j.1754-7121.2005.tb01198.x.

Cohn, Daniel. 2007. "Academic and Public Policy: Informing Policy Analysis and Policy Making." In *Policy Analysis in Canada: The State of the Art*, ed. L. Dobuzinskis, M. Howlett, and D. Laycock, 574–97. Toronto: University of Toronto Press.

Cole, Richard L., John Kincaid, and Alejandro Rodriguez. 2004. "Public Opinion in Federalism and Federal Political Culture in Canada, Mexico, and the United States." *Publius: The Journal of Federalism* 34 (3): 201–21. http://dx.doi.org/10.1093/oxfordjournals.pubjof.a005037.

Coleman, William, and Grace Skogstad, eds. 1990. *Policy Communities and Public Policies in Canada*. Toronto: Copp Clark.

Coleman, William D., Grace D. Skogstad, and Michael Atkinson. 1996. "Paradigm Shifts and Policy Networks: Cumulative Change in Agriculture." *Journal of Public Policy* 16 (03): 273–302. http://dx.doi.org/10.1017/S0143814X00007777.

Conference Board of Canada. 2004. *Expectations of Performance-Based Regulation in the Natural Gas Industry*. Conference Board of Canada Discussion Paper No. 680-04. Ottawa: Conference Board of Canada. http://www.ontarioenergyboard.ca/documents/

consultation_ontariosgasmarket_cgacbofc2_finalsub_121104.pdf (accessed February 28, 2012).

Corden, Warner M. 1984. "Booming Sector and Dutch Disease Economies: Survey and Consolidation." *Oxford Economic Papers,* New Series 36 (3): 359–80.

Cotton, Bob. 2009. "Innovation Networks: A Report on Creating a Specialist Professional Social Network, Offline and Online, to Foster Innovation in the New Media Sector." *Online Communities and Social Computing* 5621: 312–21.

Coulibaly, Aïcha L. 2010. *Does the Agreement on Internal Trade Do Enough to Liberalize Canada's Domestic Trade in Agri-Food Products?* Ottawa: Library of Parliament.

Council of the Federation. 2012. *From Innovation to Action: The First Report of the Health Care Innovation Group.* Ottawa: Council of the Federation Secretariat.

Courchene, Thomas J. 2012. *Policy Signposts in Post-War Canada.* Montreal: Institute for Research on Public Policy.

CPRN (Canadian Policy Research Networks). 2009. *The Future of Policy Capacity in Canada: A Roundtable Report.* Ottawa: Canadian Policy Research Networks. http://www.cprn.org/doc.cfm?doc=2038&l=en.

CSTO (Canadian Securities Transition Office). 2011. The Canadian Securities Transition Office. http://csto-btcvm.ca/Home.aspx.

Dahlby, Bev. 2005. *Dealing with the Fiscal Imbalances: Vertical, Horizontal, and Structural.* C.D. Howe Working Paper. Toronto: C. D. Howe Institute.

Dalton, J.E. 2006. "Aboriginal Self-Determination in Canada: Protections Afforded by the Judiciary and Government." *Canadian Journal of Law and Society* 21 (1): 11–37. http://dx.doi.org/10.1353/jls.2006.0034.

Davies, Louise. 2002. "Technical Cooperation and the International Coordination of Patentability of Biotechnological Inventions." *Journal of Law and Society* 29 (1): 137–62. http://dx.doi.org/10.1111/1467-6478.00214.

de Boer, Stephen. 2002. "Canadian Provinces, US States and North American Integration: Bench Warmers or Key Players?" *Choices: Canada's Options in North America* 8 (4): 2–24.

deLeon, Peter. 1997. *Democracy and the Policy Sciences.* Albany, NY: State University of New York Press.

deLeon, Peter, and Danielle Vogenbeck. 2007. "The Policy Sciences at the Crossroads." In *Handbook of Public Policy Analysis: Theory, Politics, and Methods,* ed. Frank Fischer, Gerald J. Miller, and Mara S. Sidney, 3–14. New York: Taylor & Francis Group.

Deschamps, Ryan. 2012. "Twitter Use and the Governance of Social Media in Canadian Federal and Provincial Government Departments." Paper presented at the 2012 Prairie Political Science Association Annual Conference, Saskatoon, September 21–22.

DiStaso, Marcia W., Tina McCorkindale, and Donald K. Wright. 2011. "How Public Relations Executives Perceive and Measure the Impact of Social Media in Their Organizations." *Public Relations Review* 37 (3): 325–28. http://dx.doi.org/10.1016/j.pubrev.2011.06.005.

Dixon, Brian E. 2010. "Towards E-Government 2.0: An Assessment Of Where E-Government 2.0 Is and Where It Is Headed." *Public Administration & Management* 15 (2): 418–54.

Dobuzinskis, Laurent, Michael Howlett, and David Laycock, eds. 2007. *Policy Analysis in Canada: The State of the Art.* Toronto: University of Toronto Press.

Dodge, David A., and Richard Dion. 2010. *Chronic Health Care Spending Disease: A Macro Diagnosis and Prognosis.* Working Paper. Ottawa: Bennett Jones LLP.

Drummond, Don. 2012. *Commission on the Reform of Ontario's Public Services.* Toronto: Queen's Printer for Ontario.

Dunn, Christopher. 1995. *The Institutionalized Cabinet: Governing the Western Provinces.* Montreal: McGill-Queen's University Press.

Dunn, Christopher. 2006a. *Provinces: Canadian Provincial Politics.* 2nd ed. Toronto: University of Toronto Press.

Dunn, Christopher, ed. 2006b. *Provincial Politics.* Toronto: University of Toronto Press.

Dutil, Patrice A. 2008. *Searching for Leadership; Cabinet Secretaries in Canada.* Toronto: University of Toronto Press.

Dutil, Patrice A., Cosmo Howard, John Langford, and Jeffrey Roy. 2008. "Rethinking Government-Public Relationships in a Digital World: Customers, Clients, or Citizens?" *Journal of Information Technology & Politics* 4 (1): 77–90. http://dx.doi.org/10.1300/J516v04n01_06.

Dyck, Rand. 1996. *Provincial Politics in Canada: Towards the Turn of the Century.* Toronto: Prentice-Hall.

Eggers, William D. 2005. *Government 2.0: Using Technology to Improve Education, Cut Red Tape, Reduce Gridlock, and Enhance Democracy.* Lanham, MD: Rowman & Littlefield Publishers.

Eid, Elisabeth. 2001. "Interaction between International and Domestic Human Rights Law: A Canadian Perspective." Paper presented at the Sino Canadian International Conference on the Ratification and Implementation of Human Rights Covenants, Beijing, China, October. http://www.icclr.law.ubc.ca/publications/reports/e-eid.pdf (accessed December 21, 2012).

Erk, Jan, and Lawrence Anderson. 2009. "The Paradox of Federalism: Does Self-Rule Accommodate or Exacerbate Ethnic Divisions." *Regional & Federal Studies* 19 (2): 191–202. http://dx.doi.org/10.1080/13597560902753388.

Erk, Jan, and Edward Koning. 2010. "New Structuralism and Institutional Change: Federalism between Centralization and Decentralization." *Comparative Political Studies* 43 (3): 353–78. http://dx.doi.org/10.1177/0010414009332143.

Fafard, Patrick. 2012. "Intergovernmental Accountability and Health Care: Reflections on the Recent Canadian Experience." In *Overpromising and Underperforming? Understanding and Evaluating New Intergovernmental Accountability Regimes*, ed. Linda White, Peter Graefe, and Julie Simmons, 31–55. Toronto: University of Toronto Press.

Feldman, Lionel D., and Katherine A. Graham. 1979. *Bargaining for Cities: Municipalities and Intergovernmental Relations—An Assessment*. Montreal: Institute for Research in Public Policy.

Fenna, Alan. 2010. *Benchmarking in Federal Systems*. Occasional Papers Series No. 6. Ottawa: Forum of Federations.

Ferris, J. Stephen, Soo-Bin Park, and Stanley L. Winer. 2006. *Political Competition and Convergence to Fundamentals: With Application to the Political Business Cycle and Size of Government*. CESifo Working Paper No. 1646. Munich: Ifo Institute, Center for Economic Studies. http://www.cesifo-group.de/ifoHome/publications/working-papers/CESifoWP/CESifoWPdetails?wp_id=14558518.

Ferris, J. Stephan, and Stanley L. Winer. 2007. "Just How Much Bigger is Government in Canada? A Comparative Analysis of the Size and Structure of the Public Sectors in Canada and the United States, 1929–2004." *Canadian Public Policy* 33 (2): 173–206. http://dx.doi.org/10.3138/cpp.33.2.173.

Frederickson, H. George, and Kevin B. Smith. 2003. *The Public Administration Theory Primer*. Boulder, CO: Westview Press.

Flanagan, Tom. 2000. *First Nations? Second Thoughts*. Montreal and Kingston, ON: McGill-Queen's University Press.

Fortin, Pierre. 2011. "Income Support in the Canadian Federation: International and Interprovincial Comparisons and Future Directions." In *New Directions for Intelligent Government in Canada: Papers in Honour of Ian Stewart*, ed. Fred Gorbet and Andrew Sharpe, 211–26. Ottawa: Centre for the Study of Living Standards.

Fortin, Sarah, Alain Noël, and France St-Hilaire. 2003. *Forging the Canadian Social Union: SUFA and Beyond*. Montreal: Institute for Research on Public Policy.

Freeman, Neil. 1996. *The Politics of Power: Ontario Hydro and Its Government, 1906–1995*. Toronto: University of Toronto Press.

Fyfe, Toby, and Paul Crookall. 2010. *Social Media and Public Sector Policy Dilemmas*. Toronto: Institution of Public Administration of Canada.

Gérard, Marcel. 2002. "Fiscal Federalism in Belgium." In *Texts Submitted for the International Symposium on Fiscal Imbalance*, 175–94. Québec, QC: Commission on Fiscal Imbalance, http://www.groupes.finances.gouv.qc.ca/desequilibrefiscal/en/document/recueil.htm.

Gilpin, Robert. 2001. *Global Political Economy: Understanding the International Economic Order*. Princeton: Princeton University Press.

Gow, James I. 1976. "Modernisation et administration publique," in *La Modernisation politique du Québec*, ed. E. Orban, 157–86. Montreal: Boreal.

Graben, Sari. 2007. "The Nisga'a Final Agreement and Negotiating Federalism." *Indigenous Law Journal* 6 (2): 63–94.

Graefe, Peter, and Andrew Bourns. 2009. "The Gradual Defederalization of Canadian Health Policy." *Publius: The Journal of Federalism* 39 (1): 187–209. http://dx.doi.org/10.1093/publius/pjn029.

Graham, Katherine A., and Susan D. Phillips. 1998. ""Who Does What" in Ontario: The Process of Provincial-Municipal Disentanglement." *Canadian Public Administration* 41 (2): 175–209.

Grant, John. 2012. "Stock and Bond Markets." *The Canadian Encyclopaedia*. http://www.thecanadianencyclopedia.com/articles/stock-and-bond-markets (accessed January 27, 2012).

Guillemette, Yvan. 2010. *Fiscal-Consolidation Strategies for Canadian Governments*. OECD Economics Department Working Paper 818. Paris: Organisation for Economic Co-operation and Development. http://www.oecd-ilibrary.org/economics/fiscal-consolidation-strategies-for-canadian-governments_5km36j7nc2g4-en.

Hajer, Maarten, and Hendrik Wagenaar, eds. 2003. *Deliberative Policy Analysis: Understanding Governance in the Network Society*. Cambridge: Cambridge University Press. http://dx.doi.org/10.1017/CBO9780511490934.

Hale, Geoffrey E. 2006. "Balancing Autonomy and Responsibility: The Politics of Provincial Fiscal and Tax Policies." In *Provinces-Canadian Provincial Politics*. 2nd ed., ed. Christopher Dunn, 373–412. Peterborough, ON: Broadview Press.

Hanick, David, David Vernon, and James Brown. 2012. *Mining in Canada in 2011*. Toronto: Osler. http://www.osler.com/NewsResources/Default.aspx?id=4143 (accessed February 28, 2012).

Hansen, Robin, and Heather Heavin. 2011. "What's "New" in the New West Partnership Trade Agreement? The NWPTA and the Agreement on Internal Trade Compared." *Saskatchewan Law Review* 73 (2): 197–235.

Harrison, Jeffrey P., and Angela Lee. 2006. "The Role of e-Health in the Changing Health Care Environment." *Nursing Economic$* 24 (6): 283–88, 279, quiz 289. Medline:17266004.

Harrison, Kathryn. 2006. "Provincial Interdependence: Concepts and Theories." In *Racing to the Bottom? Provincial Interdependence in the Canadian Federation*, ed. Kathryn Harrison, 1–24. Vancouver: University of British Columbia Press.

Harrison, Kathryn, and W.T. Stanbury. 1990. "Privatization in British Columbia: Lessons from the Sale of Government Laboratories." *Canadian Public Administration* 33 (2): 165–97. http://dx.doi.org/10.1111/j.1754-7121.1990.tb01392.x.

Helco, Hugh. 1977. *A Government of Strangers: Executive Politics in Washington*. Washington, DC: Brookings Institution.

Henderson, Ailsa. 2007. *Nunavut: Rethinking Political Culture*. Vancouver: University of British Columbia Press.

Hirschman, Albert O. 1970. *Exit, Voice, and Loyalty: Responses to Decline in Firms, Organizations, and States*. Cambridge, MA: Harvard University Press.

Hoberg, George, and Edward Morawski. 1997. "Policy Change through Sector Intersection: Forest and Aboriginal Policy in Clayoquot Sound." *Canadian Public Administration* 40 (3): 387–414. http://dx.doi.org/10.1111/j.1754-7121.1997.tb01516.x.

Hodgetts, John E. 1964. "Challenge and Response: A Retrospective View of the Public Service of Canada." *Canadian Public Administration* 7 (4): 409–21.

Hodgetts, John E. 1982. "Implicit Values in the Administration of Public Affairs." *Canadian Public Administration* 25 (4): 471–83.

Hodgetts, John E., and Onkar P. Dwivedi. 1974. *Provincial Governments as Employers* Montreal: McGill-Queen's University Press.

Hodgetts, John E., and Onkar P. Dwivedi. 1976. "Administration and Personnel." In *The Provincial Political Systems: Comparative Essays*, ed. David Bellamy, Jon H. Pammett, and Donald C. Rowat, 341–56. Toronto: Methuen.

Hood, Christopher. 1995. "'De-privileging the UK Civil Service in the 1980s: Dream or Reality." In *Bureaucracy in the Modern State*, ed. Jon Pierre, 92–117. Cheltenham, UK: Edward Elgar.

Hood, Christopher. 2005. "Public Management: The Word, the Movement, the Science." In *Oxford Handbook of Public Management*, ed. Ewan Ferlie, Laurence Lynn Jr., and Christopher Pollitt, 7–26. Oxford: Oxford University Press.

Howlett, Michael. 2002. "Do Networks Matter? Linking Policy Network Structure to Policy Outcomes: Evidence from Four Canadian Policy Sectors 1990–2000." *Canadian Journal of Political Science* 25 (2): 235–67.

Howlett, Michael. 2009a. "A Profile of B.C. Provincial Policy Analysts: Troubleshooters or Planners?" *Canadian Political Science Review* 3 (3): 50–68.

Howlett, Michael. 2009b. "Policy Analytical Capacity and Evidence-Based Policy-Making: Lessons from Canada." *Canadian Public Administration* 52 (2): 153–75.

Howlett, Michael, and Sima Joshi-Koop. 2011. "Transnational Learning, Policy Analytical Capacity, and Environmental Policy Convergence: Survey Results from Canada." *Global Environmental Change* 21 (1): 85–92. http://dx.doi.org/10.1016/j.gloenvcha.2010.10.002.

Howlett, Michael, and Evert Lindquist. 2004. "Policy Analysis and Governance: Analytical and Policy Styles in Canada." *Journal of Comparative Policy Analysis* 6 (3): 225–49. http://dx.doi.org/10.1080/1387698042000305194.

Howlett, Michael, and Evert Lindquist. 2007. "Beyond Formal Policy Analysis: Governance Context, Analytical Styles, and the Policy Analysis Movement in

Canada." In *Policy Analysis in Canada*, ed. L. Dobuzinskis, M. Howlett, and D. Laycock, 86–115. Toronto: University of Toronto Press.

Howlett, Michael, and Josh Newman. 2010. "Policy Analysis and Policy Work in Federal Systems: Policy Advice and Its Contribution to Evidence-Based Policy Making in Multi-Level Governance Systems." *Policy and Society* 29 (2): 123–36. http://dx.doi.org/10.1016/j.polsoc.2010.03.004.

Howlett, Michael, M. Ramesh, and Anthony Perl. 2009. *Studying Public Policy: Policy Cycles and Policy Subsystems.* 3rd ed. Toronto: Oxford University Press.

Howlett, Michael, and Jeremy Rayner. 1995. "Do Ideas Matter? Policy Network Configurations and Resistance to Policy Change in the Canadian Forest Sector." *Canadian Public Administration* 38 (3): 382–410. http://dx.doi.org/10.1111/j.1754-7121.1995.tb01055.x.

Hyson, Stewart. 2009. *Provincial and Territorial Ombudsman Offices in Canada.* Toronto: University of Toronto Press.

Imbeau, Louis M., Réjean Landry, Henry Milner, Francois Pétry, Jean Crête, Pierre-Gerlier Forest, and Vincent Lemieux. 2000. "Comparative Provincial Policy Analysis: A Research Agenda." *Canadian Journal of Political Science* 33 (04): 779–804.

Imbeau, Louis M., François Pétry, Jean Crête, Geneviève Tellier, and Michel Clavet. 2001. "Measuring Government Growth in the Canadian Provinces: Decomposing Real Growth and Deflator Effects." *Canadian Public Policy* 27 (1): 39–52.

IMF (International Monetary Fund). 2009. Fiscal Rules—Anchoring Expectations for Sustainable Public Finance. Fiscal Affairs Department, IMF, December 16.

Institute on Governance. 2011. "Defining Governance." Institute on Governance, Ottawa ON. http://iog.ca/defining-governance (accessed March 12, 2013).

Inwood, Gregory J., Carolyn M. Johns, and Patricia L. O'Reilly. 2004. "Intergovernmental Officials in Canada." In *Canada: The State of the Federation 2002—Reconsidering the Institutions of Canadian Federalism*, ed. J.P. Meekison, M. Telford, and H. Lazar, 249–84. Montreal and Kingston, ON: McGill-Queen's University Press for the Institute of Intergovernmental Relations.

IPAC (Institute of Public Administration in Canada). 2011. *Survey of Deputy Ministers and CAOs and Members.* Toronto: IPAC.

ITS (Internal Trade Secretariat). n.d. "Introduction." The Agreement on Internal Trade. www.ait-aci.ca/index_en.htm (accessed December 10, 2012).

Johannson, P.R. 1978. "British Columbia's Relations with the United States." *Canadian Public Administration* 21 (2): 212–33. http://dx.doi.org/10.1111/j.1754-7121.1978.tb01762.x.

Johns, Carolyn M., Patricia L. O'Reilly, and Gregory J. Inwood. 2007. "Formal and Informal Dimensions of Intergovernmental Administrative Relations in

Canada." *Canadian Public Administration* 50 (1): 21–41. http://dx.doi.org/10.1111/j.1754-7121.2007.tb02001.x.

Johnson, A.W. 2004. *Dream No Little Dreams: A Biography of the Douglas Government of Saskatchewan 1944–1961.* Toronto: University of Toronto Press.

Johnson, Peter, and Graham White. 1980. "To Everything There Is An Agency: Boards, Agencies, and Commissions." In *The Government and Politics of Ontario*, revised edition, ed. Donald C. MacDonald, 123–44. Toronto: Van Nostrand.

Johnson, Ronald, and Gary Libecap. 1994. *The Federal Civil Service System and the Problem of Bureaucracy.* Chicago: University of Chicago Press.

Jones, Laura, and Stephen Graf. 2001. *Canada's Regulatory Burden: How Many Regulations? At What Cost?* Vancouver, BC: The Fraser Institute. http://www.investorvoice.ca/Research/FraserI_RegulatoryBurden_Aug01.pdf (accessed January 27, 2012).

Juillet, Luc, and Ken Rasmussen. 2008. *Defending a Contested Ideal: Merit and the PSC of Canada, 1908–2008.* Ottawa: University of Ottawa Press.

Kahneman, Daniel, and Amos Tversky. 1979. "Prospect Theory: An Analysis of Decision under Risk." *Econometrica: Journal of the Econometric Society* 47 (2): 263–91. http://dx.doi.org/10.2307/1914185.

Kaldor, Mary, Helmut Anheier, and Marlies Glasius, eds. 2004. *Global Civil Society 2004–2005.* London: Sage. http://www2.lse.ac.uk/internationalDevelopment/research/CSHS/civilSociety/yearBook/contentsPages/2004-2005.aspx (accessed January 3, 2012).

Kanter, Beth, and Allison Fine. 2010. *The Networked Nonprofit: Connecting with Social Media to Drive Change.* San Francisco: John Wiley & Sons.

Kennedy, Suzanne, and Janine Robbins. 2003. *The Role of Fiscal Rules in Determining Fiscal Performance.* Updated version of Department of Finance Working Paper 2001-16. Ottawa: Department of Finance Canada.

Kernaghan, Kenneth. 1976. "Politics, Policy, and Public Servants: Political Neutrality Revisited." *Canadian Public Administration* 19 (3): 432–56.

Kernaghan, Kenneth. 2005. "Moving Towards the Virtual State: Integrating Services and Service Channels for Citizen-Centred Delivery." *International Review of Administrative Sciences* 71 (1): 119–31. http://dx.doi.org/10.1177/0020852305051688.

Kettl, Donald F. 2000. "The Transformation of Governance: Globalization, Devolution, and the Role of Government." *Public Administration Review* 60 (6): 488–97. http://dx.doi.org/10.1111/0033-3352.00112.

Kettl, Donald F. 2002. *The Transformation of Governance: Public Administration for Twenty-First Century America.* Baltimore, MD: Johns Hopkins University Press.

Kneebone, Ronald D. 1994. "Deficits and Debt in Canada: Some Lessons from Recent History." *Canadian Public Policy* 20 (2): 152–64. http://dx.doi.org/10.2307/3552103.

Kneebone, Ronald D. 2006. "From Famine to Feast: The Evolution of Budgeting Rules in Alberta." *Canadian Tax Journal* 54 (3): 657–73.

Kneebone, Ronald D., and Kenneth J. McKenzie. 2001. "Electoral and Partisan Cycles in Fiscal Policy: An Examination of Canadian Provinces." *International Tax and Public Finance* 8 (5/6): 753–74. http://dx.doi.org/10.1023/A:1012895211073.

Krueger, Anne O. 1974. "The Political Economy of the Rent-Seeking Society." *The American Economic Review* 64 (3): 291–303.

Kukucha, Christopher J. 2004. "The Role of the Provinces in Canadian Foreign Trade Policy: Multi-Level Governance and Sub-National Interests in the Twenty-First Century." *Policy and Society* 23 (3): 113–34. http://dx.doi.org/10.1016/S1449-4035(04)70040-5.

Kukucha, Christopher J. 2005. "From Kyoto to the WTO: Evaluating the Constitutional Legitimacy of the Provinces in Canadian Foreign Trade and Environmental Policy." *Canadian Journal of Political Science* 38 (01): 1–24. http://dx.doi.org/10.1017/S000842390505002X.

Kukucha, Christopher J. 2008. *The Provinces and Canadian Foreign Trade Policy.* Vancouver: University of British Columbia Press.

Lai, Linda S.L., and Efraim Turban. 2008. "Groups Formation and Operations in the Web 2.0 Environment and Social Networks." *Group Decision and Negotiation* 17 (5): 387–402. http://dx.doi.org/10.1007/s10726-008-9113-2.

Landon, Stuart, Melville L. McMillan, Vijay Muralidharan, and Mark Parsons. 2006. "Does Health-Care Spending Crowd Out Other Provincial Government Expenditures?" *Canadian Public Policy* 32 (2): 121–41. http://dx.doi.org/10.2307/4128724.

Langlois, Ganaele, Greg Elmer, Fenwick McKelvey, and Zachary Devereaux. 2009. "Networked Publics: The Double Articulation of Code and Politics on Facebook." *Canadian Journal of Communication* 34 (3): 415–34.

Lazar, Harvey, France St-Hilaire, and Jean-Francois Tremblay. 2004. "Vertical Fiscal Imbalance: Myth or Reality." In *Money, Politics and Health Care: Reconstructing the Federal-Provincial Partnership*, ed. Harvey Lazar and Francis St-Hilaire, 141–93. Montreal: Institute for Research on Public Policy.

Leclair, Jean. 2006. "Jane Austen and the Council of the Federation." *Constitutional Forum* 15 (2): 51–61.

Lecours, André, and Daniel Béland. 2010. "Federalism and Fiscal Policy: The Politics of Equalization in Canada." *Publius: The Journal of Federalism* 40 (4): 569–96. http://dx.doi.org/10.1093/publius/pjp030.

Leeson, Howard. 1987. "The Intergovernmental Affairs Function in Saskatchewan, 1960–1983." *Canadian Public Administration* 30 (3): 399–420. http://dx.doi. org/10.1111/j.1754-7121.1987.tb00091.x.

Lefebvre, Pierre, and Philip Merrigan. 2008. "Child-Care Policy and the Labor Supply of Mothers with Young Children: A Natural Experiment from Canada." *Journal of Labor Economics* 26 (3): 519–48. http://dx.doi.org/10.1086/587760.

Leitch, Shona, and Matthew Warren. 2009. "Security Issue Challenging Facebook." In *Proceedings of the 7th Australian Information Security Management Conference, December 1–3, Perth W.A.*, ed. Edith Cowan, 137–42. Perth, WA: Cowan University.

Lewis, Nathaniel M. 2010. "A Decade Later: Assessing Successes and Challenges in Manitoba's Provincial Immigrant Nominee Program." *Canadian Public Policy* 36 (2): 241–64.

Lindblom, Charles E. 1958. "Policy Analysis." *American Economic Review* 48 (3): 298–312.

Lindquist, Evert A. 1993. "Think Tanks or Clubs? Assessing the Influence and Roles of Canadian Policy Institutes." *Canadian Public Administration* 36 (4): 547–79. http://dx.doi.org/10.1111/j.1754-7121.1993.tb00833.x.

Lindquist, Evert A., ed. 2000. *Government Restructure and Career Public Services.* Toronto: Institute of Public Administration of Canada.

Lindquist, Evert A., and Graham White. 1994. "Streams, Springs, and Stones: Ontario Public Service Reform in the 1980s and the 1990s." *Canadian Public Administration* 37 (2): 267–301. http://dx.doi.org/10.1111/j.1754-7121.1994. tb00858.x.

Livingston, William S. 1956. *Federalism and Constitutional Change.* Oxford: Clarendon Press.

Loreto, Richard A. 1997. "Making and Implementing Decisions: Issues of Public Administration in the Ontario Government." In *The Government and Politics of Ontario*, ed. Graham White, 93–125. Toronto: University of Toronto Press.

Loukacheva, Natalia. 2007. *Arctic Promise: Legal and Political Autonomy of Greenland and Nunavut.* Toronto: University of Toronto Press.

Macmillan, Kathleen, and Patrick Grady. 2007. *A New Prescription: Can the BC-Alberta TILMA Resuscitate Internal Trade in Canada?* Toronto: C.D. Howe Institute.

MacNevin, Alex S. 2004. *The Canadian Federal-Provincial Equalization Regime: An Assessment.* Toronto: Canadian Tax Foundation.

MacRae, Duncan. 1991. "Policy Analysis and Knowledge Use." *Knowledge and Policy* 4 (3): 27–40. http://dx.doi.org/10.1007/BF02693086.

Magnusson, Warren. 2005a. "Are Municipalities Creatures of the Provinces?" *Journal of Canadian Studies / Revue d'Etudes Canadiennes* 38 (4): 5–29.

Magnusson, Warren. 2005b. "Protecting the Right of Local Self-Government." *Canadian Journal of Political Science* 38 (04): 897–922. http://dx.doi.org/10.1017/S0008423905040436.

Majone, Giandomenico. 1994. "The Rise of the Regulatory State in Europe." *West European Politics* 17 (3): 77–101. http://dx.doi.org/10.1080/01402389408425031.

Malita, Laura. 2011. "Social Media Time Management Tools and Tips." *Procedia Computer Science* 3: 747–53. http://dx.doi.org/10.1016/j.procs.2010.12.123.

Malloy, Jonathan. 2003. *Between Colliding Worlds: The Ambiguous Existence of Government Agencies for Aboriginal and Women's Issues.* Toronto: University of Toronto Press.

Manovich, Lev. 2009. "The Practice of Everyday (Media) Life: From Mass Consumption to Mass Cultural Production?" *Critical Inquiry* 35 (2): 319–31. http://dx.doi.org/10.1086/596645.

Marchildon, Gregory P. 1995. "Fin de siècle Canada: The Federal Government in Retreat." In *Disintegration or Transformation: The Crisis of the State in Advanced Industrial Countries*, ed. P. McCarthy and E. Jones, 133–51. New York: St. Martin's Press.

Marchildon, Gregory P. 1999. "Constructive Entanglement: Intergovernmental Collaboration in Canadian Social Policy." In *Collaborative Government: Is There a Canadian Way?* ed. S. Delacourt and D.G. Lenihan, 72–80. Toronto: Institute of Public Administration of Canada.

Marchildon, Gregory P. 2000. "A Step in the Right Direction." *Inroads* 9: 124–33.

Marchildon, Gregory P. 2006. *Health Systems in Transition: Canada.* Toronto: University of Toronto Press.

Marchildon, Gregory P., and K. McNutt. 2007. "Infostructure and the Revitalization of Public Health in Canada." *HealthcarePapers* 7 (3): 44–51. http://www.ncbi.nlm.nih.gov/entrez/query.fcgi?cmd=Retrieve&db=PubMed&list_uids=17476128&dopt=Abstract.

Margetts, Helen Z. 2009. "The Internet and Public Policy." *Policy & Internet* 1 (1): 1–21. http://dx.doi.org/10.2202/1944-2866.1029.

Matier, Chris. 2012. *Renewing the Canada Health Transfer: Implications for Federal and Provincial-Territorial Fiscal Sustainability.* Ottawa: Parliamentary Budget Office.

McArthur, Douglas. 2007. "Policy Analysis in Provincial Governments in Canada: From PPBS to Network Management." In *Policy Analysis in Canada: The State of the Art*, ed. L. Dobuzinskis, M. Howlett, and D. Laycock, 238–64. Toronto: University of Toronto Press.

McGregor, Deborah. 2011. "Aboriginal/non-Aboriginal Relations and Sustainable Forest Management in Canada: The Influence of the Royal Commission on Aboriginal Peoples." *Journal of Environmental Management* 92 (2): 300–10.

McGuire, Michael. 2000. "Collaborative Policy Making and Administration: The Operational Demands of Local Economic Development." *Economic Development Quarterly* 14 (3): 278–93. http://dx.doi.org/10.1177/089124240001400307.

McInnes, Simon. 1977. "Improving Legislative Surveillance of Provincial Public Expenditure: The Performance of Public Accounts Committee and Auditors General." *Canadian Public Administration* 20 (1): 36–86. http://dx.doi.org/10.1111/j.1754-7121.1977.tb01890.x.

McKenzie, Kenneth J. 2006. "A Race to the Bottom in Provincial Business Taxation in Canada?" In *Racing to the Bottom? Provincial Interdependence in the Canadian Federation*, ed. Kathryn Harrison, 25–48. Vancouver: University of British Columbia Press.

McKinnon, Janice. 2003. *Minding the Public Purse*. Montreal: McGill-Queen's University Press.

McNutt, Kathleen. 2009. *Citizen Engagement through Online Consultation A Comment on Public Involvement and E-Consultation: A New Era of Democratic Governance in Canada*. Montreal: IRPP.

McNutt, Kathleen, and Gregory P. Marchildon. 2009. "Think Tanks and the Web: Measuring Visibility and Influence." *Canadian Public Policy* 35 (2): 219–36. http://dx.doi.org/10.3138/cpp.35.2.219.

Meekison, J. Peter. 2004. "The Annual Premier's Conference: Forging a Common Front." In *Canada: The State of the Federation 2002—Reconsidering the Institutions of Canadian Federalism*, ed. J. Peter Meekison, Hamish Telford, and Harvey Lazar, 141–82. Montreal and Kingston: McGill-Queen's University Press for the Institute of Intergovernmental Relations.

Meekison, J. Peter. 2004a. "The Weakest Link? First Ministers' Conferences in Canadian Intergovernmental Relations." In *Canada: The State of the Federation 2002—Reconsidering the Institutions of Canadian Federalism*, ed. J.Peter Meekison, Hamish Telford, and Harvey Lazar, 113–40. Montreal and Kingston: McGill-Queen's University Press for the Institute of Intergovernmental Relations.

Meekison, J. Peter. 2004b. "The Western Premiers' Conference: Intergovernmental Cooperation at the Regional Level." In *Canada: The State of the Federation 2002—Reconsidering the Institutions of Canadian Federalism*, ed. J. Peter Meekison, Hamish Telford, and Harvey Lazar, 183–209. Montreal and Kingston: McGill-Queen's University Press for the Institute of Intergovernmental Relations.

Meekison, J. Peter, Hamish Telford, and Harvey Lazar, eds. 2004. *Canada: The State of the Federation 2002—Reconsidering the Institutions of Canadian Federalism*. Montreal and Kingston: McGill-Queen's University Press for the Institute of Intergovernmental Relations.

Miljan, Lydia. 2008. *Public Policy in Canada: An Introduction*. 5th ed. Toronto: Oxford University Press.

Miller, Laura. 2009. "e-Petitions at Westminster: the Way Forward for Democracy?" *Parliamentary Affairs* 62 (1): 162–77. http://dx.doi.org/10.1093/pa/gsn044.

Milne, David. 2005. *Asymmetry in Canada: Past and Present*. Asymmetric Federalism Series 1. Kingston, ON: Institute of Intergovernmental Relations, Queen's University. http://www.queensu.ca/iigr/WorkingPapers/ asymmetricfederalism/Milne2005.pdf.

Mintrom, Michael. 2007. "The Policy Analysis Movement." In *Policy Analysis in Canada*, ed. L. Dobuzinskis, M. Howlett, and D. Laycock, 145–62. Toronto: University of Toronto Press.

Mintz, Jack, and Michael Smart. 2004. "Income Shifting, Investment, and Tax Competition: Theory and Evidence from Provincial Taxation in Canada." *Journal of Public Economics* 88 (6): 1149–68. http://dx.doi.org/10.1016/ S0047-2727(03)00060-4.

Montpetit, Éric. 2003. *Misplaced Distrust: Policy Networks and the Environment in France, the United States, and Canada*. Vancouver: UBC Press.

Montpetit, Éric. 2005. "Westminster Parliamentarianism, Policy Networks, and the Behaviours of Political Actors." In *New Institutionalism: Theory and Analysis*, ed. André Lecours, 225–44. Toronto: University of Toronto Press.

Morley, J. Terrance. 1996. "The Government of the Day: The Premier and Cabinet in British Columbia." In *Politics, Policy and Government in British Columbia*, ed. R.K. Carty, 143–63. Vancouver: UBC Press.

Munro, Gary. 1989. "Ontario's Urban Transportation Development Corporation: A Case Study in Privatization." *Canadian Public Administration* 32 (1): 25–40. http://dx.doi.org/10.1111/j.1754-7121.1989.tb01341.x.

Murrell, David, and Weiqiu Yu. 2000. "The Effects of the Harmonized Sales Tax on Consumer Prices in Atlantic Canada." *Canadian Public Policy* 26 (4): 451–60. http://dx.doi.org/10.2307/3552611.

Murthy, Dhiraj. 2011. "Twitter: Microphone for the Masses?" *Media, Culture & Society* 33 (5): 779–89. http://dx.doi.org/10.1177/0163443711404744.

Musgrave, Richard A. 1959. *The Theory of Public Finance*. New York: McGraw-Hill.

Mylvaganam, Chandran, and Sandford Borins. 2005. *"If You Build It . . ." Business, Government and Ontario's Electronic Toll Highway*. Toronto: University of Toronto Press.

Native Nations Institute. 2010. *Making First Nation Law: The Listuguj Mi'gmaq Fishery*. Tucson, AZ and Vancouver, BC: Native Nations Institute for Leadership, Management and Policy and National Centre for First Nations Governance. http://fngovernance.org/publication_docs/Listuguj_Mi-gmaq_ Fishery_FINAL_Dec.15.pdf.

Norman, K. 2012. Personal communication. January 13.

Norquay, Geoff. 2011. "The Death of Executive Federalism and the Rise of the 'Harper Doctrine': Prospects for the Next Health Care Accord." *Policy Options* 33 (1): 46–50.

Nova Scotia. 2007. *Policy Excellence and the Nova Scotia Public Service: A Joint Report of the Policy Advisory Council and the Policy and Treasury Board.* Halifax: Government of Nova Scotia.

NWPTA (New West Partnership Trade Agreement). 2009. "The NWPTA—The Agreement." Official website of the New West Partnership Trade Agreement. http://www.newwestpartnershiptrade.ca/the_agreement.asp (accessed December 10, 2012).

Oates, Wallace. 1972. *Fiscal Federalism.* New York: Harcourt Brace Jovanovich.

OECD (Organisation for Economic Co-operation and Development). 1997. *Regulatory Impact Analysis: Best Practices in OECD Countries.* Paris: OECD.

Oleszkiewicz, Igor. 1994. *The Concept and Practice of Performance-Based Building Regulations. Ottawa: National Research Council of Canada.* Institute for Research in Construction Series IRC-IR-697. Ottawa: National Research Council of Canada. http://archive.nrc-cnrc.gc.ca/obj/irc/doc/pubs/ir/ir697/ir697.pdf.

Ontario-Québec Trade and Cooperation Agreement. 2011. *Backgrounder.* http://www.ontariocanada.com/ontcan/1medt/econdev/en/ed_ONQBagreement_main_en.jsp.

Ontario Workplace Tribunals Library. 2009. *Workers' Compensation Law: A Documentary History in Ontario.* Toronto: OWTL. http://www.owtlibrary.on.ca/english/print/wcl.pdf.

Orb, Jocelyn D. 2008. "The Political Economy of Public-Private Partnerships: Forestry Co-Management in Northwest Saskatchewan," MA thesis. Saskatoon: University of Saskatchewan. http://library.usask.ca/theses/available/etd-04302008-104741/.

Osborne, David, and Ted Gaebler. 1992. *Reinventing Government.* Addison-Wesley Pub. Co.

Osimo, David. 2008. *Web 2.0 in Government: Why and How? European Commission Joint Research Centre.* Luxembourg: Office for Official Publications of the European Communities.

Pal, Leslie A. 2010. *Beyond Policy Analysis: Public Issue Management in Turbulent Times.* 4th ed. Toronto: Nelson.

Palmer, Lisa, and Maureen Tehan. 2007. "Shared Citizenship and Self-Government in Canada: A Case Study of James Bay and Nunavik (Northern Quebec)." In *Settling with Indigenous People,* ed. Marcia Langton, Odette Mazel, Lisa Palmer, Kathryn Shain, and Maureen Tehan, 19–43. Sydney: The Federation Press.

Pan, Eric J. 2009. *Structural Reform of Financial Regulation: A Research Study Prepared for the Expert Panel on Securities Regulation in Canada.* Cardozo

Legal Studies Research Paper No. 250. Rochester, NY: Social Science Research Network. http://papers.ssrn.com/sol3/papers.cfm?abstract_id=1333385.

Pandey, Manish, and James Townsend. 2011. "Quantifying the Effects of the Provincial Nominee Programs." *Canadian Public Policy* 37 (4): 495–512. http://dx.doi.org/10.3138/cpp.37.4.495.

Perdikis, Nick, and William Kerr. 1999. "Can Consumer-Based Demands for Protection Be Incorporated in the WTO? The Case of Genetically Modified Foods." *Canadian Journal of Agricultural Economics* 47 (4): 457–65. http://dx.doi.org/10.1111/j.1744-7976.1999.tb00443.x.

Peters, Evelyn. 2005. "Indigeneity and Marginalisation: Planning for and with Urban Aboriginal Communities in Canada." *Progress in Planning* 63 (4): 327–404. http://dx.doi.org/10.1016/j.progress.2005.03.008.

Petry, François, Louis M. Imbeau, Jean Crête, and Michel Clavet. 2000. "Explaining the Evolution of Government Size in the Canadian Provinces." *Public Finance Review* 28 (1): 26–47. http://dx.doi.org/10.1177/109114210002800102.

Pfeil, Ulrike, Raj Arjan, and Panayiotis Zaphiris. 2009. "Age Differences in Online Social Networking—A Study of User Profiles and the Social Capital Divide among Teenagers and Older Users in MySpace." *Computers in Human Behavior* 25 (3): 643–54. http://dx.doi.org/10.1016/j.chb.2008.08.015.

Phillips, Peter. 2007. *Governing Transformative Technological Innovation: Who's in Charge?* Oxford: Edward Elgar.

Poel, Dale. 1976. "The Diffusion of Legislation Among the Canadian Provinces: A Statistical Analysis." *Canadian Journal of Political Science* 9 (04): 605–26. http://dx.doi.org/10.1017/S0008423900044723.

Pollard, Bruce G. 1986. *Managing the Interface: Intergovernmental Affairs Agencies in Canada.* Kingston: Institute for Intergovernmental Relations. http://www.queensu.ca/iigr/pub/archive/books/ManagingtheInterface1986.pdf

Posner, Richard. 1971. "Taxation by Regulation." *Bell Journal of Economics and Management Science* 2 (1): 22–50. http://dx.doi.org/10.2307/3003161.

Quantz, Darryl, and Wilfreda E. Thurston, and the Aboriginal Community Health Council. 2006. "Representation Strategies in Public Participation in Health Policy: the Aboriginal Community Health Council." *Health Policy* 75 (3): 243–50. http://dx.doi.org/10.1016/j.healthpol.2005.03.009. Medline:16399168.

Radin, Beryl A. 2000. *Beyond Machiavelli: Policy Analysis Comes of Age.* Washington, DC: Georgetown University Press.

Raphael, Dennis, Rebecca Renwick, Ivan Brown, Brenda Steinmetz, Hersh Sehdev, and Sherry Phillips. 2001. "Making the Links Between Community Structure and Individual Well-Being: Community Quality of Life in Riverdale, Toronto, Canada." *Health & Place* 7 (3): 179–96. http://dx.doi.org/10.1016/S1353-8292(01)00008-9. Medline:11439254.

Rasmussen, Ken. 1999. "Policy Capacity in Saskatchewan: Strengthening the Equilibrium." *Canadian Public Administration* 42 (3): 331–48. http://dx.doi.org/10.1111/j.1754-7121.1999.tb01554.x.

Rasmussen, Ken. 2000. "The Manitoba Civil Service: A Quiet Tradition in Transition." In *Government Restructuring and the Future of the Career Public Service in Canada*, ed. Evert Lindquist, 349–73. Toronto: IPAC.

Rasmussen, Ken. 2001. "Saskatchewan's Public Service: Converging Towards the Norm?" In *Saskatchewan Politics: Into the Twenty-First Century*, ed. Howard Leeson, 95–110. Regina: Canadian Plains Research Centre.

Redmond, David, and Associates. 2011. *Regulatory Reform: A Review of Provincial Government Approaches and Initiatives (Preliminary Report)*. Ottawa: Canadian Home Builders' Association. http://www.chba.ca/uploads/Urban_Council/Feb2011/Tab 9 - Preliminary Report on Provicial Regulatory Reform Initiatives.pdf (accessed February 28, 2012).

Requejo, Ferran. 2010. "Federalism and Democracy: The Case of Minority Nations—A Federalist Deficit." In *Federal Democracies*, ed. M. Burgess and A. Gagnon, 275–98. Routledge: London and New York.

Reynolds, Barbara. 2010. "Building Trust through Social Media. CDC's Experience During the H1N1 Influenza Response." *Marketing Health Services* 30 (2): 18–21. Medline:20550001.

Rhodes, R.A.W. 1996. "The New Governance: Governing without Government." *Political Studies* 44 (4): 652–67. http://dx.doi.org/10.1111/j.1467-9248.1996.tb01747.x.

Richards, John. 2008. "Cracks in the Country's Foundation: The Importance of Repairing Equalization." *Canadian Political Science Review* 2 (3): 68–83.

Robinson, David. 2005. *Review of the Agriculture and Food Products Chapter of the Agreement on Internal Trade*. Economics Backgrounder. Halifax: Nova Scotia Department of Agriculture and Fisheries. http://www.gov.ns.ca/agri/bde/econ/EconAITRevew05.pdf.

Robinson, James A., Ragnar Torvik, and Thierry Verdier. 2006. "Political Foundations of the Resource Curse." *Journal of Development Economics* 79 (2): 447–68. http://dx.doi.org/10.1016/j.jdeveco.2006.01.008.

Romanow, Roy, John Whyte, and Howard Leeson. 1984. *Canada Notwithstanding: The Making of the Canadian Constitution, 1976–1982*. Toronto: Carswell/Methuen.

Rose, Richard. 1991. "What is Lesson-Drawing." *Journal of Public Policy* 11 (01): 3–30. http://dx.doi.org/10.1017/S0143814X00004918.

Rosen, Harvey S., Jean-Francois Wen, Tracy Snoddon, Bev Dahlby, and Rogers S. Smith. 2008. *Public Finance in Canada*. 3rd ed. Toronto: McGraw-Hill Ryerson.

Rosen, Harvey S., Jean-Francois Wen, and Tracy Snoddon. 2012. *Public Finance in Canada*. 4th ed. Toronto: McGraw-Hill Ryerson.

Roy, Jeffrey, and John Langford. 2008. *Integrating Service Delivery Across Levels of Government: Case Studies of Canada and Other Countries*. Collaboration: Network and Partnerships Series. Washington, DC: IBM Centre for the Business of Government. http://www.businessofgovernment.org/sites/default/files/RoyLangfordReport.pdf.

Russell, Peter H. 2004. *Constitutional Odyssey: Can Canadians Become a Sovereign People?* 3rd ed. Toronto: University of Toronto Press.

Russo, Angelina, Jerry Watkins, Lynda Kelly, and Sebastian Chan. 2008. "Participatory Communication with Social Media." *Curator: The Museum Journal* 51 (1): 21–31. http://dx.doi.org/10.1111/j.2151-6952.2008.tb00292.x.

Salamon, Lester, ed. 2002. *The Tools of Government: A Guide to New Governance*. Oxford: Oxford University Press.

Sancton, Andrew. 2008. *The Limits of Boundaries: Why City-Regions Cannot be Self-Governing*. Montreal and Kingston: McGill-Queen's University Press.

Sancton, Andrew. 2011. *Canadian Local Government: An Urban Perspective*. Toronto: Oxford University Press.

Savoie, Donald J. 2003. *Strengthening the Policy Capacity of Government*. Panel on the Role of Government in Ontario Research Paper 42. Toronto: University of Toronto. http://www.law-lib.utoronto.ca/investing/reports/rp42.pdf.

Savoie, Donald J. 2004. "Searching for Accountability in a Government without Boundaries." *Canadian Public Administration* 47 (1): 1–26.

Saywell, John T. 2002. *The Lawmakers: Judicial Interpretation and the Shaping of Canadian Federalism*. Toronto: University of Toronto Press.

Séguin, Yves. 2002. *A New Division of Canada's Financial Resources*. Quebec: Commission of Fiscal Imbalance.

Siegel, David. 1980. "Provincial-Municipal Relations in Canada: An Overview." *Canadian Public Administration* 23 (2): 281–317. http://dx.doi.org/10.1111/j.1754-7121.1980.tb00058.x.

Siegel, David. 2006. Recent Changes in Provincial-Municipal Relations in Ontario: A New Era or a Missed Opportunity? In *Municipal-Federal-Provincial Relations in Canada*, ed. Robert Young and Christian Leuprecht, 181–97. Montreal: McGill-Queen's University Press.

Simmons, Julie M. 2004. "Securing the Threads of Co-operation in the Tapestry of Intergovernmental Relations: Does the Institutionalization of Ministerial Conferences Matter?" In *Canada: The State of the Federation 2002— Reconsidering the Institutions of Canadian Federalism*, ed. J.P. Meekison, M. Telford, and H. Lazar, 285–311. Montreal and Kingston, ON: McGill-Queen's University Press for the Institute of Intergovernmental Relations.

Simpson, Wayne, and Jared Wesley. 2012. "Effective Tool or Effectively Hollow? Balanced Budget Legislation in Western Canada." *Canadian Public Policy* 38 (3): 291–313. http://dx.doi.org/10.3138/cpp.38.3.291.

Skogstad, Grace. 2002. "International Trade Policy and Canadian Federalism: A Constructive Tension?" In *Canadian Federalism: Performance, Effectiveness, and Legitimacy*, ed. Herman Bakvis and Grace Skogstad, 159–77. Don Mills: Oxford University Press.

Slack, Enid, and Richard M. Bird. 2007. "Cities in Canadian Federalism." *Policy Options* 29 (1): 72–77.

Smiley, Donald. 1987. *The Federal Condition in Canada*. Toronto: McGraw-Hill Ryerson.

Smith, Bruce. 2003. *Public Policy and Public Participation: Engaging Citizens and Community in the Development of Public Policy*. Halifax: Health Canada, Population and Public Health Branch, Atlantic Regional Office.

Smith, Jennifer. 2008. "Intergovernmental Relations, Legitimacy, and the Atlantic Accords." *Constitutional Forum* 17 (3): 81–98. https://ejournals.library. ualberta.ca/index.php/constitutional_forum/article/download/10929/8426.

Smith, Sheila, Joseph P. Newhouse, and Mark S. Freeland. 2009. "Income, Insurance, and Technology: Why Does Health Spending Outpace Economic Growth?" *Health Affairs* 28 (5): 1276–84. http://dx.doi.org/10.1377/ hlthaff.28.5.1276. Medline:19738242.

Smith, Vernon L. 1976. "Experimental Economics: Induced Value Theory." *American Economic Review* 66 (2): 274–79.

Smith, Vernon L. 1982. "Microeconomic Systems as an Experimental Science." *American Economic Review* 72 (5): 923–55.

Smyth, Stuart, William Kerr, and Peter Phillips. 2011. "Recent Trends in the Scientific Basis of Sanitary and Phytosanitary Trade Rules and Their Potential Impact on Investment." *Journal of World Investment and Trade* 12 (1): 5–26.

Smyth, Stuart, Peter Phillips, and William Kerr. 2009. "Global Governance Quandaries Regarding Transformative Technologies for Bioproducts, Crops, and Foods." *Journal of World Trade* 43 (6): 1299–323.

Spears, Kimberly. 2007. "The Invisible Private Service: Consultants and Public Policy in Canada." In *Policy Analysis in Canada: The State of the Art*, ed. L. Dobuzinskis, M. Howlett, and D. Laycock, 399–422. Toronto: University of Toronto Press.

Spicker, Paul. 2006. *Policy Analysis for Practice*. Bristol: The Policy Press.

Statistics Canada. 2010. *Table 358-0132: Canadian Internet Use Survey, Internet Use at Home, by Sex and Government On-line (GOL) Activity, Every 2 Years (percent)*. CANSIM (database).

Steffen, Monika. 2005. "Comparing Complex Policies: Lessons from a Public Health Case." *Journal of Comparative Policy Analysis* 7 (4): 267–90. http://dx.doi.org/10.1080/13876980500327926.

Steunson, Don, and Richard Gilbert. 2005. "Coping with Canadian Federalism: The Case of the Federation of Canadian Municipalities." *Canadian Public*

Administration 48 (4): 528–51. http://dx.doi.org/10.1111/j.1754-7121.2005.
tb01201.x.

Stigler, George. 1971. "The Theory of Economic Regulation." *Bell Journal of
Economics and Management Science* 2 (1): 3–21. http://dx.doi.org/10.2307/
3003160.

Stone, Diane. 2007. "Recycling Bins, Garbage Cans or Think Tanks? Three Myths
Regarding Policy Analysis Institutes." *Public Administration* 85 (2): 259–78.
http://dx.doi.org/10.1111/j.1467-9299.2007.00649.x.

Stritch, Andrew. 2007. "Business Associations and Policy Analysis in Canada." In
Policy Analysis in Canada: The State of the Art, ed. L. Dobuzinskis, M. Howlett,
and D. Laycock, 443–72. Toronto: University of Toronto Press.

Supreme Court of Canada. 2011. Reference re Securities Act, 2011 SCC 66, [2011]
3 S.C.R. 837. http://scc.lexum.org/decisia-scc-csc/scc-csc/scc-csc/en/item/7984/
index.do.

Taft, Kevin. 1997. *Shredding the Public Interest: Ralph Klein and 25 Years of One
Party Government*. Edmonton: University of Alberta Press.

Tapp, Stephen. 2010. *Canadian Experiences with Fiscal Consolidations and Fiscal
Rules*. Ottawa: Parliamentary Budget Office.

TBS (Treasury Board of Canada). 1997. *Regulatory Reform through Regulatory
Impact Analysis: The Canadian Experience*. Ottawa: Treasury Board of Canada
Secretariat. http://www.tbs-sct.gc.ca/pubs_pol/dcgpubs/manbetseries/VOL14-
eng.asp (accessed December 10, 2012).

Teisman, Geert R. 2000. "Models for Research into Decision-Making Processes: On
Phases, Streams and Decision-Making Rounds." *Public Administration* 78 (4):
937–56. http://dx.doi.org/10.1111/1467-9299.00238.

Telford, Hamish. 2003. "The Federal Spending Power in Canada: Nation-Building
or Nation-Ddestroying." *Publius: The Journal of Federalism* 33 (1): 23–44.
http://dx.doi.org/10.1093/oxfordjournals.pubjof.a004976.

Tennant, Paul. 1977. "The NDP Government of British Columbia: Unaided
Politicians in an Unaided Cabinet." *Canadian Public Policy* 3 (4): 489–502.
http://dx.doi.org/10.2307/3549569.

Thomas, Christopher, and Amit Sheth. 2011. "Web Wisdom: An Essay on
How Web 2.0 and Semantic Web can Foster a Global Knowledge Society."
Computers in Human Behavior 27 (4): 1285–93. http://dx.doi.org/10.1016/
j.chb.2010.07.023.

Thomas, Paul. 2010. "Parliament and the Public Service." In *The Handbook of
Canadian Public Administration*, 2nd ed., ed. Christopher Dunn, 119–23.
Toronto: Oxford University Press.

Tiebout, Charles. 1956. "A Pure Theory of Local Expenditures." *Journal of Political
Economy* 64 (5): 416–24. http://dx.doi.org/10.1086/257839.

Tiernan, Anne. 2008. "The Council for the Australian Federation: A New Structure of Australian Federalism." *Australian Journal of Public Administration* 67 (2): 122–34. http://dx.doi.org/10.1111/j.1467-8500.2008.00576.x.

Tondeur, Jo, Ilse Sinnaeve, Mieke van Houtte, and Johan van Braak. 2011. "ICT as Cultural Capital: The Relationship between Socioeconomic Status and the Computer-Use Profile of Young People." *New Media & Society* 13 (1): 151–68. http://dx.doi.org/10.1177/1461444810369245.

Treff, Karin, and Deborah Ort. 2010. *Finances of the Nation 2010*. Canadian Tax Foundation series. Toronto: Canadian Tax Foundation.

Truman, David. 1951. *The Governmental Process: Political Interests and Public Opinion*. London: Greenwood Press.

Tupper, Allan, and Roger Gibbons. 1992. *The Government and Politics of Alberta*. Edmonton: University of Alberta Press.

Vedung, Evert. 2007. "Policy Instruments: Typologies and Theories." In *Carrots, Sticks, and Sermons: Policy Instruments and Their Evaluation*. 4th ed., ed. Marie-Louise Bemelmans-Videc, Ray C. Rist, and Evert Vedung, 21–58. New Jersey: Transaction Publishers.

Wallace, Murray D. 1974. "Budget Reform in Saskatchewan: A New Approach to Programme Based Management." *Canadian Public Administration* 17 (4): 586–99. http://dx.doi.org/10.1111/j.1754-7121.1974.tb01682.x.

Wallner, Jennifer. 2010. "Beyond National Standards: Reconciling Tension between Federalism and the Welfare State." *Publius: The Journal of Federalism* 40 (4): 646–71.

Ward, Ann, and Lee Ward, eds. 2009. *The Ashgate Companion to Federalism*. Farnham, UK: Ashgate.

Watling, Sue. 2011. "Digital Exclusion: Coming Out from Behind Closed Doors." *Disability & Society* 26 (4): 491–95. http://dx.doi.org/10.1080/09687599.2011.567802.

Watts, Ronald L. 1999. *The Spending Power in Federal Systems: A Comparative Study*. Kingston: Institute of Intergovernmental Relations.

Watts, Ronald L. 2008. *Comparing Federal Systems*. 3rd ed. Montreal and Kingston, ON: McGill-Queen's University Press for the Institute of Intergovernmental Relations.

Wellstead, Adam M., and Jeremy Rayner. 2009. "Manitoba: From Provincial-Based Planning to Localised Aboriginal Governance." *Policy and Society* 28 (2): 151–63.

Wibbels, Erik. 2000. "Federalism and the Politics of Macroeconomic Policy and Performance." *American Journal of Political Science* 44 (4): 687–702. http://dx.doi.org/10.2307/2669275.

Wiber, Melanie G., Murray A. Rudd, Evelyn Pinkerton, Anthony T. Charles, and Arthur Bull. 2010. "Coastal Management Challenges from a Community

Perspective: The Problem of 'Stealth Privatization' in a Canadian Fishery."
Marine Policy 34 (3): 598–605.

Wildavsky, Aaron. 1979. *Speaking Truth to Power: The Art and Craft of Policy Analysis*. Boston: Little Brown.

Wilson, John D., and David E. Wildasin. 2004. "Capital Tax Competition: Bane or Boon." *Journal of Public Economics* 88 (6): 1065–91. http://dx.doi.org/10.1016/S0047-2727(03)00057-4.

Winfield, Mark R. 2002. "Environmental Policy and Federalism." In *Canadian Federalism: Performance, Effectiveness, and Legitimacy*, ed. Herman Bakvis and Grace Skogstad, 124–38. Don Mills: Oxford University Press.

Wiseman, Nelson. 1996. "Provincial Political Cultures." In *Provinces: Canadian Provincial Politics*, ed. Christopher Dunn, 21–62. Ontario: Broadview Press.

Yanow, Dvora. 1999. *Conducting Interpretive Policy Analysis*. Thousand Oaks, CA: Sage.

Index

interprovincial agreements, xviii, 15, 42
interprovincial cooperation, 43
interprovincial initiatives, 14
Interprovincial Meat Trade Pilot Project, 115
interprovincial policy leadership, 18
interprovincial trade, 44, 115. *See also* internal trade
interprovincial trade regulation, 111
"intertemporal optimization" approach, 93
intragovernmental relations, 24, 42
Inuit, 158
    quest for policy autonomy, 155
Inuit self-government, 19
"investment income," 72
Iranian election (2009), 148

James Bay and Northern Québec Agreement, 18
Johnson-Shoyama Graduate School of Public Policy, xi–xii
joint provincial-federal responsibilities, 4–5, 105, 139
judicial appeal, 6

K-12 education, 38, 40
Keynesian-inspired recovery from 2008 recession, 91
knowledge, 127–28
knowledge economy, 53–54, 150
knowledge production, xxi, 124, 133, 145, 150, 158
knowledge transfer policy networks, 132

labour, 24, 41, 104, 112
"Labour Conventions case" (1937), 107
labour legislation and regulation, 106, 112
labour mobility, 1, 13, 15–16, 44, 111. *See also* migration of labour
labour training programs
    transferred from Ottawa to provincial governments, 9, 16
laissez-faire economics, 124
land management, 145
language
    Canada's official languages, 8, 136
    French language, 14
    importance to cultural identity, 12
    linguistic minorities, 12, 21
Latin America, 94

legitimacy, 133
"legitimate objectives" test, 118
"level playing field," 100, 103
LinkedIn, 135, 144
liquor distribution outlets, 24
Listuguj Mi'gmak, 114
lobbying, 39, 49
local governments. *See* municipal governments
local policy networks, 145
London Stock Exchange (LSE), 116
long-term debt (municipal bonds), 63
"long-time horizon budget," 93
loopholes (tax), 60

MacdonaldQ1 government, 112
macroeconomic theory, 94
macroeconomists, 83
management and audit boards, 49
management approaches, 130
managerial reform, xxi
managerial revolution, 32. *See also* administrative reform
mandate letters, 36
Manitoba, 85, 95, 112, 117, 144
    associations for francophone municipalities, 48
    debt, 75
    debt-to-GDP ratio, 93
    e-consultations, 139
    health care spending, 82
    Ministry of Innovation, Energy and Mines, 53
    provincial nominee program (PNP), 15
    social media use, 140
    YouTube channels featuring new legislation, 140
manufacturing, 72, 85
Maritime Economic Cooperation Agreement, 111
market, 45, 60, 126
market organizational structure, 131
marketplace of information, 127
marriage and divorce, 104–5
Martin, Paul, 87
Mavis Baker v. Canada (Minister of Citizenship), 107
Meadow Lake Tribal Council, 114
Medicare, 1–2, 13–14
Meech Lake Accord, 6

"Pareto optimum," 102
partnerships, 24, 33, 119
patents, 104
patronage appointments, 29, 31
payroll taxes, 68
peace, order, and good government, 5
peer-produced user content, 135
penitentiaries, 104
pensions, 5, 8, 40, 66
Performance Indicator Reporting
    Committee (PIRC), 13
performance- or goal-based regulation,
    114–15
personnel management, 32
pharmaceuticals, 81
planning and priorities committee of cab-
    inet, 36
policy advocacy from private and non-
    profit sectors, 50
policy ambition / policy capacity tension,
    xviii, 16, 51–52, 155
policy ambition / policy responsibility ten-
    sion, 137
policy analysis, xx, 129
    evidence-based, 142
    evidence-informed, 142–43
    purposes, 128
policy analysis movement, 125, 127–28,
    140–41
policy analysts, 129, 157, 254
policy capacity, 26, 125, 141–44, 147, 155
    lost policy capacity, 150
policy convergence, 52, 155
policy convergence and divergence among
    provinces, xviii
policy coordination mechanisms, 40
policy development, 49–52, 133, 145
policy development capacity, 49
policy diffusion, 52
policy expertise, 150
policy implementation, 133
policy innovation, 120
policy knowledge, xxi, 125, 157
policy learning, 145, 148
policy networks, xvi, xviii, xx, 130–31,
    143–47, 154–55
    idea production, 133
    implications for the Westminster sys-
        tem, 144
    innovation, 147

knowledge production agents, 124
policy regulation, 154
policy studies as a discipline, 129
policymaking
    shift from public service toward elected
        officials, 51
political culture, 4, 6, 25, 91, 130, 154
political feasibility, 127, 142
political preferences, 127
political pundits, 149
political relevance, 151
political will, 82
pollution, 102
popular uprising in Egypt (2011)
    Facebook campaign during, 148
post-Internet era, 125, 131, 149
post-secondary education, 40, 74
postal service, 104
potash, 85, 146
preeminent premier, rise of, 27, 46–47
premiers, 37, 43, 47
premier's chief of staff, 36
pressure groups, 125
price shocks, 85
prime minister, 43
Prince Edward Island, 95, 111
    departmental organization, 38
    Maritime Economic Cooperation
        Agreement, 111
    merit hiring, 30
    population, 4
prisons, 105
privacy, 136, 138, 143, 150
private investment, 80
private-sector, 32, 50
privatization, 44–45, 52
    limitations, 45–46
    of regulatory power, 118
productivity, 81
professional associations, 157
professional graduate programs in public
        policy and public administration,
        129
professional public service, xx, 26–31, 142
professional qualifications, 111
professionals recruited through PNPs, 15
property and civil rights
    protection of, 105
property taxes, 20, 48
provincial advocacy networks, 133

provincial apprenticeship training programs, 15
provincial bonds, 94
provincial collaboration (forging a united front against the federal government), 9, 42
provincial competition. *See* competition; tax competition
provincial decision making, xx, 35–37, 144
provincial differences, xxi, 25, 41, 157
provincial e-consultations, 139
provincial governments, 23, 26, 33, 55–56
  as administrative and policy laboratories, 52–54
  autonomy, 59, 153
  challenged by local and Aboriginal governments, 16, 18–20, 22–23
  changes across time, 54–55
  co-regulation of resources with First Nations, Inuit, and Métis, 114
  convergence, 53–54, 96
  debt expenditures, 75
  decision making (*See* provincial decision making)
  deficit positions after 2008 recession, 91
  departmental organization, 37–41
  development of Crown corporations, 45
  different governance priorities, 25
  expenditures, 62, 74–76, 153
  fiscal capacity of, 17, 88
  fiscal matters, xxi, 50, 91, 95, 157
  foreign trade policy, 146
  future research proposals, 55–56
  growth, 26, 37
  horizontal collaboration among, 17
  immigration, 15 (*See also* provincial nominee programs)
  jurisdiction (*See* provincial jurisdiction)
  policy ambitions, 52
  policy analytical deficits, 143
  policy capacity, 51
  policy coordination, 21, 41–42
  policy development, xv, xvi, xvii, xviii, xx, xxii, 51, 154, 156
  policy innovation, 153
  policy networks, 124, 132, 145
  policy regulation, 154
  privatization, 45
  providers of welfare benefits and services, 79–80 (*See also* provincial jurisdiction; social assistance)

public expectations, 96
regional representation by, 7, 21
as regulator, 24, 99–121, 154, 157
resistance to unilateral federal action, 44
responsibility *vs.* capacity, 16–18
revenues, 68–71, 90, 96
social media, 140, 148
structural deficits, 64, 91
vulnerable to economic downturns, 90, 92
provincial jurisdiction, 11, 19, 104, 107. *See also* concurrent jurisdiction; shared jurisdiction
intergovernmental and intragovernmental activity in, 44
provincial marketing boards, 106
provincial-municipal relations, xxi, 16, 18–20, 22–23, 47–49
provincial nominee programs (PNPs), 13–15
provincial politics, xix
provincial populations, 4
provincial priorities, 127, 142
provincial public service. *See also* public service
  growing insecurity and low morale, 35
  policy capacity, 24, 49–50
  pressures for new constraints, 24
provincial regulatory innovation, 107–17
provincial sales tax (PST), 47
provincial stock exchanges, 115–16
provincial tax capacity, 17, 90
provincial taxes on business, 65
public affairs firms, 49
public consultation, 36
public debate, 128
public education, 150
public engagement, 125, 139, 144. *See also* citizen engagement; democratic engagement
public health and safety, 102
public health information, 138
Public Health Ontario, 132
public health websites, 139
public intellectuals, 149
"the public interest," 59
public lands, 105
public management reform, 124
public mining companies, 116
public opinion, 79

electronic, 135
innovations, 52
integration across all levels of government, 137
municipalities, 48
provincial, 24
restructuring, 124
small provinces, 25
through e-government, 134, 137
Service New Brunswick, 138
Service Nova Scotia and Municipal
Relations, 138
settlement, 145
shared jurisdiction or responsibility, 4–5,
40, 105, 139
short-term debt (treasury bills), 63
skilled labourers recruited through PNPs, 15
"smart government," 149
smart regulation, 109
social assistance, 88
social assistance cutbacks, 65
social benefit spending, 74
social cohesion, 126, 150
social justice, 107
social media, 149
impact on advocacy, 148
public take-up rate, 149
social inclusion and, 150
social media campaigns, 127, 136
social media technologies
government use of, 140
social networking, 140
social networking sites (SNS), 135
social services
intergovernmental agencies for, 42
provincial budgets, 41
provincial delivery, 24
spending reductions, 76
Social Union Framework Agreement
(SUFA), 10
social union initiative (1990s), 17
social welfare, xviii, 74, 81. See also welfare state development
softwood lumber, 146
stakeholder participation, 125, 150
stakeholders, 39, 131, 133, 137
standard operating procedures, 102
state. See also government
national state relative to suprastate and
substate, 1

state responsibility for equitable distribution and redistribution, 79. See also equalization transfers
Stigler, George, 102, 117
stock exchanges, 115–16
structural deficits, 64, 91
structural fiscal imbalance, 62
subsidiarity of regulatory authority in
Canada, 103
subsidies on wages, interest, and the purchase of equipment, 66
subsidizing desired activities, 100
substate entities, xv, xx, 89. See also provincial governments
Supreme Court of Canada, 6, 18, 107, 117
surplus, 92
Switzerland, 8, 156

tax competition, 65, 69, 89, 155. See also
competition
tax exemptions (or expenditures), 60
tax fields, 68, 88
tax harmonization, 69, 90
"tax on tax," 69–70
tax relief, 78
tax system equity, 60
taxation, 8, 103
taxes and spending, xxi, 60–61, 96, 100, 153
efficiency and effectiveness, 63
GST, 90
"hidden" taxes, 69
HST, 70
income taxes, 68–69
payroll taxes, 68
property taxes, 20, 48
provincial, 17, 59
provincial sales tax (PST), 47
provincial taxes on business, 65
"race to the bottom," 65
revenues, 68–71
sales taxes, 68
vertical imbalance, 88–91
technology
health care spending and, 81
telecommunications, 118
territorial premiers, 9
territories, 59, 158
think tanks, xvi, 129, 139, 154, 157
participants in provincial policy networks, 146–47